YOUR CHINESE HOROSCOPE 2003

NEIL SOMERVILLE

What the Year of the Goat holds in store for you

Thorsons

TO ROS, RICHARD AND EMILY

Thorsons
An Imprint of HarperCollins*Publishers*
77–85 Fulham Palace Road
Hammersmith, London W6 8JB

The Thorsons website address is:
www.thorsons.com

and *Thorsons*
are trademarks of
HarperCollins*Publishers* Limited

Published by Thorsons 2002

10 9 8 7 6 5 4 3 2 1

A catalogue record for this book
is available from the British Library

ISBN 0 00 713149 6

Printed and bound in Great Britain by
Clays Ltd, St Ives plc

CONTENTS

———◆———

ABOUT THE AUTHOR

Neil Somerville is one of the leading writers in the West on Chinese horoscopes. He has been interested in Eastern forms of divination for many years and believes that much can be learnt from the ancient wisdom of the East. His annual book on Chinese horoscopes has built up an international following and he is also the author of *What's Your Chinese Love Sign?* (Thorsons, 2000) and *Chinese Success Signs* (Thorsons, 2001).

Neil Somerville was born in the Year of the Water Snake. His wife was born under the sign of the Monkey, his son is an Ox and daughter a Horse.

ACKNOWLEDGEMENTS

In writing *Your Chinese Horoscope 2003* I am grateful for the assistance and support that those around me have given.

I wish to acknowledge Theodora Lau's *The Handbook of Chinese Horoscopes* (Harper & Row, 1979; Arrow, 1981), which was particularly useful to me in my research.

In addition to Ms Lau's work, I commend the following books to those who wish to find out more about Chinese horoscopes: Kristyna Arcarti, *Chinese Horoscopes for Beginners* (Headway, 1995); Catherine Aubier, *Chinese Zodiac Signs* (Arrow, 1984), a series of 12 books; E. A. Crawford and Teresa Kennedy, *Chinese Elemental Astrology* (Piatkus, 1992); Paula Delsol, *Chinese Horoscopes* (Pan, 1973); Barry Fantoni, *Barry Fantoni's Chinese Horoscopes* (Warner, 1994); Bridget Giles and the Diagram Group, *Chinese Astrology* (Collins Gem, HarperCollins*Publishers*, 1996); Kwok Man-Ho, *Authentic Chinese Horoscopes* (Arrow, 1987), a series of 12 books; Lori Reid, *The Complete Book of Chinese Horoscopes* (Element Books, 1997); Paul Rigby and Harvey Bean, *Chinese Astrologics* (Publications Division, South China Morning Post Ltd, 1981); Ruth Q. Sun, *The Asian Animal Zodiac* (Charles E. Tuttle Company, Inc., 1996); Derek Walters, *Ming Shu* (Pagoda Books, 1987) and *The Chinese*

Astrology Workbook (The Aquarian Press, 1988); Suzanne White, *Suzanne White's Book of Chinese Chance* (Fontana/Collins, 1978), *The New Astrology* (Pan, 1987) and *The New Chinese Astrology* (Pan, 1994).

———◆◆———

As you venture forward into another year,
venture forward with hope,
determined to make the most of yourself, your talents and ideas.

There will be successes and some setbacks too,
but by venturing forward,
by making the most of yourself,
you will know you will have given the year your best,
and will in some way, large or small, have learnt and gained.

Neil Somerville

———◆◆———

INTRODUCTION

The origins of Chinese horoscopes have been lost in the mists of time. It is known that Oriental astrologers practised their art many thousands of years ago and even today Chinese astrology continues to fascinate and intrigue.

In Chinese astrology there are 12 signs named after 12 different animals. No one quite knows how the signs acquired their names, but there is one legend that offers an explanation.

According to this legend, one Chinese New Year the Buddha invited all the animals in his kingdom to come before him. Unfortunately, for reasons best known to the animals, only 12 turned up. The first to arrive was the Rat, followed by the Ox, Tiger, Rabbit, Dragon, Snake, Horse, Goat, Monkey, Rooster, Dog and finally Pig.

In gratitude, the Buddha decided to name a year after each of the animals and that those born during that year would inherit some of the personality of that animal. Therefore those born in the Year of the Ox would be hardworking, resolute and stubborn, just like the Ox, while those born in the Year of the Dog would be loyal and faithful, just like the Dog. While not everyone can possibly share all the characteristics of a sign, it is incredible what similarities do occur and this is partly where the fascination of Chinese horoscopes lies.

In addition to the 12 signs of the Chinese zodiac there are also five elements and these have a strengthening or moderating influence upon the sign. Details about the effects of the elements are given in each of the chapters on the 12 signs.

To find out which sign you were born under, refer to the tables on pages ix–xii. As the Chinese year is based on the lunar year and does not start until late January or early February, it is particularly important for anyone born in those two months to check carefully the dates of the Chinese year in which they were born.

Also included, in the Appendix, are two charts showing the compatibility between the signs for personal and business relationships, and details about the signs ruling the different hours of the day. From this it is possible to locate your ascendant and, as in Western astrology, this has a significant influence on your personality.

In writing this book, I have taken the unusual step of combining the intriguing nature of Chinese horoscopes with the Western desire to know what the future holds and have based my interpretations upon various factors relating to each of the signs. I have been pleased that over the years in which *Your Chinese Horoscope* has been published so many have found the sections on the forthcoming year of interest, and hope that the horoscope has been constructive and useful. Remember, though, that at all times you are the master of your own destiny. I sincerely hope that *Your Chinese Horoscope 2003* will prove interesting and helpful for the year ahead.

THE CHINESE YEARS

Rat	18 February	1912	to	5 February	1913
Ox	6 February	1913	to	25 January	1914
Tiger	26 January	1914	to	13 February	1915
Rabbit	14 February	1915	to	2 February	1916
Dragon	3 February	1916	to	22 January	1917
Snake	23 January	1917	to	10 February	1918
Horse	11 February	1918	to	31 January	1919
Goat	1 February	1919	to	19 February	1920
Monkey	20 February	1920	to	7 February	1921
Rooster	8 February	1921	to	27 January	1922
Dog	28 January	1922	to	15 February	1923
Pig	16 February	1923	to	4 February	1924
Rat	5 February	1924	to	23 January	1925
Ox	24 January	1925	to	12 February	1926
Tiger	13 February	1926	to	1 February	1927
Rabbit	2 February	1927	to	22 January	1928
Dragon	23 January	1928	to	9 February	1929
Snake	10 February	1929	to	29 January	1930
Horse	30 January	1930	to	16 February	1931
Goat	17 February	1931	to	5 February	1932
Monkey	6 February	1932	to	25 January	1933
Rooster	26 January	1933	to	13 February	1934
Dog	14 February	1934	to	3 February	1935
Pig	4 February	1935	to	23 January	1936

Rat	24 January	1936	to	10 February	1937
Ox	11 February	1937	to	30 January	1938
Tiger	31 January	1938	to	18 February	1939
Rabbit	19 February	1939	to	7 February	1940
Dragon	8 February	1940	to	26 January	1941
Snake	27 January	1941	to	14 February	1942
Horse	15 February	1942	to	4 February	1943
Goat	5 February	1943	to	24 January	1944
Monkey	25 January	1944	to	12 February	1945
Rooster	13 February	1945	to	1 February	1946
Dog	2 February	1946	to	21 January	1947
Pig	22 January	1947	to	9 February	1948
Rat	10 February	1948	to	28 January	1949
Ox	29 January	1949	to	16 February	1950
Tiger	17 February	1950	to	5 February	1951
Rabbit	6 February	1951	to	26 January	1952
Dragon	27 January	1952	to	13 February	1953
Snake	14 February	1953	to	2 February	1954
Horse	3 February	1954	to	23 January	1955
Goat	24 January	1955	to	11 February	1956
Monkey	12 February	1956	to	30 January	1957
Rooster	31 January	1957	to	17 February	1958
Dog	18 February	1958	to	7 February	1959
Pig	8 February	1959	to	27 January	1960
Rat	28 January	1960	to	14 February	1961
Ox	15 February	1961	to	4 February	1962
Tiger	5 February	1962	to	24 January	1963
Rabbit	25 January	1963	to	12 February	1964
Dragon	13 February	1964	to	1 February	1965
Snake	2 February	1965	to	20 January	1966
Horse	21 January	1966	to	8 February	1967

Goat	9 February	1967	to	29 January	1968
Monkey	30 January	1968	to	16 February	1969
Rooster	17 February	1969	to	5 February	1970
Dog	6 February	1970	to	26 January	1971
Pig	27 January	1971	to	14 February	1972
Rat	15 February	1972	to	2 February	1973
Ox	3 February	1973	to	22 January	1974
Tiger	23 January	1974	to	10 February	1975
Rabbit	11 February	1975	to	30 January	1976
Dragon	31 January	1976	to	17 February	1977
Snake	18 February	1977	to	6 February	1978
Horse	7 February	1978	to	27 January	1979
Goat	28 January	1979	to	15 February	1980
Monkey	16 February	1980	to	4 February	1981
Rooster	5 February	1981	to	24 January	1982
Dog	25 January	1982	to	12 February	1983
Pig	13 February	1983	to	1 February	1984
Rat	2 February	1984	to	19 February	1985
Ox	20 February	1985	to	8 February	1986
Tiger	9 February	1986	to	28 January	1987
Rabbit	29 January	1987	to	16 February	1988
Dragon	17 February	1988	to	5 February	1989
Snake	6 February	1989	to	26 January	1990
Horse	27 January	1990	to	14 February	1991
Goat	15 February	1991	to	3 February	1992
Monkey	4 February	1992	to	22 January	1993
Rooster	23 January	1993	to	9 February	1994
Dog	10 February	1994	to	30 January	1995
Pig	31 January	1995	to	18 February	1996
Rat	19 February	1996	to	6 February	1997
Ox	7 February	1997	to	27 January	1998

Tiger	28 January	1998	to	15 February	1999
Rabbit	16 February	1999	to	4 February	2000
Dragon	5 February	2000	to	23 January	2001
Snake	24 January	2001	to	11 February	2002
Horse	12 February	2002	to	31 January	2003
Goat	1 February	2003	to	21 January	2004

Note: The names of the signs in the Chinese zodiac occasionally differ in the various books on Chinese astrology, although the characteristics of the signs remain the same. In some books the Ox is referred to as the Buffalo or Bull, the Rabbit as the Hare or Cat, the Goat as the Sheep and the Pig as the Boar.

For the sake of convenience, the male gender is used throughout this book. Unless otherwise stated, the characteristics of the signs apply to both sexes.

WELCOME TO THE
YEAR OF THE GOAT

Whether clambering over mountain rocks or grazing in lush green pastures, there is an air of contentment about the Goat. Unless troubled by some threat, he is happy in himself and his genial nature will have a marked effect upon his own Chinese year.

After the tribulations of the last two years, the Goat year will offer hope, reconciliation and healing. The process will not be easy, and sudden events will lead to some anxious moments, but major attempts will be made to settle disputes and bring peace to troubled areas. This has been seen in previous Goat years, for example with the historic Camp David peace treaty, the SALT II agreement, the ending of the Gulf War and the abolition of apartheid in South Africa. This pattern of resolution will certainly be a major feature of 2003, with the accent very much on diplomacy and dialogue.

In addition there will be a coming together of certain powers and communities which will lead to closer co-operation and sharing of resources. In some cases nations will negotiate significant bilateral treaties, while organizations such as NATO and the European Union are likely to grow as further countries join or pledge a greater commitment.

Leaders on the world stage will certainly be fully

occupied during the year, but internally too there will be major upheavals in certain countries. In some cases well-established leaders will suddenly lose power and new figures will enter the political arena, often with sweeping agendas of their own. It was, for example, in the previous Goat year that Mikhail Gorbachev, President Kaunda and Australia's Bob Hawke all fell from power and this pattern of transition will again be seen in 2003.

As in recent years, the world will not, unfortunately, be free from natural disasters, some arising from the climatic changes that have been experienced of late. In some parts there will be drought, flooding and severe weather conditions. In the worst-affected areas major relief operations will be mounted and in addition to aid, attention will be given to ways of preventing future disasters. Again, the emphasis will be on humanitarian matters and attempts to relieve suffering. And even if some of the measures decided upon now only prove to be 'the tip of the iceberg', at least a start will have been made.

The Goat's humanitarian concerns will also filter through to the world of medicine, with some major advances being made. It was in a Goat year that the first human heart transplant took place and further headway will be made in surgery, treatment and medicines in 2003. Also, in the Goat year many people will decide to take a greater interest in their own well-being and, as a result, more attention will be paid to diet, exercise and general lifestyle. Some may recognize that their demanding schedules have been making too many incursions into their life and there will be more emphasis on the importance of the family unit as well as on balancing activities.

This will also be an excellent year for culture and the arts. In addition to major exhibitions being held in many countries and, in some cases, record prices being paid for works of art, new styles and fashions will attract many followers. The Goat is all for colour, style and innovation. The world of entertainment too will serve up some notable delights and on stage and screen 2003 will see the premieres of what will become much-loved classics. *Casablanca,* hailed as 'one of the outstanding entertainment experiences of cinema history', was released in a Goat year and so too was the Beatles' novel and groundbreaking album *Sgt Pepper's Lonely Hearts Club Band.* For creativity, the Goat year is one of the best. And it will also see some fine sporting achievements.

In so many respects 2003 is a year of both hope and potential. There will be the chance for politicians and world leaders to bring about a greater understanding between nations, while for the individual, the Goat year is often a time for reappraisal and for appreciating the importance of the family and of leading a richer and more balanced lifestyle.

I hope that by following through your ideas and using your strengths, you will prosper as well as find a greater contentment under the kindly and supportive influence of the Goat year.

Good luck and good fortune.

31 JANUARY 1900 ⌒ 18 FEBRUARY 1901   *Metal Rat*

18 FEBRUARY 1912 ⌒ 5 FEBRUARY 1913   *Water Rat*

5 FEBRUARY 1924 ⌒ 23 JANUARY 1925   *Wood Rat*

24 JANUARY 1936 ⌒ 10 FEBRUARY 1937   *Fire Rat*

10 FEBRUARY 1948 ⌒ 28 JANUARY 1949   *Earth Rat*

28 JANUARY 1960 ⌒ 14 FEBRUARY 1961   *Metal Rat*

15 FEBRUARY 1972 ⌒ 2 FEBRUARY 1973   *Water Rat*

2 FEBRUARY 1984 ⌒ 19 FEBRUARY 1985   *Wood Rat*

19 FEBRUARY 1996 ⌒ 6 FEBRUARY 1997   *Fire Rat*

THE
RAT

THE PERSONALITY OF THE RAT

Cherish your visions, your ideals, the music that stirs in your heart. If you remain true to them, your world will at last be built.

James Allen, a Rat

The Rat is born under the sign of charm. He is intelligent, popular and loves attending parties and large social gatherings. He is able to establish friendships with remarkable ease and people generally feel relaxed in his company. He is a very social creature and is genuinely interested in the welfare and activities of others. He has a good understanding of human nature and his advice and opinions are often sought.

The Rat is a hard and diligent worker. He is also very imaginative and is never short of ideas. However, he does sometimes lack the confidence to promote his ideas as much as he should and this can often prevent him from securing the recognition and credit he so often deserves.

The Rat is very observant and many Rats have made excellent writers and journalists. The Rat also excels at personnel and PR work and any job which brings him into contact with people and the media. His skills are particularly appreciated in times of crisis, for he has an incredibly strong sense of self-preservation. When it comes to finding a way out of an awkward situation, the Rat is certain to be the one who comes up with a solution.

The Rat loves to be where there is a lot of action, but should he ever find himself in a very bureaucratic or restrictive environment he can become a stickler for discipline and routine.

He is also something of an opportunist and is constantly on the lookout for ways in which he can improve his wealth and lifestyle. He rarely lets an opportunity go by and can become involved in so many plans and schemes that he sometimes squanders his energies and achieves very little as a result. He is also rather gullible and can be taken in by those less scrupulous than himself.

Another characteristic of the Rat is his attitude to money. He is very thrifty and to some he may appear a little mean. The reason for this is purely that he likes to keep his money within his family. He can be most generous to his partner, his children and close friends and relatives. He can also be generous to himself, for he often finds it impossible to deprive himself of any luxury or object he fancies. The Rat is also very acquisitive and can be a notorious hoarder. He hates waste and is rarely prepared to throw anything away. He can also be rather greedy and will rarely refuse an invitation for a free meal or a complimentary ticket to some lavish function.

The Rat is a good conversationalist, although he can occasionally be a little indiscreet. He can be highly critical of others – for an honest and unbiased opinion, the Rat is a superb critic – and sometimes will use confidential information to his own advantage. However, as the Rat has such a bright and irresistible nature, most are prepared to forgive him for his slight indiscretions.

Throughout his long and eventful life, the Rat will make many friends and will find that he is especially well suited to those born under his own sign and those of the Ox,

Dragon and Monkey. He can also get on well with those born under the signs of the Tiger, Snake, Rooster, Dog and Pig, but the rather sensitive Rabbit and Goat will find the Rat a little too critical and blunt for their liking. The Horse and Rat will also find it difficult to get on with each other – the Rat craves security and will find the Horse's changeable moods and rather independent nature a little unsettling.

The Rat is very family-orientated and will do anything to please his nearest and dearest. He is exceptionally loyal to his parents and can himself be a very caring and loving parent. He will take an interest in all his children's activities and will see that they want for nothing. The Rat usually has a large family.

The female Rat has a kindly, outgoing nature and involves herself in a multitude of different activities. She has a wide circle of friends, enjoys entertaining and is an attentive hostess. She is also conscientious about the upkeep of her home and has superb taste in home furnishings. She is most supportive to the other members of her family and, due to her resourceful, friendly and persevering nature, can do well in practically any career she enters.

Although the Rat is essentially outgoing and something of an extrovert, he is also a very private individual. He tends to keep his feelings to himself and while he is not averse to learning what other people are doing, he resents anyone prying too closely into his own affairs. He also does not like solitude and if he is alone for any length of time he can easily get depressed.

The Rat is undoubtedly very talented, but he does sometimes fail to capitalize on his many abilities. He has a tendency to become involved in too many schemes and chase after too many opportunities all at once. If he were to slow down and concentrate on one thing at a time he could become very successful. If not, success and wealth could elude him. But the Rat, with his tremendous ability to charm, will rarely, if ever, be without friends.

THE FIVE DIFFERENT TYPES OF RAT

In addition to the 12 signs of the Chinese zodiac, there are five elements and these have a strengthening or moderating influence on the sign. The effects of the five elements on the Rat are described below, together with the years in which the elements were exercising their influence. Therefore all Rats born in 1960 are Metal Rats, those born in 1912 and 1972 are Water Rats, and so on.

Metal Rat: 1960

This Rat has excellent taste and certainly knows how to appreciate the finer things in life. His home is comfortable and nicely decorated and he likes to entertain or mix in fashionable circles. He has considerable financial acumen and invests his money well. On the surface the Metal Rat appears cheerful and confident, but deep down he can be troubled by worries that are quite often of his own making. He is exceptionally loyal to his family and friends.

Water Rat: 1912, 1972

The Water Rat is intelligent and very astute. He is a deep thinker and can express his thoughts clearly and persuasively. He is always eager to learn and is talented in many different areas. He is usually very popular, but his fear of loneliness can sometimes lead him into mixing with the wrong sort of company. He is a particularly skilful writer, but he can get side-tracked very easily and should try to concentrate on just one thing at a time.

Wood Rat: 1924, 1984

The Wood Rat has a friendly, outgoing personality and is most popular with his colleagues and friends. He has a quick, agile brain and likes to turn his hand to anything he thinks may be useful. His one fear is insecurity, but given his intelligence and capabilities, this fear is usually unfounded. He has a good sense of humour, enjoys travel and, due to his highly imaginative nature, can be a gifted writer or artist.

Fire Rat: 1936, 1996

The Fire Rat is rarely still and seems to have a never-ending supply of energy and enthusiasm. He loves being involved in the action – be it travel, following up new ideas or campaigning for a cause in which he fervently believes. He is an original thinker and hates being bound by petty restrictions or the dictates of others. He can be forthright in his views, but can sometimes get carried away in the excitement of the moment and commit himself to various undertakings without checking all the implications. Yet he has a resilient nature and with the right support can often go far in life.

Earth Rat: 1948

This Rat is astute and very level-headed. He rarely takes unnecessary chances and while he is constantly trying to improve his financial status, he is prepared to proceed slowly and leave nothing to chance. The Earth Rat is probably not as adventurous as the other types of Rat and prefers to remain in familiar areas rather than rush headlong into something he knows little about. He is talented, conscientious and caring towards his loved ones, but at the same time can be self-conscious and worry a little too much about the image he is trying to project.

PROSPECTS FOR THE RAT IN 2003

The Chinese New Year starts on 1 February 2003. Until then, the old year, the Year of the Horse, is still making its presence felt.

The Rat can heave a great sigh of relief. After two sometimes tricky and indifferent years, his prospects are about to receive a major boost. However, in the meantime, he will need to proceed with some care.

In the Horse year (12 February 2002 to 31 January 2003) the Rat will have found progress difficult and not everything will have gone his way. However, the Rat is resourceful and will have made the most of the situations that have arisen. As the year draws to a close, he should take any chance to add to his skills and should be more forward looking in his outlook. With the aspects about to turn his way, what he accomplishes now can have a favourable impact on his future prospects.

The Rat also needs to remain aware of the views and feelings of those around him at this time. He is particularly adept in handling his relations with others, but he must not take support for granted or assume charm alone will be enough to sway others. He will need to work hard for results and to liaise closely with others both in his working and domestic life. Also, the Rat should avoid becoming so preoccupied that he does not spend as much time with his loved ones as he should. He does need to balance his activities.

In the closing months of the Horse year the Rat's social life is likely to become busier, especially from mid-November onwards, and this will help lift the Rat's spirits and in some cases lead to a widening of his social circle.

An area that requires care, though, is finance and the Rat should watch his outgoings, especially any new commitments that he takes on. This is not a time for risks, complacency or overspending.

The last two years will not have been the easiest for the Rat, but every cloud has a silver lining, and from mid-October onwards the clouds will at last begin to clear away.

The Year of the Goat starts on 1 February and is one which very much suits the Rat's drive, enterprise and creative approach. The experience he has gained during the preceding rather mixed years will now serve him well.

As the Goat year starts, the Rat should aim to draw a line under any past disappointments and failures. Now is the time to move forward. With a positive approach, renewed determination and his resourceful spirit, the Rat can set his own agenda and make this a rewarding and progressive year.

Work aspects are particularly encouraging for the Rat and whether he is in work or seeking it, he will find opportunities aplenty. This is a time when the Rat can make significant strides.

Any Rats who may be currently disillusioned in their present role will find that by using their initiative and looking for a position more in line with what they now want to do, they can bring about the improvement they seek. The onus rests with the Rat himself, but with so much going his way over the year, action taken now is likely to start a sequence of events favourable to him.

The Goat year favours creative pursuits and Rats whose work is in any way creative could enjoy some pleasing successes. Again, these Rats should not be fettered by past disappointments, but hold faith with their talents and promote their ideas. In 2003 initiative and enterprise *will* be well rewarded.

For work opportunities, the early months of the Goat year, May, June and the last quarter will all present some interesting opportunities.

The Rat will also gain considerable satisfaction from his own personal interests over the year, especially as they often represent a complete change from his everyday concerns. Despite the many demands on his time, he should make sure he sets a regular period aside to spend on activities he enjoys and which allow him to relax and unwind. If, because of other preoccupations, he has let his interests lapse, he should make it his resolution to rekindle them or take up something different this year. His personal interests really can bring a balance to his life as well as be a valuable tonic for him.

The Rat should also give some consideration to his well-being and if he does not get much exercise or is reliant on convenience foods, he should try to make some modifications. Medical guidance will help here. With the year holding such promise, the Rat should try to keep himself on good form.

The progress that the Rat will make in his work during the year will also lead to an improvement in his finances. In addition, many Rats could enjoy some financial good fortune, perhaps through a gift, the fruition of a policy or an unexpected bonus. Despite this upturn, the Rat would do well to manage his money carefully. Rather than be tempted to spend too hastily – and, despite his thriftiness, the Rat can be indulgent – he should set funds aside for specific purposes and, if he has borrowed, aim to reduce his debts. By using his money wisely, by the end of the year the Rat will find his financial situation healthier than it has been for some while. Also, if he is able to set funds aside for his future, he will, in time, come to appreciate this.

With his sociable and outgoing manner, the Rat particularly values his relations with others and in this respect too the Goat year will be a happier one for him. The Rat can look forward to many special and meaningful occasions with those dear to him. And although sometimes his domestic life may seem busy, with many demands upon his time, he can be particularly effective in drawing his family together and enjoying a good rapport. Family bonds are important to the Rat and by giving his time and making that all-important effort, he can make his family life both rich and rewarding.

The Rat can also enjoy a marked improvement in his social life over the year and for any Rats who may be feeling lonely, the year holds great promise. By going out more and perhaps joining interest groups, these Rats will find their social circle increasing, with many meeting someone who will quickly become special. March, April, August and September will all be favourable months for social matters, but the Goat year as a whole will represent a new and much brighter chapter in the Rat's social and personal life. As with other areas of his life, if the Rat has experienced some personal sadness or difficulty in recent times, 2003 is a year to move on and look forward.

With his resourceful nature, quick wits and considerable charm, the Rat has a great deal in his favour and the Goat year will see him once again come into his own and display some of his many fine qualities. It is a year for enterprise, action and progress, and by giving of his best and taking steps to improve his present position, the Rat can make it a rewarding and enjoyable time.

As far as the different types of Rat are concerned, the Goat year will see the *Metal Rat* in fine form. He will more than make up for any recent disappointments and will once again be able to use his skills and talents to good effect. For any Metal Rats who start the year disillusioned with their present situation, this is very much be time to draw a line under the past and move forward. The prospects are most encouraging and the Metal Rat should make the most of them.

The Goat year will offer considerable opportunity, particularly where work is concerned. For those Metal Rats who have been in the same position for a long time, promotion will beckon or there will be chances to take on different responsibilities. These Rats will also find that their experience, the contacts they have built up and often their good in-house knowledge will serve them well and allow them to make the progress they have been seeking for some time. With the aspects being so favourable, some Metal Rats will also find that the advances they make will quickly open up other possibilities as well. May and June will be two particularly interesting months and will set the pattern for further developments to follow on quickly.

Similarly, for those Metal Rats seeking work or wanting to move to a different type of position, the Goat year will present some excellent opportunities. However, to benefit, these Metal Rats should take the time to consider the sort of role they want and how they feel they can best use their skills. By following through their ideas, they will see some interesting possibilities emerging and, once given a chance, these Metal Rats will revel in their new role. For some, this might be a complete career change, but it is one they will relish. One of the key messages for the Metal Rat in 2003 is that it is a year which offers new opportunities and a chance to move forward.

With the aspects being so favourable, the Metal Rat could also benefit from any chance to widen or refresh his skills. He will find that this will not only help in the performance of his duties but also enhance his prospects. This is particularly true for those Metal Rats who may have been seeking work for some time.

The progress that the Metal Rat makes in his work will also lead to an upturn in his income. However, while this will be welcome, he does need to manage his finances with prudence. Rather than spend too readily, he should take the time to get his finances in order, looking at his obligations (and sometimes trying to reduce them) and checking that all his outgoings are really necessary as well as setting funds aside for specific purposes. The time the Metal Rat spends reviewing his finances will not only lead to some surprises as he discovers where some of his money actually does go, but will also help him to manage his money that much better. Also, with their resourceful nature, some Metal Rats may be able to supplement their income by putting a skill or interest they have to profitable use.

As far as his relations with others are concerned, this will be a much improved year for the Metal Rat and if any recent difficulties or differences of opinion have arisen, he will find a willingness to talk and address problems will do much to ease or resolve them. As so many Metal Rats will find, by setting aside time to be with their loved ones and encouraging interests that can be shared and enjoyed – including special treats and holidays – the year will bring some treasured times. As far as his domestic life is concerned, the Metal Rat's input, encouragement and thoughtfulness will be greatly appreciated. For those who may be alone or desiring companionship, the Goat year can mark the start of an exciting new chapter in their life, with a chance meeting resulting in a significant new friendship and much happiness. The months of April and May can be particularly interesting ones socially, but at any time the Goat year can spring agreeable surprises.

In so many respects, 2003 is a positive and progressive year for the Metal Rat. He has so much in his favour that he should use his abilities, personality and ideas to excellent effect. He should also not feel fettered by past disappointments or reversals. This is a year to make the most of himself and his opportunities.

TIP FOR THE YEAR
Be prepared to look forward and make the most of your strengths and talents. This is a progressive and favourable time.

The *Water Rat* has a very deep faith in himself and his abilities. He knows he has some unique talents and is capable of doing well in certain areas. And despite some of the setbacks and disappointments of recent years, his belief in himself will come into its own in the Goat year. It is a time for the Water Rat to emerge from the shadows and reach for new heights.

However, as the Goat year starts, the Water Rat would do well to look closely at his present position and consider how he would like to progress. Workwise, for some Water Rats this will mean advancing to a more responsible position within the organization in which they are based, while others will look elsewhere and, in some cases, completely change career. Whatever he decides upon, by following up his ideas, the Water Rat can make considerable headway this year and his experience, personable manner and belief in himself will all help him move forward. Those Water Rats seeking work should actively follow up any openings that interest them, even if they involve something totally new. And, if initial attempts do not go his way, the Water Rat will find that with persistence, new doors will be opened. For many, what happens in 2003 will start them off on a new track, one which offers a much brighter future. The message for all Water Rats in the Goat year is to decide what they want and then go after it in determined fashion.

Another factor which will help is the Water Rat's ability to get on well with others. In his quest, whether for work, promotion or a possible career change, if there is someone he knows who can help him, he should ask for advice. Often those he approaches will be delighted to assist and he will benefit from what he is told, the practical support he is given or a good word being put in for him. Throughout the year, the Water Rat must not forget that he does have some influential friends who can offer help should he need it.

The Water Rat's progress in his work will also lead to an improvement in his financial situation. As a result, he will feel able to go ahead with some purchases he has been considering, including an overhaul of his wardrobe (some-thing he will enjoy) and items for his home and loved ones. With this being a year of positive change, some Water Rats will also decide to move. However, while money will flow in, it will also flow out, and this is an area the Water Rat does need to watch. Despite the favourable aspects, this is not a year to become financially complacent. If he is able, the Water Rat should try to set a certain amount of money aside for the longer term. Regular savings, however small, will accumulate over the years and when he is older he may be thankful for them.

As far as the Water Rat's personal life is concerned, this will be a busy but rewarding year. His home life in particular will see much activity and whether he moves or remains in his present accommodation, there will often seem a very great deal for him to do. However busy, the Water Rat's home is a special place for him and he should make sure he takes time to appreciate it. In addition, by sharing interests and carrying out domestic projects with others in his household, the Water Rat will find these can be very satisfying to all concerned. This is especially true for some of the more practical projects which improve or add comfort to the home. Should the Water Rat find household tasks mounting up at any time, he should not hesitate to ask for further assistance. This particularly applies to those Water Rats with young children.

The Water Rat can also look forward to a pleasing social life and will value the support and camaraderie offered by his friends. He will not only enjoy meeting up and talking with them, but also some of the parties and social occasions that he attends. For those Water Rats who are seeking new friends and perhaps love, especially after some of disappointments of late, the Goat year offers great promise, with a chance meeting or introduction quickly becoming very special. For social matters the months of March, April, August and September are well aspected.

In so many respects, the Goat year will mark a major upturn in the Water Rat's fortunes and by making the most of himself and going after what he wants, he can make it a successful and personally rewarding year.

Do not be held back by past mistakes or reversals but resolve to move ahead, seize the initiative and make the most of your talents and ideas.

This will be an important year for the *Wood Rat* and can be a successful one too, but a great deal depends upon his attitude and organization. Over the year a lot will be demanded of him and in order to cope he will need to organize his time well and set about all he has to do in determined fashion.

For those Wood Rats in education, there will be a great deal of work to be covered. By setting about this at a steady and consistent pace, however, the Wood Rat will be pleased with his progress and results. In addition, by rising to the challenges, he will not only gain a great deal from what he learns but also discover new strengths, and he will be able to build on these, as well as the qualifications he obtains, in the years ahead.

For those Wood Rats in work or seeking work, again this will be an important year. Wood Rats already in a job should learn as much as they can about their duties and continue to build up their experience. By showing willing and initiative the young Wood Rat can greatly impress and mark himself out for future progress when opportunities do fall available. Wood Rats who are seeking work or who do not feel fulfilled in their present role should actively follow up other positions that they feel could be more interesting or offer better prospects. Admittedly, it may take the Wood Rat several attempts to secure an opening and what he is initially offered may be more routine than he might have liked, but it can form a useful platform on which to build. Also, whether in work or seeking it, the Wood Rat should take full advantage of any training opportunities he is given or ways in which he can extend his skills. What he learns now can help his future progress a great deal.

As far as money matters are concerned, with enterprise the Wood Rat can improve his position over the year. However, he still needs to be careful. He will want to do a lot on often limited means and will need to watch his outgoings. In some cases, economies will be called for and the Wood Rat may have to think carefully about certain items he may wish to acquire. However, by remaining aware of his position and avoiding unnecessary risks, he will be generally pleased with how he is able to manage.

This will be a favourable year for personal matters, with the Wood Rat finding himself much in demand with his friends and with many parties and other social occasions to attend. In addition to the good times he will have, he will be grateful for the support and camaraderie his friends offer. Wood Rats who may not feel as involved in the social scene as they would like will find that a friendship made early in the year will soon take on a special significance as well as raise their spirits and esteem. As the Wood Rat will find, the Goat year does have a very positive influence on many aspects of his life.

Domestically, too, the Wood Rat will value the support and advice of those around him. While he may sometimes feel that an age gap prevents a true understanding, those older than him have often experienced similar pressures and uncertainties and can give useful advice and encouragement. Also, if the Wood Rat has any ideas he is thinking about, particularly relating to travel or developing his personal interests, he should mention these, as those around him can offer helpful advice as well as sometimes assist in ways that the Wood Rat may not have envisaged.

The Goat year is a favourable one for the Wood Rat and by setting about his activities in a positive spirit and a consistent and organized way, he will be able to prepare for the future as well as greatly enjoy himself.

TIP FOR THE YEAR
Aim to build on your experience and if possible add to your qualifications. What is achieved in 2003 can be a great asset in years to come.

This can be a rewarding year for the *Fire Rat*, although to make the most of its encouraging aspects, he should give some thought to what he wants to do over the next 12 months. Drawing up plans will give more structure to the year as well as give him something purposeful to aim for. The plans can relate to almost any area of the Fire Rat's life, although those that will concern him most will probably be domestic and accommodation matters, travel and personal interests.

Domestically, this will certainly be an active year for the Fire Rat and he may well decide to tackle various projects in his home, including altering certain rooms as well as sorting through accumulated papers and belongings and so making his home better organized and more efficient. What is accomplished will bring him – and others – considerable satisfaction. Some Fire Rats will also decide to move in 2003, feeling that their present accommodation is not so suitable to their needs. The process will be time-consuming and put the Fire Rats under pressure, but once installed in their new accommodation, they will often find it easier to manage as well as enjoy finding out about their new area.

While accommodation matters will take up much time, the Fire Rat's domestic life will still be a source of considerable pleasure. He will enjoy following the progress of younger relations, including grandchildren or great-grandchildren, if he has them. Similarly, any interests he can share with others will also mean a great deal to him, with the late summer and last quarter of the year being a particularly gratifying time for domestic matters.

Another feature of the Goat year is the travel possibilities it offers and the many Fire Rats who enjoy visiting places of interest would do well to discuss their ideas and see what can be arranged. Some will also enjoy finding out more about their local area and visiting neighbouring parts. Whatever he decides to do, the Goat year will certainly give the Fire Rat every chance to satisfy his inquisitive nature and, if he wishes, to travel too. In addition, the Fire Rat will derive much satisfaction from his personal interests during the Goat year and should aim to develop them in some way. By doing something that will challenge him, whether tackling a new project or taking up something new, he will add another enjoyable element to the year, one which can help keep him sharp and pleasantly occupied.

The Fire Rat will also value his social life in 2003, particularly meeting up with others and some of the events he attends. Any Fire Rats who may be feeling lonely, perhaps after moving to a new area, should make every effort to go out and make contact with those of similar age and interests. Sometimes a local society or group would be worth joining. By taking action, these Fire Rats can do much to bring a new light into their lives and in many cases forge significant new friendships.

The Goat year does offer considerable promise for the Fire Rat, but to benefit he will need to give some thought to what he wants to do and then work towards it. With planning, though, this can be a rewarding, constructive and often enjoyable year.

TIP FOR THE YEAR
Make plans and set them in motion. By using your time well, you can make this a productive as well as satisfying year.

A lot will have happened to the *Earth Rat* in recent years. There will have been pressures and disappointments and at times he may have despaired of his situation and prospects. However, the Goat year will usher in a much more positive and settled phase and for quite a few Earth Rats it will be the start of a new chapter in their life.

Particularly interesting developments will occur in the Earth Rat's work. Many Earth Rats will have seen considerable change over the last 12 months, but the Goat year will allow them to build on that change and take the course of their career more into their own hands. Those Earth Rats in a comparatively new position will find the Goat year will give them a chance to become more established in their role and by carrying out their duties with enterprise and commitment, they will feel more inspired and motivated than for some time. Other Earth Rats will regard the

Goat year as the right time to take up a fresh challenge and to do something more in line with what they have been considering for some time. By making enquiries, they will find some interesting developments will follow. Not all the Earth Rat's attempts will go his way, however, and in the early part of the Goat year he does need to keep faith with his ideas and be aware of what is achievable. Some Earth Rats may decide to take early retirement or to switch to a position involving fewer hours and so will have the opportunity of pursuing personal activities they have wanted to do for some time. Indeed, one overriding characteristic of the Goat year is that it will offer the Earth Rat more control over his situation and so lead to a greater sense of satisfaction.

The Goat year also encourages the Earth Rat to make the most of his talents. He does possess creative skills and whether he uses them in his work or leisure time, he should make full use of them as well as promote his work. Whether he is keen on writing, art, music, photography, design or some other creative sphere, he can obtain some interesting and satisfying results this year.

This is also a favourable time for money matters, with the added bonus that many Earth Rats will receive some additional funds during 2003. As a result, the Earth Rat will often choose to spend money on himself, on travel and on replacing certain items in his home. However, while he will often be pleased with his purchases, he should avoid being too hasty. By taking the time to consider his options, he will often end up with a better deal than if he were to rush his purchases.

As far as the Earth Rat's personal life is concerned, again the year offers much promise. Domestically, many Earth

Rats can look forward to being involved in a family celebration and whether this is the marriage of a close relation or the birth of a grandchild, it will be a source of much pride and excitement. In addition, family members will often look to the Earth Rat for support and advice and his assistance will be much appreciated. As always, family matters will mean much to the Earth Rat and domestically the Goat year will be characterized by some special and often meaningful occasions.

The Earth Rat's social life too will be busier than for some while, with opportunities to go out and meet friends as well as go to a range of functions and gatherings. Any Earth Rats who may have kept themselves to themselves in recent years should make the effort to go out and enjoy themselves. This will add a whole new dimension to the year and many Earth Rats will find their social circle widening quite appreciably. For the lonely and unattached, there could also be a significant new friendship and the chance of romance.

In so many respects, the Goat year holds excellent prospects for the Earth Rat. However, to benefit, the Earth Rat should decide on how he would like his life to develop over the next 12 months and set about realizing his aims. With the aspects on his side, he can make this a pleasant and constructive year.

TIP FOR THE YEAR

Make the most of your interests, ideas and personal strengths. If they are put to good use, this can be a rewarding and positive time.

FAMOUS RATS

Ben Affleck, Alan Alda, Ursula Andress, Louis Armstrong, Charles Aznavour, Lauren Bacall, James Baldwin, Shirley Bassey, Kathy Bates, Irving Berlin, Silvio Berlusconi, Kenneth Branagh, Marlon Brando, Charlotte Brontë, Jackson Browne, Chris de Burgh, George H. Bush, Glen Campbell, David Carradine, Jimmy Carter, Maurice Chevalier, Aaron Copland, Cameron Diaz, David Duchovny, T. S. Eliot, Colin Firth, Clark Gable, Liam Gallagher, Gareth Gates, Hugh Grant, Geri Halliwell, Daryl Hannah, Thomas Hardy, Prince Harry, Vaclav Havel, Haydn, Charlton Heston, Buddy Holly, Mick Hucknall, Engelbert Humperdinck, Henrik Ibsen, Jeremy Irons, Jean-Michel Jarre, Danny Kaye, Gene Kelly, Kris Kristofferson, Lawrence of Arabia, Gary Lineker, Lord Andrew Lloyd Webber, Claude Monet, Richard Nixon, Sean Penn, Terry Pratchett, the Queen Mother, Lou Rawls, Vanessa Redgrave, Burt Reynolds, Rossini, William Shakespeare, Yves St Laurent, Tommy Steele, Donna Summer, James Taylor, Leo Tolstoy, Henri Toulouse-Lautrec, Spencer Tracy, Anthea Turner, the Prince of Wales, George Washington, Dennis Weaver, Richard Wilson, the Duke of York, Emile Zola.

19 FEBRUARY 1901 ⁓ 7 FEBRUARY 1902   *Metal Ox*

6 FEBRUARY 1913 ⁓ 25 JANUARY 1914   *Water Ox*

24 JANUARY 1925 ⁓ 12 FEBRUARY 1926   *Wood Ox*

11 FEBRUARY 1937 ⁓ 30 JANUARY 1938   *Fire Ox*

29 JANUARY 1949 ⁓ 16 FEBRUARY 1950   *Earth Ox*

15 FEBRUARY 1961 ⁓ 4 FEBRUARY 1962   *Metal Ox*

3 FEBRUARY 1973 ⁓ 22 JANUARY 1974   *Water Ox*

20 FEBRUARY 1985 ⁓ 8 FEBRUARY 1986   *Wood Ox*

7 FEBRUARY 1997 ⁓ 27 JANUARY 1998   *Fire Ox*

THE
OX

THE PERSONALITY OF THE OX

Somehow I can't believe that there are any heights that can't be scaled by a person who knows the secret of making his dreams come true. This special secret, it seems to me, can be summarized in four 'C's. They are Curiosity, Confidence, Courage and Constancy, and the greatest of these is confidence. When you believe in a thing, believe in it all the way.

Walt Disney, an Ox

The Ox is born under the signs of equilibrium and tenacity. He is a hard and conscientious worker and sets about everything he does in a resolute, methodical and determined manner. He has considerable leadership qualities and is often admired for his tough and uncompromising nature. He knows what he wants to achieve in life and, as far as possible, will not be deflected from his ultimate objective.

The Ox takes his responsibilities and duties very seriously. He is decisive and quick to take advantage of any opportunity that comes his way. He is also sincere and places a great deal of trust in his friends and colleagues. He is, nevertheless, something of a loner. He is a quiet and private individual and often keeps his thoughts to himself. He also cherishes his independence and prefers to set about things in his own way rather than be bound by the dictates of others or be influenced by outside pressures.

The Ox tends to have a calm and tranquil nature, but if something angers him or he feels that someone has let him down, he can have a fearsome temper. He can also be stubborn and obstinate and this can lead him into conflict with others. Usually the Ox will succeed in getting his own way, but should things go against him, he is a poor loser and will take any defeat or setback extremely badly.

The Ox is often a deep thinker and rather studious. He is not particularly renowned for his sense of humour and does not take kindly to new gimmicks or anything too innovative. The Ox is too solid and traditional for that and he prefers to stick to the more conventional norm.

His home is very important to him and in some respects he treats it as a private sanctuary. His family tends to be closely knit and the Ox will make sure that each member does their fair share around the house. The Ox tends to be a hoarder, but he is always well organized and neat. He also places great importance on punctuality and there is nothing that infuriates him more than to be kept waiting – particularly if it is due to someone's inefficiency. The Ox can be a hard taskmaster!

Once settled in a job or house the Ox will quite happily remain there for many years. He does not like change and he is also not particularly keen on travel. He does, however, enjoy gardening and other outdoor pursuits and he will often spend much of his spare time out of doors. The Ox is usually an excellent gardener and whenever possible he will always make sure he has a large area of ground to maintain. He usually prefers to live in the country rather than the town.

Due to his dedicated and dependable nature, the Ox will usually do well in his chosen career, providing he is given enough freedom to act on his own initiative. He invariably does well in politics, agriculture and in careers which need specialized training. The Ox is also very gifted in the arts and many Oxen have enjoyed considerable success as musicians or composers.

The Ox is not as outgoing as some and it often takes him a long time to establish friendships and feel relaxed in another person's company. His courtships are likely to be long, but once he is settled he will remain devoted and loyal to his partner. The Ox is particularly well suited to those born under the signs of the Rat, Rabbit, Snake and Rooster. He can also establish a good relationship with the Monkey, Dog, Pig and another Ox, but he will find that he has little in common with the whimsical and sensitive Goat. He will also find it difficult to get on with the Horse, Dragon and Tiger – the Ox prefers a quiet and peaceful existence and those born under these three signs tend to be a little too lively and impulsive for his liking.

The female Ox has a kind and caring nature, and her home and family are very much her pride and joy. She always tries to do her best for her partner and can be a most conscientious and loving parent. She is an excellent organizer and also a very determined person who will often succeed in getting what she wants in life. She usually has a deep interest in the arts and is often a talented artist or musician.

The Ox is a very down-to-earth character. He is sincere, loyal and unpretentious. He can, however, be rather reserved and to some he may appear distant and aloof. He has a quiet nature, but underneath he is very strong-willed and ambitious. He has the courage of his convictions and is often prepared to stand up for what he believes is right, regardless of the consequences. He inspires confidence and trust and throughout his life he will rarely be short of people who are ready to support him or who admire his strong and resolute manner.

THE FIVE DIFFERENT TYPES OF OX

In addition to the 12 signs of the Chinese zodiac, there are five elements and these have a strengthening or moderating influence on the sign. The effects of the five elements on the Ox are described below, together with the years in which the elements were exercising their influence. Therefore all Oxen born in 1901 and 1961 are Metal Oxen, those born in 1913 and 1973 are Water Oxen, and so on.

Metal Ox: 1901, 1961

This Ox is confident and very strong-willed. He can be blunt and forthright in his views and is not afraid of speaking his mind. He sets about his objectives with a dogged determination, but he can become so involved in his various activities that he is oblivious to the thoughts and feelings of those around him, and this can sometimes be to his detriment. He is honest and dependable and will never promise more than he can deliver. He has a good appreciation of the arts and usually has a small circle of very good and loyal friends.

Water Ox: 1913, 1973

This Ox has a sharp and penetrating mind. He is a good organizer and sets about his work in a methodical manner. He is not as narrow-minded as some of the other types of Ox and is more willing to involve others in his plans and aspirations. He usually has very high moral standards and is often attracted to careers in public service. He is a good judge of character and has such a friendly and persuasive manner that he usually experiences little difficulty in securing his objectives. He is popular and has an excellent way with children.

Wood Ox: 1925, 1985

The Wood Ox conducts himself with an air of dignity and authority and will often take a leading role in any enterprise in which he becomes involved. He is very self-confident and is direct in his dealings with others. He does, however, have a quick temper and has no hesitation in speaking his mind. He has tremendous drive and will-power and has an extremely good memory. The Wood Ox is particularly loyal and devoted to the members of his family and has a most caring nature.

Fire Ox: 1937, 1997

The Fire Ox has a powerful and assertive personality and is a hard and conscientious worker. He holds strong views and has very little patience when things do not go his own way. He can also get carried away in the excitement of the moment and does not always take into account the views of those around him. He nevertheless has many leadership qualities and will often reach positions of power, eminence and wealth. He usually has a small group of loyal and close friends and is very devoted to his family.

Earth Ox: 1949

This Ox sets about everything he does in a sensible and level-headed manner. He is ambitious, but also realistic in his aims and is often prepared to work long hours in order to secure his objectives. He is shrewd in financial and business matters and is a very good judge of character. He has a quiet nature and is greatly admired for his sincerity and integrity. He is also very loyal to his family and friends and his views and opinions are often sought.

PROSPECTS FOR THE OX IN 2003

The Chinese New Year starts on 1 February 2003. Until then, the old year, the Year of the Horse, is still making its presence felt.

The Horse year (12 February 2002 to 31 January 2003) will have been a variable one for the Ox and while it will not have been without its successes, the Ox will have had to work hard for them. The Horse year does require the Ox to be on his mettle as well as show some flexibility in his outlook.

In what remains of the Horse year, the Ox will need to proceed carefully and cautiously. In his work he should concentrate on the areas he knows best while remaining aware of any changes under consideration and of the attitudes of others. The Ox might like to retain a certain independence in what he does, but taken too far it can result in him becoming isolated and missing out on chances to progress. In the Horse year the Ox does need to show some team spirit. However, there will be chances to take on new responsibilities as the year draws to a close. The Horse year does reward the worker, but for the Ox, the rewards in this particular year can be late in coming.

The Ox will also need to handle his finances with care. Although he is usually meticulous in keeping track of his financial position, the closing months of the Horse year can be a demanding time. To help ease some of the burden, the Ox should consider spreading out some of his seasonal purchases as well as saving for specific expenses. Fortunately, his usual prudence will work to his advantage, but financially the Horse year does require careful management.

The latter part of the Horse year will be a pleasing time for personal matters, however, and the Ox will have good reason to value the support of his friends and loved ones. If he is forthcoming about his ideas, he will gain much from the input of others at this time. He can also look forward to enjoying some fine domestic and social occasions, with the period from mid-October onwards marking an upturn in his social life.

The Ox should, however, give some consideration to his well-being as the Horse year draws to a close. In the face of pressure, he does tend to drive himself hard, and while he may be blessed with a strong constitution, he should make sure he has sufficient rest and balances his activities.

Although the Horse year will have demanded much from the Ox, his efforts and diligence will have allowed him to make pleasing progress as well as widen his experience. And amid the pressures, there will have been occasions that will have meant a great deal to him personally.

The Year of the Goat starts on 1 February and is another one which will test the Ox. However, while the aspects may be mixed, the Ox will nevertheless gain much from the year and will enjoy some worthy successes. Indeed, part of his character is his redoubtable spirit. The Ox likes to work for his results, believing it rests with him to secure what he wants.

One area which will particularly challenge the Ox is his work. In 2003 many Oxen will see changes taking place and will feel uneasy with some of the developments under consideration. The Ox likes stability and definite decisions, not the 'maybe' and 'might happen' which he will frequently hear over the year.

However, the Ox is never one to stand idly by and over the year he will often consider his options. Some Oxen will decide to remain where they are and adapt as well as they can to any changes. While sometimes uneasy, these Oxen will find their specialist skills and in-house knowledge will serve them well and place them in a good position for any new openings that arise. Also, colleagues will often look to the Ox for advice and assistance, and by co-operating he will not only win the gratitude of many but also enhance his longer-term prospects. Other Oxen will decide to move from their present position and seek new challenges. For these Oxen, as well as those currently looking for work, the way ahead may not be straightforward. In some cases, competition for posts could be fierce or the Oxen could lack the necessary skills. However, they should not lose heart. By persisting and considering *all* the possibilities, they will often be able to find a position which is just right for them, one which will not only be an interesting challenge (something which always brings out the best in the Ox) but will also allow them to extend their skills and offer potential for future development. Although some parts of 2003 will be disheartening, when the Ox is given a chance, he will find the way ahead can suddenly become brighter and full of possibility. The months of April, July and October could, in particular, see interesting developments.

In view of the variable aspects and the uncertainties he will face, it is important that the Ox looks after himself during the Goat year. Difficult though it might sometimes be, he should not let himself become totally preoccupied by work matters, but actively involve himself in other pursuits. It is important that he has a release valve. In some cases, a completely new interest could be the ideal tonic. Regular exercise could also be of benefit, allowing the Ox to let off steam as well as maintain his fitness. Whether this exercise comes in the form of sport, yoga or tai chi, jogging, swimming or a brisk walk, the Ox can find it satisfying and beneficial. However, before starting any new physical activity, he should obtain medical guidance on the best way to proceed.

As far as personal interests are concerned, many Oxen have a good appreciation of music and for those who wish to develop this, by learning an instrument, adding to their musical skills or even composing and performing, the Goat year can be particularly supportive. The year does favour the arts and will certainly contain opportunities for the Ox to further his more creative talents, whether in music or some other sphere.

As far as financial matters are concerned, this will be another year in which the Ox will need to remain careful. During 2003 he could face several expensive periods, especially in connection with his accommodation, and if he borrows, he will need to check the obligations he is taking on and that he is getting the best terms. If he has any doubts, he should seek advice. And while the Ox is not usually disposed towards risks, if he is considering any speculative venture or investment, again he needs to be clear about the implications. Without such care, money could well be lost. Oxen, take note.

One of the more favourably aspected areas of the year, however, will concern the Ox's relations with others. The Ox does choose his friends and associates with care and while he may not be particularly outgoing, those around him do mean a great deal to him and their love and respect will prove important throughout the year.

The Ox's home life in particular will bring him much contentment. Not only will he be grateful for the support he is given, but he will also appreciate the opportunity to discuss any concerns and decisions that he has to take. If he is forthcoming, he will be able to benefit from the assistance and advice of others. He will though as usual, play a full and valuable role in homelife, encouraging others, arranging activities and ensuring his home is run in an efficient and orderly way. The Ox's organizational skills, together with his caring and considerate attitude, will contribute to what can be a satisfying and rewarding domestic life.

The Ox's social life too holds much promise. Although the Ox may not always be the most active of socializers, preferring the company of those he knows well, some occasions he attends in the first quarter of the Goat year will give his social life a much needed fillip. Some Oxen will find themselves starting to go out more regularly and will enjoy widening their social circle. For those who have kept themselves to themselves in the past, a new friendship or romance could add an exciting new dimension to the year. February and March can be particularly good months for meeting others, with April, November and December seeing considerable social activity. For those Oxen who start the year in low spirits, hope, happiness and in many cases a new start are all on offer.

Although the Goat year will be a variable one for the Ox and will see uncertainties connected with his work, the Ox's redoubtable qualities will enable him to emerge with much to his credit. Many Oxen will be able to use the events of the year to their advantage, particularly by taking on new challenges. And all Oxen will find that their personal life will do much to brighten the year. For all its difficulties, the Goat year is actually one which holds some interesting possibilities for the Ox.

As far as the different types of Ox are concerned, this will be an important year for the *Metal Ox*. Although not all his activities may go as well as he may like, the year will certainly not be without its value. In addition, what the Metal Ox achieves now can do much to prepare for the success he will enjoy over the next few years. In this respect the Goat year can often mark the beginning of a much brighter chapter in his life.

One area which will see considerable activity will be the Metal Ox's work. Changes will be in the offing and for one who so likes stability, the year could contain periods of uncertainty. Despite this, some Metal Oxen will decide to remain in their existing position, concentrating on what they know and do best. While their expertise and commitment will continue to impress, these Metal Oxen should still remain aware of any proposals under consideration and give thought to how they would like their career to progress. This is just not a time to immerse themselves in their own duties so much that they ignore what is going on around them or fail to give adequate consideration to their future. Something they accomplish or think of now can have significant consequences in the latter part of 2003 and the more progressive Monkey year that follows.

Other Metal Oxen will decide the time has come to try a different type of work and for these Oxen, as well as those currently seeking work, the Goat year will hold some interesting developments. When they see a vacancy that interests them, they should make an application and await results. While not all their attempts may go their way, many will find themselves being given constructive advice, alerted to other possibilities or able to strengthen their interview technique. To make headway in 2003 *will* require patience and persistence, but the Metal Ox will gain a great deal by venturing forth. Opportunities will often arise through a curious twist in circumstances and once the Metal Ox has been offered a position, he will find it an important base for the future. March, April, July and October are all favoured for promoting ideas and making applications.

Throughout the year the Metal Ox does need to be his careful self when dealing with money matters. Some parts of 2003 will be expensive and could involve the Metal Ox entering into new commitments and agreements. Although he is usually thorough, he does need to check the terms and make allowances for the obligations involved. Financial matters and paperwork do need care. This is not a time for risks.

The Metal Ox's personal life is well aspected, however, and he will be thankful for the love and support of those around him, and grateful for their advice when he has important decisions or matters concerning him. In some respects, being so resolute and independent-minded, the Metal Ox can be a loner, but those who are important to him are very much his prop and he will have good reason to be thankful for their assistance and love during the Goat year. The Metal Ox can also look forward to some important family events which will mean a great deal to him. And while there will be many demands on him, he should always make sure he devotes sufficient time to his loved ones and to encouraging mutual and meaningful activities.

The Metal Ox's social life is also favourably aspected, with some of the events that he attends often surpassing expectations and in some cases leading to a wider social circle. Although some Metal Oxen have a tendency to keep themselves to themselves, in 2003 they would do well to lower their reserve a little and go out more. An interest that brings them into contact with others, a new friendship or a new romance can do so much to brighten up their life that they really should make the effort.

Although the Goat year will not be without its difficulties and pressures, what the Metal Ox accomplishes now can do much to usher in a particularly successful and progressive chapter in his life, with his prospects brightening from October onwards.

TIP FOR THE YEAR
Take careful note of developing situations and be prepared to adapt. With care and a flexible outlook, what occurs can have important and far-reaching benefits.

This will mark the thirtieth year of the *Water Ox* and it will find many in reflective mood and feeling unfulfilled in some way. In the Goat year all Water Oxen should decide to take concerted action to make more of themselves. As the Water Ox has realized for some time, achieving his aims does depend upon his own efforts and the Goat year will be very much a time of reappraisal and venturing forth in sometimes different directions.

One area which will figure prominently will be work. Here many Water Oxen will be looking to advance and to make changes. However, before taking any irrevocable steps, the Water Ox should look closely at his present position and work out how he can build on it. Rather than abandon the valuable experience he has gained, he should investigate other ways of putting this to good use. In some cases, by talking to senior colleagues or seeking out those in the type of work he wants to enter, he can be given some useful advice as well as be altered to possible openings. For all Water Oxen, the message of the Goat year is to consider possibilities and then take action. Admittedly, progress will not come automatically and the Water Ox will need to remain persistent, but his efforts and initiative will be rewarded in the end. This also applies to those Water Oxen currently seeking work and those who have a particular ambition or goal they wish to reach. By remaining determined and going after the opportunities that interest them, they will often gain a new platform on which to build. The months of April, June, July and October will see some particularly interesting developments as far as work matters are concerned.

The Goat year does call for care when dealing with finance, however. Although many Water Oxen will see an increase in their income, they will still have many commitments to meet and 2003 will require careful budgeting. Fortunately, the Water Ox's methodical and disciplined manner will help, but he would do well to keep an account of his income and outgoings and make early allowance for forthcoming expenses. With careful management, problems can be avoided, but this is certainly a year for restraint and watchfulness.

More positively aspected is the Water Ox's personal life, with both his home and social life bringing him much pleasure over the year. Domestically, the Water Ox will do much to support those close to him and he will often be called upon to advise or help others in some way. The Water Ox does indeed have a special place in the hearts of many and the assistance he gives to his family will be valued in more ways than he may realize. Also, if any practical projects he has in mind for his home and garden can be carried out jointly, it will help to make the end result more satisfying for all concerned. In the Goat year, the Water Ox's domestic life will be busy but rewarding.

As for his social life, although the Water Ox may be selective about the events he attends, when he does go out he can look forward to some fine times. Any Water Oxen who may have been leading sometimes lonely existences really should make the effort to socialize more and perhaps consider joining a local group or society. By making the effort, they will soon find themselves building up new friendships and bringing a brighter dimension into their life. For the lonely, 2003 does hold good prospects.

Another area the Water Ox should not ignore is his own personal interests, especially those that draw on his more creative talents. Although he will have many demands on his time, these can bring an important balance to his life as well as help him to relax and unwind.

Overall, this will be an important year for the Water Ox, with what he achieves now helping to set him on the road to some fine successes over the next few years. The Water Ox knows he has much to give and in 2003 his faith in himself will certainly start to propel him forward. And this is only the beginning...

TIP FOR THE YEAR
Begin to set your thoughts and ideas in motion. Although results may not be immediately forthcoming, what is started now can unlock great possibilities in the near future.

This will be a variable year for the *Wood Ox*. It will contain some pleasing and memorable moments, but mixed in with these will be some demanding situations. However, although the year will ask a great deal of the Wood Ox, he will emerge from it with some useful gains to his credit and will be able to build upon these in the next few years. With his conscientious nature and likeable manner the Wood Ox has a great future ahead of him and in the Goat year he will be preparing the way for the successes he will soon enjoy.

For the many Wood Oxen in education, there will be important exams to take, with the results often determining their more immediate future. With so much at stake, these Wood Oxen should aim to study consistently and give adequate time to revision and course work. Although the workload will often be great and there will be many other things the Wood Ox might prefer to be doing, by making the effort, especially in the time leading up to exams, his diligence and discipline will be rewarded. Also, when studying, the Wood Ox could find it helpful to keep the end result in mind and remember the benefits that certain qualifications can bring.

In addition to exams, many Wood Oxen will be giving thought to their future, with some deciding to continue their education while others will look for work. Those Wood Oxen deciding to study further should give thought to the profession they wish to enter and the most appropriate course for them to take. In some cases, professional organizations or advisers will be able to assist. If the Wood Ox has not yet have decided on a particular career, as will often be the case, he should follow his inclination and select courses which interest him. He is still at a young age and showing a willingness to learn will in itself prepare him for when he does decide to seek employment.

Also, with important decisions to take over the year, the Wood Ox should be prepared to discuss his options with his family and tutors rather than keep his thoughts to himself, as may be the case with some more reclusive Wood Oxen. By being forthcoming, the Wood Ox will not only receive more support and input but will also feel reassured to some extent.

For those Wood Oxen in work or seeking it, the Goat year will also contain some interesting developments, though there may be some false starts as well. Sometimes the positions these Wood Oxen are offered will not develop in the manner they wanted. Also, certain types of work may prove harder to enter than they envisaged. In 2003 the Wood Ox will learn some difficult lessons as well as sometimes rethink his aims. However, at no time should he lose heart. He is just starting out on his career and it will take him time to find his niche. The particular value of the Goat year is that it will allow the Wood Ox to try his hand at several different things and give him an indication of where his future lies. June, July, October and November will see some interesting opportunities as far as his work is concerned.

The Wood Ox will need to be careful in money matters during the year and at times will find his resources considerably stretched. He should be wary of taking any risks and dubious about any 'get rich quick' schemes. Also, when taking on any new agreement, he needs to check the small print and be sure of the obligations he is taking on.

Money matters do need careful management throughout the year.

The aspects concerning the Wood Ox's personal life are, though, much brighter and he will enjoy some great times with his friends. For those Wood Oxen who move during the year, perhaps for work or education, the prospects are especially good for making new and in some cases important friends. Although many Wood Oxen are quiet and sometimes reserved, their likeable personality will shine through over the year and, in some cases, serious romance or a livelier social life will beckon. During the year the Wood Ox will find himself much in demand, with February, March and last quarter being especially active socially.

There will also be some Wood Oxen who decide to travel over the year, in some cases quite widely. In order to make the most of their time away, they should plan their itinerary, finding out about the places they intend to visit and making sure they are leaving adequately equipped. Travelwise, the Goat year can provide some wonderful experiences and the better prepared the Wood Ox is, the better his time away will be.

In fact preparation is very much the key word for the Wood Ox in 2003. Through careful preparation in all he does, he can look forward to some pleasing accomplishments as well as future progress. And while the Goat year will contain some difficult decisions as well as be a tricky one financially, the Wood Ox will be well supported by others and can look forward to a rewarding social life and often romance as well.

Be adventurous, inquisitive and bold. By following through ideas and trying things out, you can discover a great deal.

The *Fire Ox* has a very determined nature and sets about his activities in an orderly and precise way. However, the Goat year is one which will test his patience, which is not one of his strong points! In 2003 he could find that some of his activities are beset by niggling problems and that not all his plans work out as he envisaged.

The Goat year will certainly have its troublesome aspects, but there is much the Fire Ox can do to limit them. When he has ideas he wants to try out, no matter what area of his life they concern, he should discuss them with those around him. Although, in true Fire Ox fashion, he may be keen to get things moving, prior consultation can do much to prevent possible misunderstandings and subsequent problems. Also, the Fire Ox should be receptive to any feedback he is given. In 2003 it is essential that he acts as far as possible with the support of others.

One area which will see considerable activity will be accommodation. The Fire Ox is likely to carry out some alterations, including replacing some furnishings and equipment and generally smartening certain rooms. By considering the possibilities with those in his household, he will find the changes that much easier to make. However, in keeping with the variable aspects, the Fire Ox could find certain plans do take longer to achieve than he anticipated, and where practical activities are concerned, he would be wise not to set too tight a deadline on their completion. Also, should he make any major purchases or authorize any work to be carried out, he should make sure his instructions are clearly understood and that he is aware of any obligations he might be taking on. This is a year for vigilance.

As always, however, the Fire Ox will take a fond interest in the activities of his loved ones and some of their successes will mean a great deal to him. He will find that any advice and support he can offer will be particularly valued.

Although some of the Fire Ox's activities will prove time-consuming, especially in relation to his home, he should still make sure that he sets a regular time aside for his own personal interests, especially if they allow him to draw on his creative or practical talents or develop his skills in any way. If there has been a new interest that has been intriguing him or a skill he is keen to develop, this would be an excellent year in which to take action. In the Goat year, the Fire Ox's personal interests can provide him with much pleasure and he should not neglect them. Also, for the many Fire Oxen who are fond of gardening, this will be a good year for enjoying the garden.

With finance and important paperwork, however, care is needed. Throughout the year the Fire Ox should keep his records in order, deal promptly with forms and correspondence and check up on anything that may be giving him concern or is not clear. Admittedly, the Fire Ox's careful manner can prevent problems from arising in this area, but vigilance is necessary. Also, if he is able, he would do well to set some money aside for a holiday later in 2003. Not only will he benefit from the break, but he could also be very taken with some of the places he visits.

Although the Goat year will have its difficulties for the Fire Ox, it will not be without its pleasures. By consulting and carrying out activities with others, devoting time to personal interests and taking advantage of travel opportunities, the Fire Ox will certainly have some agreeable and personally rewarding times.

TIP FOR THE YEAR
Liaise with others. Much can happen as a result and this can also help strengthen the rapport with those around.

The *Earth Ox* likes to set about his activities in an orderly and organized way but, as he will soon experience, the Goat year is one which will bring unexpected developments. Plans may not materialize as he anticipated and he could face delays as well as niggling concerns. However, although the Goat year will be frustrating at times, by making the best of the situations that arise, the Earth Ox can still achieve a great deal.

Many Earth Oxen will see important developments in their work and will be required to adjust to new practices and procedures or to take on greater duties. Although the Earth Ox may have some misgivings about this, by being willing to adapt and learn, he will find some of what he is asked to take on will work in his favour, especially as it will often allow him to draw on his skills and experience in a new way. The changes can indeed open up new possibilities and work out far better than the Earth Ox may have initially thought.

Those Earth Oxen who decide to change jobs or are seeking employment will also see some interesting developments over the year. Not only should they follow up any openings that particularly interest them, but also any training they are eligible for. By learning new skills and keeping their existing ones up to date, they can enhance their prospects. While sometimes difficult, the Goat year can serve the Earth Ox well, but he must be receptive to the possibilities that exist. The Goat year also favours creativity and any Earth Ox who has a creative interest, whether vocationally or as a hobby, should promote his ideas. By taking the initiative, he may achieve some interesting results. If he feels inclined to write about his experiences or pass on some specialist knowledge, he could find this too could become an absorbing occupation.

The Earth Ox is generally careful in money matters, but in the Goat year he must not to let his vigilance slip. Sometimes his outgoings could prove greater than he thought, or failure to read small print or deal promptly with finance or tax-related forms could be to his detriment. In financial matters, the Earth Ox needs to be both thorough and cautious.

The Earth Ox's personal life is, though, more favourably aspected and he can enjoy some happy times with his loved ones. However, this does require input from the Earth Ox himself and he should be careful not to become so involved in his own activities that he does not pay as much attention to those around him as he should. In some cases tackling domestic projects jointly or taking up a new interest with a loved one can lead to rewarding times.

The Earth Ox should also make sure that his social life does not get squeezed out because of other demands. Time spent with friends can help him unwind and do him good. While some Earth Oxen can be reclusive, by making the effort to go out, they can give a lift to the year. For those who are feeling lonely, the Goat year holds great promise, but to find new friends or romance, the Earth Ox *must* mix with others. Socially, the months from February to April and the last quarter of the year are favourably aspected.

Although the Goat year will contain its frustrations, provided the Earth Ox is prepared to adapt to the situations that arise, he will not only do well but also sow the seeds for the more successful times that await in the following year. So much does, though, depend upon his own attitude.

TIP FOR THE YEAR
By being accommodating and showing a willing spirit, you can strengthen your position and prospects and considerably enhance your reputation.

FAMOUS OXEN

Robert Altman, Hans Christian Andersen, Johann Sebastian Bach, Warren Beatty, Kate Beckinsale, Napoleon Bonaparte, Rory Bremner, Benjamin Britten, Albert Camus, Jim Carrey, Johnny Carson, Barbara Cartland, Charlie Chaplin, Melanie Chisholm, George Clooney, Martin Clunes, Jean Cocteau, Natalie Cole, Bill Cosby, Tom Courtenay, Tony Curtis, Diana, Princess of Wales, Marlene Dietrich, Walt Disney, Patrick Duffy, Harry Enfield, Jane Fonda, Gerald Ford, Edward Fox, Michael J. Fox, Richard Gere, Maurice Gibb, Robin Gibb, Handel, King Harald V of Norway, Adolf Hitler, Dustin Hoffman, Anthony Hopkins, Saddam Hussein, Billy Joel, Don Johnson, Lionel Jospin,

King Juan Carlos of Spain, B. B. King, Mark Knopfler, Burt Lancaster, k. d. Lang, Jessica Lange, Jack Lemmon, Nicholas Lyndhurst, Kate Moss, Alison Moyet, Eddie Murphy, Paul Newman, Jack Nicholson, Leslie Nielsen, Billy Ocean, Gwyneth Paltrow, Oscar Peterson, Colin Powell, Robert Redford, Lionel Richie, Rubens, Greg Rusedski, Meg Ryan, Monica Seles, Jean Sibelius, Sissy Spacek, Bruce Springsteen, Rod Steiger, Meryl Streep, Lady Thatcher, Scott F. Turow, Dick van Dyke, Vincent van Gogh, Gore Vidal, Minette Walters, Zoë Wanamaker, Sigourney Weaver, the Duke of Wellington, Barbara Windsor, W. B. Yeats.

8 FEBRUARY 1902 〜 28 JANUARY 1903   *Water Tiger*

26 JANUARY 1914 〜 13 FEBRUARY 1915   *Wood Tiger*

13 FEBRUARY 1926 〜 1 FEBRUARY 1927   *Fire Tiger*

31 JANUARY 1938 〜 18 FEBRUARY 1939   *Earth Tiger*

17 FEBRUARY 1950 〜 5 FEBRUARY 1951   *Metal Tiger*

5 FEBRUARY 1962 〜 24 JANUARY 1963   *Water Tiger*

23 JANUARY 1974 〜 10 FEBRUARY 1975   *Wood Tiger*

9 FEBRUARY 1986 〜 28 JANUARY 1987   *Fire Tiger*

28 JANUARY 1998 〜 15 FEBRUARY 1999   *Earth Tiger*

THE
TIGER

THE PERSONALITY OF THE TIGER

We all have ability. The difference is how we use it.
Stevie Wonder, a Tiger

The Tiger is born under the sign of courage. He is a charismatic figure and usually holds very firm views. He is strong-willed and determined, and sets about most of his activities with tremendous energy and enthusiasm. He is very alert and quick-witted and his mind is forever active. He is a highly original thinker and is nearly always brimming with new ideas or full of enthusiasm for some new project or scheme.

The Tiger adores challenges and loves to get involved in anything which he thinks has an exciting future or which catches his imagination. He is prepared to take risks and does not like to be bound either by convention or the dictates of others. The Tiger likes to be free to act as he chooses and at least once during his life he will throw caution to the wind and go off and do the things he wants to do.

The Tiger does, however, have a somewhat restless nature. Even though he is often prepared to throw himself wholeheartedly into a project, his initial enthusiasm can soon wane if he sees something more appealing. He can also be rather impulsive and there will be occasions in his life when he acts in a manner which he later regrets. If the Tiger were to think things through or be prepared to persevere in his various activities, he would almost certainly enjoy a greater degree of success.

Fortunately, the Tiger is lucky in most of his enterprises, but should things not work out as he had hoped, he is liable to suffer from severe bouts of depression and it will often take him a long time to recover. His life often consists of a series of ups and downs.

The Tiger is, however, very adaptable. He has an adventurous spirit and rarely stays in the same place for long. In the early stages of his life he is likely to try his hand at several different jobs and he will also change his residence fairly frequently.

The Tiger is very honest and open in his dealings with others. He hates any sort of hypocrisy or falsehood. He is also well known for being blunt and forthright and has no hesitation in speaking his mind. He can be most rebellious at times, particularly against any form of petty authority, and while this can lead him into conflict with others, he is never one to shrink from an argument or avoid standing up for what he believes is right.

The Tiger is a natural leader and can invariably rise to the top of his chosen profession. He does not, however, care for anything too bureaucratic or detailed and he also does not like to obey orders. He can be stubborn and obstinate, and throughout his life he likes to retain a certain amount of independence in his actions and be responsible to no one but himself. He likes to consider that all his achievements are due to his own efforts and unless he cannot avoid it, he will rarely ask for support from others.

Ironically, despite his self-confidence and leadership qualities, the Tiger can be indecisive and will often delay making a major decision until the very last moment. He can also be sensitive to criticism.

Although the Tiger is capable of earning large sums of money, he is rather a spendthrift and does not always put his money to its best use. He can also be most generous and will often shower lavish gifts on friends and relations.

The Tiger cares very much for his reputation and the image that he tries to project. He carries himself with an air of dignity and authority and enjoys being the centre of attention. He is very adept at attracting publicity, both for himself and for the causes he supports.

The Tiger often marries young and he will find himself best suited to those born under the signs of the Pig, Dog, Horse and Goat. He can also get on well with the Rat, Rabbit and Rooster, but will find the Ox and Snake a bit too quiet and too serious for his liking, and he will be highly irritated by the Monkey's rather mischievous and inquisitive ways. The Tiger will also find it difficult to get on with another Tiger or a Dragon – both partners will want to dominate the relationship and could find it difficult to compromise on even the smallest of matters.

The Tigress is lively, witty and a marvellous hostess at parties. She is usually most attractive and takes great care over her appearance. She can be a very doting mother and while she believes in letting her children have their freedom, she makes an excellent teacher and will ensure that her children are well brought up and want for nothing. Like her male counterpart, she has numerous interests and likes to have sufficient independence and freedom to go off and do the things that she wants to do. She also has a most caring and generous nature.

The Tiger has many commendable qualities. He is honest, courageous and often a source of inspiration for others. Providing he can curb the wilder excesses of his restless nature, he is almost certain to lead a most fulfilling and satisfying life.

THE FIVE DIFFERENT TYPES OF TIGER

In addition to the 12 signs of the Chinese zodiac, there are five elements and these have a strengthening or moderating influence on the sign. The effects of the five elements on the Tiger are described below, together with the years in which the elements were exercising their influence. Therefore all Tigers born in 1950 are Metal Tigers, those born in 1902 and 1962 are Water Tigers, and so on.

Metal Tiger: 1950
The Metal Tiger has an assertive and outgoing personality. He is very ambitious and, while his aims may change from time to time, he will work relentlessly until he has obtained what he wants. He can, however, be impatient for results and also become highly strung if things do not work out as he would like. He is distinctive in his appearance and is admired and respected by many.

Water Tiger: 1902, 1962
This Tiger has a wide variety of interests and is always eager to experiment with new ideas or satisfy his adventurous nature by exploring distant lands. He is versatile,

shrewd and has a kindly nature. He tends to remain calm in a crisis, although he can be annoyingly indecisive at times. He communicates well with others and through his many capabilities and persuasive nature he usually achieves what he wants in life. He is also highly imaginative and is often a gifted orator or writer.

Wood Tiger: 1914, 1974

The Wood Tiger has a very friendly and pleasant personality. He is less independent than some of the other types of Tiger and is more prepared to work with others to secure a desired objective. However, he does have a tendency to jump from one thing to another and can easily become distracted. He is usually very popular, has a large circle of friends and invariably leads a busy and enjoyable social life. He also has a good sense of humour.

Fire Tiger: 1926, 1986

The Fire Tiger sets about everything he does with great verve and enthusiasm. He loves action and is always ready to throw himself wholeheartedly into anything which catches his imagination. He has many leadership qualities and is capable of communicating his ideas and enthusiasm to others. He is very much an optimist and can be most generous. He has a likeable nature and can be a witty and persuasive speaker.

Earth Tiger: 1938, 1998

This Tiger is responsible and level-headed. He studies everything objectively and tries to be scrupulously fair in all his dealings. Unlike other Tigers, he is prepared to specialize in certain areas rather than get distracted by other matters, but he can become so involved in what he is doing that he does not always take into account the opinions of those around him. He has good business sense and is usually very successful in later life. He has a large circle of friends and pays great attention to both his appearance and his reputation.

PROSPECTS FOR THE TIGER IN 2003

The Chinese New Year starts on 1 February 2003. Until then, the old year, the Year of the Horse, is still making its presence felt.

The Year of the Horse (12 February 2002 to 31 January 2003) is a generally favourable one for the Tiger and in most respects he will fare well. Particularly well aspected is the closing quarter, with the period from mid-October to the end of the Horse year seeing a great deal of activity.

At this time if there is something that the Tiger wants to achieve at work, he should actively pursue any opportunities to advance his ideas. Concerted effort in the closing months will be well rewarded.

In addition to making headway in his work, if the Tiger has a personal interest or skill he can use to his advantage, he should do so. As the proverb states, 'Nothing ventured nothing gained' and if the Tiger ventures, some interesting results can ensue. The Horse year does favour those who are prepared to take the initiative and this suits the Tiger personality well.

The progress that the Tiger makes in his work will lead to an improvement in his finances, but while he will find this welcome, he does need to watch his spending. With many temptations, and with the last quarter of the year being a traditionally expensive time, his outgoings could become considerable. Where possible, he should plan his purchases and set money aside for forthcoming expenses. Careful management can make a considerable difference.

Travel is well aspected and if there are places the Tiger would like to visit or distant friends or relations he would like to see, he should follow up his ideas.

The Tiger's personal life will be pleasant, with those close to him being generally supportive. However, he would do well to listen closely to any advice they may offer, remembering that they do speak with his best interests at heart. For the unattached Tiger or those who would like more companionship, the Horse year can often bring new friends and new love, sometimes in an unexpected but glorious way. As far as personal relations are concerned, September could be significant, either for existing relationships or for new ones.

In many respects, the Horse year holds a lot of promise for the Tiger and by making the most of his talents and his rich personality, he can make it a pleasing and rewarding time.

The Year of the Goat starts on 1 February and will be a reasonable one for the Tiger. Although he will be able to build on some of his more recent achievements, Goat years sometimes lack the colour and pace that the Tiger so enjoys. The Tiger likes action, and in 2003 his adventurous and pioneering spirit could be somewhat quenched. However, while at times frustrating, the quieter nature of the year will offer the chance to consolidate his recent gains as well as give some thought to future activities.

At work this will be a year of steady progress. Tigers who have recently changed their job or are undertaking comparatively new duties should use the first months of the year to establish themselves in their new position, build up contacts and learn more about the various aspects of their work. By showing initiative, they can make an impression and place themselves in line for further responsibilities as they become available. Similarly, those Tigers who have been in the same position for some time will find that by using their skills and in-house knowledge to advantage they too will be well placed for promotion opportunities or other openings. This may not be a year of swift or unprecedented progress, but by being committed and using his experience, the Tiger can make reasonable headway, with the months of April, May and September holding particularly interesting possibilities.

All Tigers, whether in work or seeking it, would do well to give thought to how they would like their future to develop and if it would help them to learn new skills, undertake training or obtain further qualifications, they should find out what is available. In this way the Tiger will not only enhance his prospects but also open up other possibilities. Tigers who have been looking for work for some time will find that widening the scope of jobs they are prepared to consider will bring the offer of a position which will give them training and useful experience in a new area. This can set them off in a new direction, one with interesting prospects. The Tiger's achievements in 2003, while at first sight appearing modest, can indeed turn out to be significant.

Also, the Tiger possesses an imaginative and creative streak and creativity is very much to the fore in Goat years. So, throughout 2003, the Tiger should aim to put forward his ideas and if he has a creative hobby or interest, he should devote time to it and, if applicable, promote what he does. This could bring forth a pleasing response and, in some cases, open up interesting possibilities. In addition, if there is a particular interest that has been intriguing the Tiger, he should follow it up. As he will find, this is a good year to add to his knowledge and further his skills.

The Tiger should also give some consideration to his well-being and if he is sedentary for much of the day, consider taking some exercise. With regular exercise and a balanced diet, he will feel better in himself and possess more energy and stamina. Also, as he will discover, life does not always need to be conducted at a breakneck pace and time spent enjoying some of the quieter pleasures can be time well spent.

An area which the Tiger could enjoy is travel and if possible he should aim to get away at some time over the year. A break from his usual routine will do him good and by choosing his destination carefully, he will get to see some interesting and in some cases beautiful areas.

As far as his relations with others are concerned, this will be a quiet but pleasant year for the Tiger. In his home life he will follow the activities of his loved ones with much interest. He will offer assistance and advice and often be heartened by the effect his input has, particularly from those much younger and more senior than himself. He will also spend some time over the year tackling practical projects on his home. While these may be more disruptive and complex than initially envisaged, the Tiger will be satisfied with the results, especially as they can be appreciated by all in his household.

However, while the Tiger's domestic life will generally bring him contentment, there could be a few issues which do cause concern. Rather than let these simmer in the background, the Tiger should try talking things through. With compromise and understanding, any disagreements can often be amicably defused. Also, the slower pace of the Goat year will allow the Tiger to spend more time with those who are important to him and by encouraging interests that can be shared, he can enjoy some meaningful occasions as well as help maintain a good rapport.

The Tiger's social life will also be quieter than in some years, but although he may not go out as much as usual he will still appreciate meeting up with friends and the various social occasions he does attend. The first quarter of the year is likely to see the most activity and, for the unattached, a friendship made in the closing months of the Horse year or early in 2003 could come to mean a great deal. Socially, this can be a pleasant year, even if not an overly active one.

In many respects the Goat year can be a beneficial one for the Tiger, particularly regarding his own development.

Although his progress may not be as swift as he would like, what he learns now will be to his future benefit.

As far as the different types of Tiger are concerned, this will be an agreeable year for the *Metal Tiger*. Although his actual progress may not be easy or substantial, he will have more time to devote to the activities he wants to do rather than conducting his life at a frantic pace. In many ways this will be a year to consolidate, take stock and savour. As it starts, though, the Metal Tiger would do well to give some thought to what he would like to achieve over the year. He could find himself coming up with some interesting notions!

One area which is well aspected is the Metal Tiger's personal interests and if there is something he wants to take up or to develop further, he should take steps to do so. By doing something purposeful – and possibly also creative – he can make this a satisfying year for himself. Those Metal Tigers who do choose to take up a new interest will also find the challenge a stimulating and absorbing use of their time. They may even unlock some hidden talents.

Partly related to this is personal development and, again with an eye to the future, if there is a skill the Metal Tiger feels it would be useful to learn, he should investigate what is on offer. Whether this involves enrolling on a course or studying on his own, he will find that it will give him a greater sense of fulfilment and of moving forward.

As far as the Metal Tiger's work is concerned, the Goat year will offer more stability than some. Over the year the Metal Tiger should concentrate on the areas he knows, while taking advantage of training opportunities or of any other ways to widen his experience. By being willing and co-operative he can do much to enhance his standing as well as prepare the way for future advances. For any Metal Tiger seeking work or keen to move on from their present position, the Goat year will hold some interesting developments. Although obtaining a new position will not necessarily be easy, any opening the Metal Tiger is given will give him a chance to develop different skills and set him an interesting personal challenge.

In financial matters, the Metal Tiger should keep a close watch over his position and if he is aware of any heavy expenses looming, make adequate provision beforehand. This is not a year to proceed on an ad hoc basis or take too relaxed an attitude. Similarly, the Metal Tiger needs to be vigilant when completing important forms (including tax) if problems are to be avoided.

This need for care also extends to his relations with others. Although both the Metal Tiger's domestic and social life will contain some truly happy occasions, throughout the Goat year he does need to consult those close to him and listen to their views. If he remains too independent-minded or engrossed in his own concerns, he could find a certain edginess creeping into some of his relationships. Both domestically and socially this can be a fine year, but it does need input from the Metal Tiger himself. Spending time on mutual interests, joint family activities, an occasional trip out or a short break could lead to some pleasing occasions. In addition, the Metal Tiger will watch with fondness the progress of a much younger relation and any help he feels able to give will be much appreciated. Overall, his domestic life can be enjoyable and meaningful, but it does require attention and input for it to go well.

The Metal Tiger should also make sure he sets time aside for socializing. Again, there could be the temptation for him to neglect this side of his life because he is engaged in other pursuits (including personal interests), but his social life can give his life balance as well as enable him to relax and unwind.

Although the Goat year may lack the activity of some, by developing himself and his interests, the Metal Tiger can make it a satisfying time, with what he achieves now often having long-term benefits.

TIP FOR THE YEAR
Plan and use your time wisely. Enjoy the company of others, spend time on personal interests and aim to develop yourself and your skills.

The *Water Tiger* possesses a keen and determined nature. Ever eager to progress and make the most of his abilities, he likes action. However, despite his best intentions, he could find the Goat year frustrating and at times awkward. His plans and ideas could be difficult to carry out and his actual progress limited. But even though some aspects of the year may be difficult, the Water Tiger can gain much value from it and can prepare the way for future progress.

In his work the Water Tiger should aim to consolidate his position, particularly if he is new to his present role or if changes have taken place recently. By developing the various aspects of his work and building on his experience as well as adding to his circle of contacts, the Water Tiger will find his standing will increase considerably and this will be especially useful when opportunities do become available, particularly late in 2003 and in 2004. Although the Water Tiger may sometimes feel uneasy with certain developments or aspects of his role, he should avoid appearing too inflexible or acting in a manner which could leave him isolated or undermine his position. This is a year for care, discretion and building up experience.

All Water Tigers should take advantage of any training opportunities that become available or, if there are certain skills they feel it would be helpful to acquire, see what is possible. This especially applies to those who may be seeking work or are disillusioned with their present position. By adding to their skills or training in a different area, they will find new possibilities will become available to them. The months of April and May could see some interesting opportunities, but the last quarter of the year will see the greatest activity.

The Water Tiger will need to exercise care in financial matters over the year, as he could face some expensive periods, especially in connection with family and accommodation. Where possible, he should try to make allowance for this in advance and if he takes on any new commitment, he should check the terms and obligations involved. This is a year which requires vigilance and careful management. However, while some of the year will be costly, the Water Tiger should still aim to set some funds aside for a holiday. Not only will a change of scene do him good but some of the places he visits will appeal to his adventurous side.

Domestically, there will be much activity, with many Water Tigers celebrating a key event, perhaps the marriage of a close relation or the birth of a grandchild. The Goat year will certainly bring some pleasing family occasions and, as always, the Water Tiger will play an important and supportive role. Family life can bring him both joy and contentment in 2003 although, throughout the year, he does need to take the time to consult others, especially where important arrangements and domestic activities are concerned.

With his active and outgoing nature, the Water Tiger values his social life and while this may sometimes lack the sparkle and activity of some years, he can still look forward to some interesting social occasions as well as meeting up with friends. Any Water Tigers who would like more companionship will find that joining a club or interest group is a good way to get to know others. Similarly, for any Water Tiger who may in recent years have become so immersed in his work that his social life has lapsed, this will be a good time to try to redress the balance and set a regular time aside to enjoy social activities. This can be one of the main benefits of the Goat year. 2003 will give the Water Tiger the opportunity to develop himself and his activities in the way that he wants and, by taking advantage of the chances available, what he accomplishes will often prove significant in the years ahead.

TIP FOR THE YEAR
Make the most of the situations that arise and be prepared to adapt, learn and show commitment. What is accomplished now can be of great future benefit.

This will be an important year for the *Wood Tiger* and while it will not be without its pressures or difficult moments, what he sets in motion can have far-reaching effects. In recent years many Wood Tigers will have seen a great deal of change in their lives, both personally and in their work. The Goat year will give them the chance to enjoy what they have achieved so far and plan for the future. Rather than being a year of progress and major developments, it will be a time of consolidation, learning and preparing for future advances.

As far as his domestic life is concerned, the Goat year can bring the Wood Tiger much contentment. Those Wood Tigers with children will watch over their development with much interest and, with the Wood Tiger's ability to empathize with others and build their confidence, young ones will look up to him and learn a great deal from him. Similarly, the Wood Tiger will also do much to assist other close relations, with a more senior relation particularly valuing the practical support and advice he is able to give. The Wood Tiger will also enjoy many of the domestic and family activities that take place, including mutual interests, breaks as well as projects carried out together to improve home comforts. By devoting time to his home and to those who mean much to him, he will find this a meaningful time and one which will contain some treasured moments. Admittedly, there will be occasions when he is tired, under pressure or irritated by some matter. At such times, rather than take his vexations out on others, he should let those around him know how he feels and take advantage of any offers of help. He should not feel that certain household tasks or matters are just his preserve and if others can assist in any activity, particularly at busy times, he should let them.

For any Wood Tiger who has had some difficulty in his personal life in recent years, the Goat year offers real hope. In some cases former differences can, with understanding and dialogue, be healed, while in other cases it will be a time to draw a line under the past and look forward. Wood Tigers who find themselves on their own might like to immerse themselves in a new interest, join a society or just go out more. By taking action, they can usher in a new chapter in their personal life, and many will, often by chance, meet someone who becomes important to them. One of the benefits of the Goat year is that it will help the Wood Tiger reappraise his situation and attend to the aspects of his life that really matter.

As far as his work is concerned, however, this will be a mixed year. Sometimes there will be daunting challenges and targets to be met and the Wood Tiger could find it difficult to obtain the responses and results he would like. However, he *is* tenacious and by persisting in his endeavours and drawing on his skills, what he does manage to achieve – sometimes under difficult conditions – will often impress. In addition, the year will contain some valuable lessons for him and will not only allow him to broaden his experience but also discover some strengths which he can draw on in the future, particularly in 2004.

For those Wood Tigers seeking work or eager to change their present position, again the year will not be easy and opportunities will not always be available. However, by making the most of any position he is able to obtain, even if it is not quite what he wants, the Wood Tiger will find that it can pave the way for some interesting possibilities in the future.

The Wood Tiger will also need to take care in money matters over the year. He will have many demands on his resources and will want to do or acquire a great deal. In view of this, he should be wary of taking unnecessary risks or committing his money to ventures or schemes he may not have fully investigated. He would do better to keep account of his outgoings and, in some cases, set aside certain amounts for specific purposes. The better he can manage his money, the better he will fare.

Although the Wood Tiger may sometimes feel his progress in the Goat year is not all that he would like it to be, he will be building on his experience and doing much to prepare for his future success, while on a personal level his family and friends will bring him much joy.

TIP FOR THE YEAR
Enjoy the support of those who are important to you and also look ahead. Deciding upon your future aims will give you a greater sense of direction.

This will be an interesting year for the *Fire Tiger* and while it will not be without its pressures, what he gains, both in experience and qualifications, can have far-reaching effects.

For the many Fire Tigers in education, this will be a demanding year with a great deal of material to be covered as well as course work and exam preparation. However, while it may all seem daunting, with steady and persistent work the Fire Tiger will accomplish a great deal and his efforts will be well rewarded. He could also find it useful to remember the words of Henry Ford: 'Nothing is particularly hard if you divide it into small jobs.' Splitting study and revision into more manageable sections will often make the tasks much easier to cope with. The Fire Tiger will also be well supported and although he may like to keep his thoughts to himself, by being more open and prepared to discuss matters, he will find that those around him will be able to offer useful assistance. They really do want to see him do his best and he should not hesitate to draw on the help they are so willing to give.

The Fire Tiger's domestic life can go well, although there could be certain issues which give rise to differences of opinion. At such times the Fire Tiger should be prepared to talk these through, putting his views across but also listening to others. Sometimes a compromise can be found or a discussion can help diffuse the matter or put it into perspective. In any event, talking things over will certainly help all involved. In addition, the Fire Tiger will find that helping with household tasks will be appreciated as well as often satisfying to do.

On a social level, the Fire Tiger will be much in demand. There will be parties and plenty of other events for him to go to and in the closing quarter of the year his social life will be especially full. Romance, too, will beckon for some Fire Tigers and while some romances will fade after a short time, as the year progresses many Fire Tigers will find a certain friendship will blossom and bring much happiness.

Although with an often busy social life as well as everything else he has to do the Fire Tiger's free time may be limited, he should still maintain his personal interests. Not only will these bring some balance to his life but they will also allow him to relax and enjoy himself and, for those keen on sporting and outdoor pursuits, offer additional exercise. The Goat year is also favourable for more creative endeavours and the aspiring musician or artist should take every opportunity to further their talents.

For those Fire Tigers in work or looking for work for the first time, the Goat year will offer some useful experience. Certain positions may not turn out as the Fire Tiger imagined or may not suit him, but once he has a foot on the employment ladder, he will find this a useful base from which to progress. Some Fire Tigers will change jobs several times over the year, but with each move they will be finding out about another aspect of work as well as discovering where their strengths lie. For some it will take time before they feel settled and fulfilled – and this will not necessarily be in the Goat year – but they should remember that this is the start of their working life and they need to discover, often by trial and error, their true forte. Deep down they will know that with their ideas, enterprise and zest, they do have a bright future ahead of them.

As far as finance is concerned, the Fire Tiger will need to keep a close watch over his outgoings and avoid unnecessary risks. Some of the year will call for economies and careful management, but with care and resourcefulness the Fire Tiger will often be surprised by what he can do on a relatively tight budget.

Although the Goat year will demand a lot of the Fire Tiger, it will certainly not be without its brighter side, with his personal life especially well aspected.

TIP FOR THE YEAR

Rise up to the challenges the year will provide. By making the most of your strengths and being persistent, whether in academic study or seeking work, you can learn a great deal.

The quieter nature of the Goat year will suit the *Earth Tiger*, especially as it will give him more chance to pursue his interests and develop some of his ideas. The Earth Tiger has always been one to use his time well and much of what he does in 2003 will bring him satisfaction.

Particularly well aspected are the Earth Tiger's personal interests, especially those of a creative and practical nature. Over the year he should aim to develop these, either by setting himself new projects, getting in contact with fellow enthusiasts or, in some cases, teaching himself a new skill. He will find his interests can give rise to some absorbing times. The Goat year favours creativity and those who enjoy photography, writing, art, drama or some other form of creative expression should further what they do. By being bolder and experimenting with their talents, they can achieve some impressive results. The year also favours self-development and if there is a subject that the Earth Tiger wishes to pursue, he would do well to set some time aside for this, whether by reading up on it or enrolling on a course. Some Earth Tigers might decide to improve their computer or Internet skills, while others may prefer areas such as keep-fit, but whatever the Earth Tiger decides upon, his personal interests can be a meaningful aspect of his life during the Goat year.

The Earth Tiger will also be well supported by family members and in some cases receive help from an unexpected quarter regarding a personal interest. He will also enjoy some of the activities he can carry out with those in his household both in pleasurable and practical pursuits, including home improvements. Some Earth Tigers too will delight in time spent in the garden, perhaps redesigning certain areas or adding new features or plants. Tasks which have visible results will bring everyone a great deal of satisfaction. As always, the Earth Tiger will follow the activities of close relations with fond interest and while he may not wish to be appear interfering, some help he gives to someone younger will be of more value than he may realize.

Although the Earth Tiger's social life may be quieter than some years, he will enjoy meeting up with friends and attending some functions. Earth Tigers who desire more companionship would do well to consider joining a local society that would bring them into contact with those who share similar interests. Positive action on their part will be rewarded and in some cases lead to some important new friendships.

As far as work matters are concerned, the Earth Tiger will find his skills and experience will serve him well over the year. There could be some unexpected developments as well as the chance for the Earth Tiger to put his expertise to satisfying use. Some Earth Tigers may take on a special project, while those who have recently retired or reduced their work commitments could find their knowledge will give rise to some new opportunities.

As far as finance is concerned, there will be some good fortune for many Earth Tigers, perhaps through an additional bonus or gift. And provided the Earth Tiger manages his finances well and plans his expenditure rather than proceeds on too much of an ad hoc basis, he will find he is able to do much more. He would certainly do well to set some money aside for a holiday later in the year, as travel is well aspected and will bring him much pleasure.

In many respects, this will be a satisfying year for the Earth Tiger. It may lack the activity of some years, but it will allow the Earth Tiger to devote time to activities of his own choosing and to enjoy himself.

TIP FOR THE YEAR

Make the most of your ideas and personal interests, as you can look forward to some satisfying results.

FAMOUS TIGERS

Debbie Allen, Kofi Annan, Sir David Attenborough, Queen Beatrix of the Netherlands, Victoria Beckham, Beethoven, Tony Bennett, Tom Berenger, Chuck Berry, Jon Bon Jovi, Sir Richard Branson, Emily Brontë, Garth Brooks, Mel Brooks, Isambard Kingdom Brunel, Agatha Christie, Charlotte Church, Helen Clark, Phil Collins, Robbie Coltrane, Sheryl Crow, Tom Cruise, Charles de Gaulle, Leonardo DiCaprio, Emily Dickinson, David Dimbleby, Isadora Duncan, Dwight Eisenhower, Queen Elizabeth II, Enya, Roberta Flack, E. M. Forster, Frederick Forsyth, Jodie Foster, Connie Francis, Crystal Gayle, Elliott Gould, Buddy Greco, Alan Greenspan, Germaine Greer, Ed Harris, Hugh Hefner, Tim Henman, William Hurt, Natalie Imbruglia, Ray Kroc, Stan Laurel, Jay Leno, Groucho Marx, Karl

Marx, Marilyn Monroe, Demi Moore, Eric Morecambe, Alanis Morissette, Neil Morrissey, Jeremy Paxman, Marco Polo, Beatrix Potter, John Prescott, Renoir, Kenny Rogers, the Princess Royal, Dame Joan Sutherland, Dylan Thomas, Liv Ullman, Jon Voight, Julie Walters, H. G. Wells, Oscar Wilde, Robbie Williams, Tennessee Williams, Terry Wogan, Stevie Wonder, William Wordsworth.

29 JANUARY 1903 ⌣ 15 FEBRUARY 1904   *Water Rabbit*

14 FEBRUARY 1915 ⌣ 2 FEBRUARY 1916   *Wood Rabbit*

2 FEBRUARY 1927 ⌣ 22 JANUARY 1928   *Fire Rabbit*

19 FEBRUARY 1939 ⌣ 7 FEBRUARY 1940   *Earth Rabbit*

6 FEBRUARY 1951 ⌣ 26 JANUARY 1952   *Metal Rabbit*

25 JANUARY 1963 ⌣ 12 FEBRUARY 1964   *Water Rabbit*

11 FEBRUARY 1975 ⌣ 30 JANUARY 1976   *Wood Rabbit*

29 JANUARY 1987 ⌣ 16 FEBRUARY 1988   *Fire Rabbit*

16 FEBRUARY 1999 ⌣ 4 FEBRUARY 2000   *Earth Rabbit*

THE
RABBIT

THE PERSONALITY OF THE RABBIT

The talent of success is nothing more than doing what
you can well, and doing well whatever you do.
Henry Wadsworth Longfellow, a Rabbit

The Rabbit is born under the signs of virtue and prudence.
He is intelligent, well-mannered and prefers a quiet and
peaceful existence. He dislikes any sort of unpleasantness
and will try to steer clear of arguments and disputes. He is
very much a pacifist and tends to have a calming influence
on those around him. He has wide interests and usually
has a good appreciation of the arts and the finer things in
life. He also knows how to enjoy himself and will often
gravitate to the best restaurants and night spots in town.

The Rabbit is a witty and intelligent speaker and loves
being involved in a good discussion. His views and advice are
often sought by others and he can be relied upon to be
discreet and diplomatic. He will rarely raise his voice in anger
and will even turn a blind eye to matters which displease him
just to preserve the peace. The Rabbit likes to remain on good
terms with everyone, but he can be rather sensitive and takes
any form of criticism very badly. He will also be the first to
get out of the way if he sees any form of trouble brewing.

The Rabbit is a quiet and efficient worker and has an
extremely good memory. He is very astute in business and
financial matters, but his degree of success often depends
on the conditions that prevail. He hates being in a situation
which is fraught with tension or where he has to make
sudden decisions. Wherever possible he will plan his

various activities with the utmost care and a good deal of caution. He does not like to take risks and does not take kindly to changes. Basically, he seeks a secure, calm and stable environment, and when conditions are right he is more than happy to leave things as they are.

The Rabbit is conscientious in most of the things he does and because of his methodical and ever-watchful nature can often do well in his chosen profession. He makes a good diplomat, lawyer, shopkeeper, administrator or priest and he excels in any job where he can use his superb skills as a communicator. He tends to be loyal to his employers and is respected for his integrity and honesty, but if he ever finds himself in a position of great power he can become rather intransigent and authoritarian.

The Rabbit attaches great importance to his home and will often spend much time and money maintaining and furnishing it and fitting it with all the latest comforts – the Rabbit is very much a creature of comfort! He is also something of a collector and there are many Rabbits who derive much pleasure from collecting antiques, stamps, coins, *objets d'art* or anything else which catches their eye or particularly interests them.

The female Rabbit has a friendly, caring and considerate nature, and will do all in her power to give her home a happy and loving atmosphere. She is also very sociable and enjoys holding parties and entertaining. She has a great ability to make the maximum use of her time and although she involves herself in numerous activities, she always manages to find time to sit back and enjoy a good read or a chat. She has a great sense of humour, is very artistic and is often a talented gardener.

The Rabbit takes considerable care over his appearance and is usually smart and very well turned out. He also attaches great importance to his relations with others and matters of the heart are particularly important to him. He will rarely be short of admirers and will often have several serious romances before he settles down. The Rabbit is not the most faithful of signs, but he will find that he is especially well suited to those born under the signs of the Goat, Snake, Pig and Ox. Due to his sociable and easy-going manner he can also get on well with the Tiger, Dragon, Horse, Monkey, Dog and another Rabbit, but will feel ill at ease with the Rat and Rooster as both these signs tend to speak their mind and be critical in their comments, and the Rabbit just loathes any form of criticism or unpleasantness.

The Rabbit is usually lucky in life and often has the happy knack of being in the right place at the right time. He is talented and quick-witted, but he does sometimes put pleasure before work and wherever possible will tend to opt for the easy life. He can at times be a little reserved and suspicious of the motives of others, but generally will lead a long and contented life and one which – as far as possible – will be free of strife and discord.

THE FIVE DIFFERENT TYPES OF RABBIT

In addition to the 12 signs of the Chinese zodiac, there are five elements and these have a strengthening or moderating influence on the sign. The effects of the five elements on the Rabbit are described below, together with the years in which the elements were exercising their influence. Therefore all Rabbits born in 1951 are Metal Rabbits, those born in 1903 and 1963 are Water Rabbits, and so on.

Metal Rabbit: 1951

This Rabbit is capable, ambitious and has very definite views on what he wants to achieve in life. He can occasionally appear reserved and aloof, but this is mainly because he likes to keep his thoughts to himself. He has a very quick and alert mind and is particularly shrewd in business matters. He can also be very cunning in his actions. The Metal Rabbit has a good appreciation of the arts and likes to mix in the best circles. He usually has a small but very loyal group of friends.

Water Rabbit: 1903, 1963

The Water Rabbit is popular, intuitive and keenly aware of the feelings of those around him. He can, however, be rather sensitive and tends to take things too much to heart. He is very precise and thorough in everything he does and has an exceedingly good memory. He tends to be quiet and at times rather withdrawn, but he expresses his ideas well and is highly regarded by his family, friends and colleagues.

Wood Rabbit: 1915, 1975

The Wood Rabbit is likeable, easy-going and very adaptable. He prefers to work in groups rather than on his own and likes to have the support of others. He can, however, be rather reticent about expressing his views and it would be in his own interests to become a little more open and let others know how he feels on certain matters. He usually has many friends, enjoys an active social life and is noted for his generosity.

Fire Rabbit: 1927, 1987

The Fire Rabbit has a friendly, outgoing personality. He likes socializing and being on good terms with everyone. He is discreet and diplomatic and has a very good understanding of human nature. He is also strong-willed and provided he has the necessary backing he can go far in life. He does not, however, suffer adversity well and can become moody and depressed when things are not working out as he would like. He has a particularly good manner with children, is very intuitive and there are some Fire Rabbits who are even noted for their psychic ability.

Earth Rabbit: 1939, 1999

The Earth Rabbit is a quiet individual, but he is nevertheless very astute. He is realistic in his aims and is prepared to work long and hard in order to achieve his objectives. He has good business sense and is invariably lucky in financial matters. He also has a most persuasive manner and usually experiences little difficulty in getting others to fall in with his plans. He is held in very high esteem by his friends and colleagues and his views are often sought and highly valued.

PROSPECTS FOR THE RABBIT IN 2003

The Chinese New Year starts on 1 February 2003. Until then, the old year, the Year of the Horse, is still making its presence felt.

The Horse year (12 February 2002 to 31 January 2003) will have been a busy and generally positive one for the Rabbit, with the closing months seeing much activity. Particularly well aspected is the Rabbit's personal life and he will find himself much in demand with both family and friends. He can look forward some pleasing news concerning a family member as well as some enjoyable get-togethers. However, with so much happening, the Rabbit needs to stay well organized and plan ahead.

In addition to a full domestic life, his social life will be active, with a variety of parties and social occasions to attend. The Rabbit will thoroughly enjoy himself, especially as he will be able to re-establish contact with people he has not seen for some while. And a romance or newfound friendship can take on a special significance as the year draws to a close.

The Horse year also favours travel and if the Rabbit receives invitations to visit those living some distance away or has the chance to take a break, he should take advantage of it. August, September and December will bring some interesting travel opportunities.

As far as work matters are concerned, the closing months of the Horse year will be a demanding time and again require good organization. However, the Rabbit's experience and perceptive nature will help him to cope and to win the gratitude of others, including some influential colleagues. What he accomplishes in the Horse year will serve him well in the more auspicious Goat year.

The Year of the Goat starts on 1 February and is a favourable one for the Rabbit. He will feel at ease with his general situation, unlike more volatile years, and will be able to make progress. The Goat year provides the stability for the Rabbit to thrive and, as a result, he will enjoy pleasing developments in many areas of his life.

The Rabbit's work prospects are especially well favoured and while some Rabbits may have been disappointed with recent progress or feel uncomfortable in their present position, this will change over the year. The prospects *are* promising and will allow the Rabbit to make more effective use of his skills and expertise. However, to benefit, he does need to give some thought to how he would like his career to develop and then follow his ideas through. The aspects are favourable, but it does rest with the Rabbit to take the initiative. For some Rabbits, excellent possibilities will arise within the organization in which they are currently based and by using their contacts, in-house knowledge and experience, they will find themselves strong candidates for promotion or will be offered the chance to take on further responsibilities. For the keen and enterprising, the opportunities will certainly be there.

For those Rabbits who are disillusioned with their present role, consider themselves in a rut or are seeking work, again the Goat year will bring some excellent opportunities to make progress. To benefit, though, the Rabbit does need to decide on the type of position he is seeking and to see what is available. In some cases he will find openings which will be ideal or will be alerted to possibilities he has not seriously considered but which offer great scope for development. Almost all Rabbits will be able to make headway in their work and in some cases start off on an exciting new career path. The months of March, May, September and November could see some interesting opportunities.

It is also a favourable year for creative pursuits and Rabbits whose work involves an element of creativity should promote their talents. With their flair and yet subtle and refined approach, they could make an impression and find their ideas being well received. Those Rabbits who have interests they would one day like to turn into a vocation should also take advantage of any chance to develop their skills and bring their work to the attention of others. Once again, if the Rabbit takes action, the Goat year will reward him.

As far as financial matters are concerned, this will be a reasonable year, although the Rabbit will need to remain his usual careful self. Over the year he will face several expensive periods, often involving accommodation and transport costs, and he does need to allow for these. While he may be keen to make some of the purchases he has in mind, rather than proceed too hastily, he should take the time to fully investigate the ranges and terms available. This is a year for keeping control over the purse strings. It is also a time for caution – the Rabbit cannot afford to become involved in risky undertakings or schemes which he has not fully investigated. In 2003 he needs to remain his careful and prudent self.

With his quiet, kindly and genial manner, the Rabbit does value his relations with others and in the Goat year he will find both his domestic and social life meaning a great deal to him. In his home life he will, as always, play an important and appreciated role, doing much to support and encourage those close to him. Others (particularly more senior relations) will look to him to advise and assist in some matter, and his help will be greatly valued.

The Rabbit will also delight in some of the domestic projects that he decides to tackle over the year. For quite a few Rabbits these will include improving home comforts and the décor of certain rooms. The Rabbit's taste and eye for colour and quality will be appreciated. However, while he will be keen to launch projects, he should resist the sometimes strong temptation of starting too many all at once.

The Rabbit will also delight in some of the more general family activities that take place and should make sure that he and his loved ones go away at some time over the year. The change of scene and break from routine will do everyone good and lead to some enjoyable occasions.

The Rabbit's social life will bring him a great deal of pleasure as well and he will value meeting up with friends. In addition he will attend some particularly fine social occasions during the Goat year.

The prospects are excellent too for romance and an existing relationship or one formed following a chance encounter could quickly become meaningful. The Goat year can offer some wonderful and heady days, with quite a few unattached Rabbits meeting their future partner during the course of the year. The first and last quarters are especially well aspected for the Rabbit's personal and social life.

In many respects, the Goat year will mark a significant upturn in the Rabbit's fortunes. In addition to benefiting from the favourable aspects, the Rabbit himself will feel determined to take the action necessary to bring about what he wants. The year holds great prospects for him, and with his talents, ideas and amiable personality, he really does have much in his favour.

As far as the different types of Rabbit are concerned, this will be an interesting year for the *Metal Rabbit*. Always keen to make the most of himself and his ideas, he can look forward to some heartening successes over the year.

In his work the Metal Rabbit can make considerable headway. With his experience and contacts, he may be considered for promotion and if he sees a position which interests him, he should certainly put himself forward. This is very much a year for the Metal Rabbit to make the most of his abilities and of the chances available.

For those Metal Rabbits who are looking for work or feeling disenchanted with their present role, the Goat year also offers bright prospects, and once successful in getting a new job, even though it may be different from what he has previously been doing, the Metal Rabbit will find it will give him a greater sense of purpose than in more recent times. In some cases, new duties will enable the Metal Rabbit to make better use of his strengths as well as discover new ones. And with the year so favourably aspected, he should put forward any ideas he has related to his work or any enterprise he has been considering. The

Goat year will reward his initiative. Opportunities could arise throughout the year, but March, May and the last quarter could see the most activity.

The Metal Rabbit will also derive much pleasure from his personal interests and those that allow him to draw on his creativity are particularly favoured. Metal Rabbits who are keen on art, writing, photography or something similarly expressive should aim to develop their skills. If the Metal Rabbit does not have a particular interest or hobby at the moment, perhaps because work or other commitments have dominated so much of his time recently, he should make a resolution to take one up. He will often find that it will give his lifestyle a greater balance.

In addition, all Metal Rabbits should take advantage of any chance to go away for a break at some time over the year and by choosing their destination carefully, they can look forward to visiting some interesting places.

The Metal Rabbit's domestic life is also well aspected. As always, he will do much to assist family members and the support and advice he is able to give to younger relations will be greatly appreciated. The Metal Rabbit should also involve those around him in his own interests as well as any domestic projects he has in mind. Not only will their contribution make a difference, but it will also help maintain the rapport that the Metal Rabbit values so much.

Over the year he could also find his social circle widening quite appreciably. For those Metal Rabbits who would like more companionship and perhaps are seeking someone special in their life, the Goat year holds wonderful promise. Quite unexpectedly many of these Metal Rabbits will form a friendship with someone who will not only appreciate their own special qualities but also help to put the fun and sparkle back into their lives. Personally, the Goat year can be a significant and encouraging time for the Metal Rabbit.

The one tricky aspect of the year relates to finance, particularly important paperwork. Although usually so meticulous, the Metal Rabbit must not let his careful nature slip and if he has any uncertainties over forms he has to complete, he would do well to check. It would also be to his advantage to deal with such matters promptly. To delay or miss deadlines could be to his detriment. Metal Rabbits, do take note.

This warning apart, this will be a splendid year for the Metal Rabbit and by promoting himself, using his skills and drawing on the richness of his personality, he will find this a satisfying and often special year.

TIP FOR THE YEAR
Move ahead and make the most of your personal strengths and experience. This is a time to make progress and enjoy yourself.

This marks the fortieth year of the *Water Rabbit* and it promises to be a significant one. In recent years much will have happened both personally and professionally. There will have been triumphs but also disappointments and in some cases bitter blows. However, the Goat year is very much one for moving forward, building on skills and past successes and drawing a firm line under past failures.

In his work the Water Rabbit will see some particularly important developments. Although many will have seen changes over the last year, further change is imminent. Some Water Rabbits will find that their conscientious nature, experience and good standing with colleagues will single them out for promotion and further responsibilities. Those Water Rabbits who are particularly interested in moving ahead should keep alert for any openings. Similarly, those who are keen to do something different should also follow up any vacancies that interest them. Although not all their applications will go their way, one door will eventually open and it will often lead to interesting duties and the discovery of new strengths. The Goat year holds particularly good prospects for the Water Rabbit, but to benefit he does need to take action and make the most of the chances that arise. In addition, some Water Rabbits could find that further training, whether to refresh existing skills or learn new ones, will enhance their prospects. For work opportunities March and May will be important, although throughout 2003 there will be many chances for the Water Rabbit to demonstrate his sterling qualities and make progress.

As with most Rabbits, the Water Rabbit possesses a creative streak and those who have interests that allow them to express this should aim to further what they do this year, perhaps by tackling more ambitious projects or getting in contact with fellow enthusiasts. In this way their interest can take on new meaning as well as be a satisfying use of their time. Many Water Rabbits will also enjoy outdoor pursuits over the year, including gardening, visiting local areas of interest or practising a sport or keep-fit activity. By using his time purposefully, the Water Rabbit will benefit from his activities.

Some Water Rabbits will decide to mark their fortieth birthday in a special way and this could prove a memorable occasion. With his outgoing nature, the Water Rabbit always sets much store by his relations with others and his friends and family will again mean much to him over the year. His domestic life will be particularly busy, with many calls upon his time. While the Water Rabbit will be keen to be involved, he must not feel that he should take on everything himself, as well as deal with what may appear to be an ever-increasing number of domestic chores. In 2003 he must make sure that everyone does their fair share of household tasks. Busy though it will be at times, the Water Rabbit's domestic life will nevertheless bring him much happiness, especially concerning the successes of his loved ones.

Water Rabbits who may start the year with clouds over their personal life will often find these will depart during the first months of the year and that 2003 will usher in a much happier and more settled time, with former rifts sometimes being healed or new friendships taking the place of old ones. On a personal level, this is a promising year.

It is also a good time for social matters and as usual the Water Rabbit will enjoy meeting up with his friends on a regular basis. In busy periods, he could also be grateful for practical help from his friends.

The one area which does require care is finance. While usually so thorough, the Water Rabbit could find his outgoings heavy and that succumbing to too many temptations depletes his resources. This is a time for moderation.

This warning apart, the Goat year is a favourable one for the Water Rabbit and by making the most of his ideas, skills and the opportunities that arise, he can make his fortieth year both a successful and fulfilling one.

TIP FOR THE YEAR

Be positive and earnest. This is a year to pursue your aims and make the most of the chances available.

This will be a rewarding year for the *Wood Rabbit* and he can look forward to pleasing developments in many areas of his life. In his work he will be able to build on his experience and achievements, while his personal life will bring him much contentment. Also, the Wood Rabbit will be well supported, and knowing he has the love and backing of others, he will feel better able to venture forward and realize some of his aspirations.

As the year starts, though, the Wood Rabbit would do well to consider his present position and decide what he wants to accomplish. Where his work interests are concerned, if he has some idea of his direction he will find himself becoming more focused as well as generally more enthused. Some Wood Rabbits, particularly those who are relatively new to their position, will decide to spend time establishing themselves, learning more about their various duties and building up useful contacts. By setting about what they do in their usual conscientious manner, they will not only impress but often find themselves being rewarded with more interesting duties as the year progresses. For those Wood Rabbits who may have been in the same job for some time and feel in a rut, the Goat year will bring some exciting opportunities. Contacts may advise them of openings to try for or they may discover, almost by chance, a new position which will not only represent a refreshing change but also allow them to extend their experience. The Goat year is a time for moving forward and it will offer the Wood Rabbit the chance to develop his skills to excellent effect.

This also applies to those Wood Rabbits seeking work. Again, by following up openings that interest them, many will find themselves being offered a position which has potential for the future. In some cases, this will start the Wood Rabbit off on a new and often more rewarding career path. The Goat year *will* bring opportunities and it rests with the Wood Rabbit to make the most of them.

The progress that he makes in his work will also lead to an improvement in his income, but while this will be welcome, the Wood Rabbit does still need to budget carefully. He has many commitments and to prevent financial problems and shortfalls, he should always take account of his outgoings and make allowance for his commitments. The better he can manage his resources, the better he will fare. He too should aim to set some money aside for travel, as going away will not only do him much good, but will also lead to some enjoyable times.

The Wood Rabbit's personal life is favourably aspected and those with young children will follow their progress with much fondness. The Wood Rabbit will enjoy many of the family activities that take place, including some home projects and shared interests. He should, though, be mindful of any advice given him, particularly by his partner and by more senior relations. They do speak with his best interests at heart and some of what he is told will prove especially helpful. In addition, with the pressures of his work, the Wood Rabbit could sometimes feel tired and tense. At such times he should not hesitate to draw on the help of others, particularly with some household tasks, as well as avoid becoming too preoccupied with work matters. His home life *is* precious and he should not let it suffer.

Neither should the Wood Rabbit let his social life become squeezed out because of other commitments. Not only will it give him the chance to unwind and enjoy himself but he will also gain a great deal from the camaraderie of his friends. And for any Wood Rabbit who has had some recent personal difficulties, the Goat year will generally be a much brighter and happier time. For those who are alone, it can bring the gift of a significant new friendship.

In 2003 the Wood Rabbit is in the ascendancy. In almost all areas of his life, he can look forward to positive and pleasing developments.

TIP FOR THE YEAR

Ensure your life has balance. Work hard, but enjoy the rewards. Spend time with those who are important and develop your personal interests.

This will be a busy but rewarding year for the *Fire Rabbit*. For the many Fire Rabbits in education there will be some important exams to take as well as decisions regarding the future. As a result, there will be pressures and times of uncertainty. However, the Fire Rabbit can emerge from the year with some impressive gains to his credit and can lay the foundations for a sound future. He is indeed blessed with some fine qualities and by drawing on these and taking advantage of the opportunities around him, he can make 2003 an important *and* successful year.

In setting about his studies the Fire Rabbit should aim to work consistently and start revision for exams early rather than leave it to the last moment. The more prepared he is, the more he will be able to take the exams in his stride. He will also be well supported by those around him and should any particular subject areas be giving him difficulty, he should ask for help. Similarly, he should resist the temptation of closing his mind to subjects in which he has little interest. By adopting a more open approach, he could find he is able to understand more as well as possibly gain an additional qualification. The aspects will support the Fire Rabbit, but much does depend upon his own attitude.

During the year many Fire Rabbits will also need to select subjects for further study. In making these choices, they should consult their tutors as well as bear in mind the vocations they may wish to follow. By carefully considering their options and selecting the subjects in which they have most interest, these Fire Rabbits will be pleased with their decisions.

There will, though, be some Fire Rabbits who will decide to seek employment rather than continue their education. For these, the Goat year will again bring forth significant developments. Although some of the positions these Fire Rabbits will be offered will be routine and junior, they will nevertheless give them a useful footing on the employment ladder and by showing commitment, the young Fire Rabbits will soon mark themselves out for further responsibilities. Some may find themselves changing their position several times over the year, such are the progressive aspects that prevail, but all the time they will be adding to their experience as well as discovering where their strengths lie. The months of March, September and November could see some interesting work opportunities.

Those Fire Rabbits who remain in education might themselves find that a holiday or weekend job will lead to some interesting experiences as well as allow them to earn something extra. The Goat year does reward the enterprising and by showing willing, the Fire Rabbit can gain a great deal.

The one word of warning that does need to be sounded concerns finance. Money does need to be handled with care and with everything that he wants to do, the Fire Rabbit will sometimes need to economize and decide upon his priorities. He should be wary of taking risks and remain dubious of any 'get rich quick' schemes he may come across. Although he may be eager to improve his lot, he could, if he is not careful, find himself losing rather than making money.

More positively, though, the Fire Rabbit's relations with others will go well, particularly on a social level. During the year the Fire Rabbit will find himself in demand and can look forward to many fun occasions, including parties and other social events. For many Fire Rabbits there will also be the excitement of romance and new friendships, and for any who may, for some reason, not feel as part of the social scene as they would like, the Goat year can bring new happiness. By devoting time to their interests and getting in contact with other enthusiasts, they may meet someone who will become a very good friend.

Domestically, the Fire Rabbit will also benefit from the support of those around them. Admittedly, views may sometimes clash, but with understanding and a willingness to both talk and listen, the Fire Rabbit will benefit from the advice offered. Also, if he is able to join in more with general family activities and help with household tasks, he will find his home life that much more rewarding.

Generally, the Goat year holds fine prospects for the Fire Rabbit and by setting about his activities in his usual conscientious and willing manner, he can achieve a great deal as well as prepare the way for future advances. And he will greatly enjoy himself.

TIP FOR THE YEAR
Be willing to learn. It is through positive effort that you will make the greatest gains.

This will be a pleasing year for the *Earth Rabbit* and unlike more active years, it will give him the chance to concentrate on activities of his own choosing. In addition, he can look forward to a rewarding personal life with some memorable occasions.

The Goat year does favour cultural pursuits and the Earth Rabbit will get a great deal of satisfaction from his various interests. Those who enjoy art, craftwork, writing, music or some other form of creativity should aim to develop their talents. Furthering their interests will lead to some absorbing and rewarding times. They might also like to get in touch with fellow enthusiasts, perhaps through a local society or even over the Internet. By making contacts and exchanging views and ideas, the Earth Rabbit will find his interests often taking on a new meaning. Any Earth Rabbits who may, because of other commitments, have let their personal interests lapse should resolve to devote more time to them in the Goat year and even take up new ones. They will feel much more fulfilled by doing so.

The Earth Rabbit will also busy himself with domestic projects over the year, including improving certain areas of his home and changing the décor. Some Earth Rabbits may decide to mount an efficiency drive and rid themselves of accumulated papers and other items they no longer need. Such projects can prove most satisfying. However, when tackling practical projects, either in his home or garden, the Earth Rabbit should take care if attempting anything hazardous or strenuous. If not, he could run the risk of a strain or injury. Earth Rabbits, take note.

Paperwork likewise calls for care, particularly any forms regarding finance, benefits or tax. Although usually so careful, the Earth Rabbit does need to check the small print and should not hesitate to contact helplines or advisers if he has any uncertainties. It is better to ask than make sometimes costly errors by jumping to conclusions. Similarly, when making large purchases or entering into agreements, the Earth Rabbit should check the paperwork and make himself fully aware of any obligations he is taking on. Bureaucratic problems could be the one difficult area in an otherwise pleasing year.

More positively, the Earth Rabbit can look forward to a rewarding domestic and social life. He will follow the activities of his loved ones with much fondness, often helping those with young families or who may be under pressure. Several times his assistance and advice will mean far more than he may realize. He will also enjoy many activities with those close to him. Whether joint interests, practical projects or outings, they can lead to some meaningful occasions. The Earth Rabbit's family life does mean a great deal to him and in the Goat year it will contain some truly special times.

The Earth Rabbit also has a circle of very good friends and will enjoy socializing, including entertaining in his own home. Added to this, there will be some pleasurable social events for him to attend, with February to May and the last quarter of the year seeing the most activity.

For any Earth Rabbit who is starting the year in low spirits or has experienced some recent sadness, the Goat year offers real hope. These Earth Rabbits should aim to put the past behind them and turn their attention to the present. It may take time, but by venturing out more, making contact with others (perhaps through a local group) and discovering new interests, they can put some brightness back into their lives. For some, there is also the prospect of a significant new friendship.

In many respects, the Goat year will be a satisfying one for the Earth Rabbit. His family and social life are especially well aspected and with this, together with time he spends on his personal interests, will make this an enjoyable and fulfilling year.

TIP FOR THE YEAR
Follow up ideas and activities that appeal to you. Time spent on purposeful pursuits really can bring great pleasure.

FAMOUS RABBITS

Bertie Ahern, Drew Barrymore, David Beckham, Harry Belafonte, Ingrid Bergman, St Bernadette, Gordon Brown, Melanie Brown, Emma Bunton, James Caan, Nicolas Cage, Lewis Carroll, Fidel Castro, John Cleese, Confucius, Marie Curie, Johnny Depp, Albert Einstein, George Eliot, W. C. Fields, James Fox, Sir David Frost, James Galway, Cary Grant, Edvard Grieg, Oliver Hardy, Seamus Heaney, Bob Hope, Whitney Houston, John Howard, Helen Hunt, John Hurt, Anjelica Huston, Chrissie Hynde, Enrique Inglesias, Clive James, Henry James, David Jason, Angelina Jolie, Michael Jordan, Michael Keaton, John Keats, Judith Krantz, Danny La Rue, Cheryl Ladd, Patrick Lichfield, Gina Lollobrigida, Ali MacGraw, Sir Trevor McDonald, George Michael, Arthur Miller, Colin Montgomerie, Roger Moore, Mike Myers, Brigitte Nielsen, Christina Onassis, George Orwell, John Peel, Edith Piaf, Sidney Poitier, Romano Prodi, Ken Russell, Mort Sahl, Elisabeth Schwarzkopf, Neil Sedaka, Jane Seymour, Neil Simon, Frank Sinatra, Fatboy Slim, Sting, J. R. R. Tolkien, Arturo Toscanini, Tina Turner, Luther Vandross, Queen Victoria, Orson Welles, Walt Whitman, Robin Williams, Kate Winslet, Tiger Woods.

16 FEBRUARY 1904 ⌒ 3 FEBRUARY 1905   *Wood Dragon*

3 FEBRUARY 1916 ⌒ 22 JANUARY 1917   *Fire Dragon*

23 JANUARY 1928 ⌒ 9 FEBRUARY 1929   *Earth Dragon*

8 FEBRUARY 1940 ⌒ 26 JANUARY 1941   *Metal Dragon*

27 JANUARY 1952 ⌒ 13 FEBRUARY 1953   *Water Dragon*

13 FEBRUARY 1964 ⌒ 1 FEBRUARY 1965   *Wood Dragon*

31 JANUARY 1976 ⌒ 17 FEBRUARY 1977   *Fire Dragon*

17 FEBRUARY 1988 ⌒ 5 FEBRUARY 1989   *Earth Dragon*

5 FEBRUARY 2000 ⌒ 23 JANUARY 2001   *Metal Dragon*

THE
DRAGON

THE PERSONALITY OF THE DRAGON

> The people who get on in this world are the people who get up and look for the circumstances they want, and, if they can't find them, make them.
>
> *George Bernard Shaw, a Dragon*

The Dragon is born under the sign of luck. He is a proud and lively character and has a tremendous amount of self-confidence. He is also highly intelligent and very quick to take advantage of any opportunities that occur. He is ambitious and determined and will do well in practically anything he attempts. He is also something of a perfectionist and will always try and maintain the high standards he sets himself.

The Dragon does not suffer fools gladly and will be quick to criticize anyone or anything that displeases him. He can be blunt and forthright in his views and is certainly not renowned for being either tactful or diplomatic. He does, however, often take people at their word and can occasionally be rather gullible. If he ever feels that his trust has been abused or his dignity wounded he can sometimes become very bitter and it will take him a long time to forgive and forget.

The Dragon is usually very outgoing and is particularly adept at attracting attention and publicity. He enjoys being in the limelight and is often at his best when he is confronted by a difficult problem or tense situation. In some respects he is a showman and he rarely lacks an audience. His views are very highly valued and he invariably has something interesting – and sometimes controversial – to say.

He has considerable energy and is often prepared to work long and unsocial hours in order to achieve what he wants. He can, however, be rather impulsive and does not always consider the consequences of his actions. He also has a tendency to live for the moment and there is nothing that riles him more than to be kept waiting. The Dragon hates delay and can get extremely impatient and irritable over even the smallest of hold-ups.

The Dragon has an enormous faith in his abilities, but he does run the risk of becoming over-confident and unless he is careful he can sometimes make grave errors of judgement. While this may prove disastrous at the time, the Dragon does have the tenacity and ability to bounce back and pick up the pieces again.

The Dragon has such an assertive personality, so much will-power and such a desire to succeed that he will often reach the top of his chosen profession. He has considerable leadership qualities and will do well in positions where he can put his own ideas and policies into practice. He is usually successful in politics, show business, as the manager of his own department or business, and in any job which brings him into contact with the media.

The Dragon relies a tremendous amount on his own judgement and can be scornful of other people's advice. He likes to feel self-sufficient and there are many Dragons who cherish their independence to such a degree that they prefer to remain single throughout their lives. However, the Dragon will often have numerous admirers and many will be attracted by his flamboyant personality and striking looks. If he does marry, the Dragon will usually marry young and will find himself particularly well suited to those born under the signs of the Snake, Rat, Monkey and Rooster. He will also find that the Rabbit, Pig, Horse and Goat make ideal companions and will readily join in with many of his escapades. Two Dragons will also get on well together, as they understand each other, but the Dragon may not find things so easy with the Ox and Dog, as both will be critical of his impulsive and somewhat extrovert manner. He will also find it difficult to form an alliance with the Tiger, for the Tiger, like the Dragon, tends to speak his mind, is very strong-willed and likes to take the lead.

The female Dragon knows what she wants in life and sets about everything she does in a very determined and positive manner. No job is too small for her and she is often prepared to work extremely hard until she has secured her objective. She is immensely practical and somewhat liberated. She hates being bound by routine and petty restrictions and likes to have sufficient freedom to be able to go off and do whatever she wants. She will keep her house tidy but is not one for spending hours on housework – there are far too many other things that she prefers to do. Like her male counterpart, she has a tendency to speak her mind.

The Dragon usually has many interests and enjoys sport and other outdoor activities. He also likes to travel and often prefers to visit places that are off the beaten track rather than head for popular tourist attractions. He has a very adventurous streak in him and providing his financial circumstances permit – and the Dragon is usually sensible with his money – he will travel considerable distances during his lifetime.

The Dragon is a very flamboyant character and while he can be demanding of others and in his early years rather precocious, he will have many friends and will nearly always be the centre of attention. He has charisma and so much confidence in himself that he can often become a source of inspiration for others. In China he is the leader of the carnival and he is also blessed with an inordinate share of luck.

THE FIVE DIFFERENT TYPES OF DRAGON

In addition to the 12 signs of the Chinese zodiac, there are five elements and these have a strengthening or moderating influence on the sign. The effects of the five elements on the Dragon are described below, together with the years in which the elements were exercising their influence. Therefore all Dragons born in 1940 and 2000 are Metal Dragons, those born in 1952 are Water Dragons, and so on.

Metal Dragon: 1940, 2000
This Dragon is very strong-willed and has a particularly forceful personality. He is energetic, ambitious and tries to be scrupulous in his dealings with others. He can also be blunt and to the point and usually has no hesitation in speaking his mind. If people disagree with him, or are not

prepared to co-operate, he is more than happy to go his own way. The Metal Dragon usually has very high moral values and is held in great esteem by his friends and colleagues.

Water Dragon: 1952

This Dragon is friendly, easy-going and intelligent. He is quick-witted and rarely lets an opportunity slip by. However, he is not as impatient as some of the other types of Dragon and is more prepared to wait for results than to expect everything to happen at once. He has an understanding nature and is prepared to share his ideas and co-operate with others. His main failing is a tendency to jump from one thing to another rather than concentrate on the job in hand. He has a good sense of humour and is an effective speaker.

Wood Dragon: 1904, 1964

The Wood Dragon is practical, imaginative and inquisitive. He loves delving into all manner of subjects and can quite often come up with some highly original ideas. He is a thinker and a doer and has sufficient drive and commitment to put many of his ideas into practice. He is more diplomatic than some of the other types of Dragon and has a good sense of humour. He is very astute in business matters and can also be most generous.

Fire Dragon: 1916, 1976

This Dragon is ambitious, articulate and has a tremendous desire to succeed. He is a hard and conscientious worker and is often admired for his integrity and forthright nature. He is very strong-willed and has considerable leadership qualities. He can, however, rely a bit too much on his own judgement and fail to take into account the views and feelings of others. He can also be rather aloof and it would certainly be in his own interests to let others join in more with his various activities. The Fire Dragon usually enjoys music, literature and the arts.

Earth Dragon: 1928, 1988

The Earth Dragon tends to be quieter and more reflective than some of the other types of Dragon. He has a wide variety of interests and is keenly aware of what is going on around him. He also has clear objectives and usually has no problems in obtaining support for his ventures. He is very astute in financial matters and is often able to accumulate considerable wealth. He is a good organizer, although he can at times be rather bureaucratic and fussy. He mixes well with others and has a large circle of friends.

PROSPECTS FOR THE DRAGON IN 2003

The Chinese New Year starts on 1 February 2003. Until then, the old year, the Year of the Horse, is still making its presence felt.

The Horse year (12 February 2002 to 31 January 2003) will have been an active one for the Dragon and despite its many pressures, it will have allowed him to learn and accomplish a great deal. The remaining months of the year will continue to see much activity and also some well-deserved successes.

The Dragon is blessed with a determined spirit and in the Horse year his energy and resourcefulness will have made a great impression. In his work he will have been able to put his ideas and experience to good use and although he will have had to deal with pressure and often considerable change, he will have done his reputation much good. Indeed, activity and challenge do bring out the best in the Dragon and the Horse year will have allowed him to use his qualities to good effect. For those Dragons keen to make further progress or to seek another position, October 2002 could be significant.

The Dragon will also get much satisfaction from practical activities in the Horse year. Whether these concern his personal interests or domestic projects, he will be pleased with what he accomplishes. However, if he starts any new undertaking late in the year, he should allow plenty of time for its completion. As the Horse year ends he will have many demands on his time and to prevent overload he would do well to keep his commitments to sensible levels.

The Dragon will gain much from both his domestic and social life during the Horse year, although he should be mindful of any advice he receives from those around him. The Dragon likes to be independent, but to close his mind to the words of those who are willing to help could cause ill-feeling and be to his disadvantage. The Dragon will find his domestic and social life becoming busier as the Horse year draws to a close and with so much to do, arrange and fit in, he would find it helpful to spread some of his commitments and start some of the more seasonal preparations early. Otherwise he could find the latter part of the year becoming a whirl and have little time left for himself.

Although the Horse year will have been a busy one for the Dragon, by managing his time and making the most of the situations that arise, he will emerge from it with much to his credit.

The Year of the Goat starts on 1 February and will be a generally pleasing one for the Dragon. However, the Goat year does require a certain care and adaptability and a lot does depend upon the Dragon's attitude.

The Goat year can have far-reaching consequences for the Dragon's work, and here his attitude will be crucial. He should continue to set about his duties in his usual conscientious way and if asked to take on new responsibilities or alter his role, he should consider what is involved rather than appear too inflexible. He should also take advantage of any training opportunities he may be offered or other ways in which he can extend his experience. What the Dragon learns in the Goat year can have important long-term consequences, but to benefit he does need to show willing and be prepared to adapt. Also, if there is a particular skill or qualification he believes it would be helpful to obtain, he should follow this up. This is very much a year for self-development and preparing the way for future advances.

For those Dragons who are eager to move on from their present position or are seeking work, again the Goat year will see some interesting developments. By widening the scope of positions they are prepared to consider, many will find themselves being offered the chance to take on duties which are a distinct and welcome change from their previous work. And although a new role may demand a great deal, particularly in view of all that needs to be learnt, the Dragon will enjoy rising to the challenge and in the process will often discover new strengths. In addition, by mastering their new duties, these Dragons will find new possibilities opening up for the future. The months of March, July, September and November could all see important developments regarding the Dragon's work and prospects.

The Goat year is also one which favours creativity and with their powerful imagination, taste and style, those Dragons whose work involves design or allows them to express themselves in some way should actively further what they do. This is a year which rewards originality and the more creative Dragon can make quite an impact. Any Dragons who have a hobby or interest which they would like to develop will find this an excellent year in which to do so. For the enterprising Dragon writer, artist, musician or craftsperson, projects started or promoted in the Goat year will not only be satisfying to complete but could also have interesting consequences.

Over the year the Dragon should also aim to give some thought to his general well-being and if he is sedentary for much of the day or feels he does not get as much exercise as he should, he should try to remedy this. With some medical guidance on the best way to proceed, the Dragon could find activities such as swimming, cycling, aerobics, yoga not only enjoyable but also of considerable benefit.

The Dragon will need to take care with his finances over the year, as he will experience several periods of considerable expense, particularly related to family and accommodation. With these matters and any other ideas and activities he wants to carry out, he will have many demands on his finances and he does need to manage his money with care and make allowance for forthcoming expenses. He should be wary of taking risks or committing funds to schemes he has not fully investigated. Without vigilance money could be lost or returns not prove as good as the Dragon may have been led to believe. Dragons, take note.

Travel is, though, more favourably aspected and the Dragon should aim to set some funds aside for a holiday or break over the year as well as take up invitations to visit family or friends who may live some distance away. A holiday or trip can lead to some happy experiences and do the Dragon a lot of good.

The Dragon will also obtain much contentment from his personal life. Domestically, this will be a reasonably settled year and while both the Dragon himself and the various members of his household will be involved with their own individual concerns, by encouraging a spirit of openness, everyone will gain from the support, encouragement and advice they can offer each other. The one word of warning that does need to be sounded is that the Dragon should avoid becoming so engrossed in his work or other activities that his contribution to family life is not as great as it could be. Even at busy times, he *must* ensure that his life has balance and that he gives time to those who are important to him. In this respect, he could find it helpful to encourage activities that everyone can enjoy. If he does so, the

Dragon's family life can be rich and rewarding and can give rise to some special times.

This also applies to his social life. Again, despite the many demands on him, the Dragon will find that if he devotes time to going out regularly and meeting up with friends, his social life can go well. Also, due to changes in his work, he could have the opportunity to build up some new contacts and some of these will become part of his social circle. The months of May and June and last quarter of the year are likely to see the most social activity, but throughout the Goat year the Dragon will have a variety of interesting social occasions to look forward to.

For the unattached or those seeking companionship, the Goat year is superbly aspected. A chance introduction or meeting will quickly come to mean a great deal and can certainly bring a new happiness into the Dragon's life. Many of those currently enjoying romance will marry or settle down with their partner in the Goat year, such are the aspects that prevail. For the Dragon, the Goat year can be a romantic and joyous time.

Overall, the Goat year will be a constructive one for the Dragon. His personal life holds much promise and the ways in which he can develop both himself and his work will be to his future benefit, with the aspects being particularly encouraging in the Monkey year that follows.

As far as the different types of Dragon are concerned, this will be a reasonable year for the *Metal Dragon*. Some aspects of his life will go well, bringing him considerable pleasure, while other parts could be troublesome and result in a good deal of aggravation.

One area which is poorly aspected is paperwork. Over the year the Metal Dragon will need to deal with several important forms and when these relate to financial matters, benefits or tax, he needs to approach them with care, even though he may feel they are unnecessarily detailed or burdensome. To miss out details or delay returning important paperwork could result in some protracted correspondence and be to his detriment. Should the Metal Dragon have any uncertainties over the questions asked or facts required, he should seek guidance. In some cases helplines or professional advice will prevent problems from arising, but where important forms and correspondence are concerned, care *is* required. The Metal Dragon should be wary of taking financial risks or becoming involved in speculations he knows little about. Also, if he makes any major purchase over the year or enters into an agreement, he should check the paperwork carefully and keep any guarantees secure. Where finance and officialdom are concerned, caution is *very* much the key word in 2003.

In other areas, however, the aspects are considerably better for the Metal Dragon. His personal interests will bring him particular satisfaction and he will find them a pleasing and constructive use of his time. If there is a particular subject that has been intriguing him for some time or there is something he feels it would be useful to learn or become more proficient in, he should take steps to follow up his ideas this year. By furthering his interest in some way, whether by enrolling on a course, reading up on a subject or joining an appropriate society, he will be satisfied with what he is able to achieve.

The Goat year also favours travel and if possible the Metal Dragon should aim to go away at some time during the year. By choosing his destination with care and reading up about it before he leaves, he can make his time away all the more interesting. In addition, some Metal Dragons could form a particularly good friendship while travelling.

The Metal Dragon will also derive much pleasure from his home life. Many Metal Dragons will decide to tackle projects they have had in mind for a long time. These could include redecorating and refurbishing certain rooms or having a major sort out and so making particular areas tidier and better organized. If the Metal Dragon is able to tackle such projects with the rest of his family, it will bring both him and others greater satisfaction. The Metal Dragon will also take a fond interest in the activities of family members and those close to him will often seek his views and advice. Similarly, if there is any matter concerning the Metal Dragon himself, he would find it helpful to discuss it with those around him rather than dwelling upon it all by himself. In many instances he will be encouraged by the advice and assistance given and his loved ones will be pleased to reciprocate his many kindnesses.

The Metal Dragon will also delight in his social life over the year, particularly in the chances he gets to meet up with his friends. Metal Dragons who decide to enrol on a course or join a special interest group or society could find that this adds a new element to their social life and leads to some new friendships. Those who are lonely or would appreciate more company will also find that by going to places where they will meet others with similar interests, they can do much to brighten their social life. In some cases this will lead to a valuable new friendship. March, June and the latter part of the year are especially favoured for social matters.

In many respects the Goat year does hold good prospects for the Metal Dragon and by using his time well and following up his ideas, he will be pleased with what he accomplishes, particularly in the way of new skills and interests. However, bureaucratic matters *do* need care and the Metal Dragon would do well to remember the maxim 'When in doubt, ask.' Overall, though, this will be a satisfying year.

TIP FOR THE YEAR
Aim to develop yourself and your interests, as this will often give a real sense of achievement as well as be something you can benefit from.

This will be a pleasing year for the *Water Dragon*, allowing him to build on some of the more recent changes that have taken place as well as put his skills to good use.

Over the last year some Water Dragons will have changed their job, while others will have taken new responsibilities or had to adjust to new practices. Some of this will not have been easy, but the Water Dragon will have gained from the experience as well as built up new strengths. The Goat year will usher in a more settled period and give the Water Dragon the opportunity to establish himself and to use his talents to good effect. Also, having gained the confidence of those in more senior positions, he will be encouraged to develop certain skills as well as make more use of his ideas, and this will be something he will appreciate.

For those Water Dragons seeking work or anxious to move from their current position, again the Goat year will offer some interesting possibilities. By widening the scope of what they are prepared to consider and perhaps looking to use their talents in a different way, they could be given an opening that will prove an interesting challenge and will have potential for the future. For work opportunities March, July, September and November are favoured and this year will often prepare the way for the even better times that lie ahead in 2004.

The Water Dragon should also aim to extend his personal interests in the Goat year, perhaps by setting himself a new project, mastering a particular skill or starting up a new activity. By setting time aside for something which he finds satisfying and enjoyable, he will find his interests can do him much good as well as bring him considerable pleasure. Also, with the Goat year's strong emphasis on culture and creativity, if the Water Dragon has an interest which allows him to create something or to express himself in some way, he could find it draws an appreciative response from others.

The Water Dragon does, though, need to be careful with money matters over the year, particularly as some months could see heavy outlay. As far as possible the Water Dragon should budget in advance for known expenses as well as keep a careful control over his general expenditure. Without care, too many impulsive buys will quickly mount up and in some instances cause the Water Dragon to regret his haste. In 2003 finance does need careful handling.

The Water Dragon will value his personal life, however, and his family will support him in his various undertakings.

By being prepared to discuss his ideas, he will find those close to him can assist in far more ways than he may have envisaged. The Water Dragon will also enjoy some of the more general family activities that take place, whether these are joint projects in the home or garden, mutual interests or family gatherings. The year will certainly provide some fine and pleasant occasions and as ever, the Water Dragon's role will be appreciated.

The Water Dragon's social life is also well aspected and he will enjoy the interesting and sometimes more unusual social events that the Goat year will bring. Any Water Dragon who feels his social life is getting a little flat or staid will find that by making the effort to go out more and meet people with similar interests, perhaps through a local group or society, his social life will become more rewarding as the year progresses. The months of April to June and last quarter could see a noticeable upturn in social matters and, for the unattached, new romance could beckon.

Generally, the Goat year is favourably aspected for the Water Dragon, particularly in allowing him to develop his skills in a purposeful way. Unlike some more frenzied years, this year will give the Water Dragon the chance to enjoy his achievements and, with his personal life well aspected, he will have fun too.

TIP FOR THE YEAR
Aim to develop yourself and your skills. By using your time well, you can make this a personally rewarding year.

This will be a satisfying year for the *Wood Dragon*, particularly as it will give him a greater chance to develop his skills as well as enjoy a rewarding personal life. In addition, the Wood Dragon will be encouraged by the general support he receives and, with this backing, he will find he is setting about his activities with a greater energy and confidence. What he accomplishes now, particularly in his work, will indeed prove significant over the next few years.

One valuable aspect of the year is that it will allow the Wood Dragon to build on his current duties and learn about other aspects of his work. By being willing to extend himself and his experience, he will find he is well placed for promotion and new positions when they become available. Over the year many Wood Dragons will indeed be able to move ahead and take on greater and often more interesting roles, but the real rewards will come later in the year and particularly in 2004.

For those Wood Dragons who are seeking work or anxious to change their job, the Goat year will develop in a curious way. It may take these Wood Dragons several attempts to secure a position, and they *will* need to remain persistent, but they will eventually secure an opening, often one in marked contrast to what they have been doing. This will, however, allow them to develop new skills and in the process open up more possibilities for the future. Workwise, 2003 can be a significant year for almost all Wood Dragons.

The Wood Dragon will, though, need to be careful in money matters and with family expenses and many obligations to meet, he does need to manage his outgoings carefully and avoid becoming involved in anything risky. Where money is concerned, this is a year for caution.

As far as his domestic life is concerned, however, this will be a pleasing year. In addition to benefiting from the support and general encouragement he receives, the Wood Dragon will particularly delight in activities he can carry out with others. These will include interests he can share with his partner as well as projects they can do together. In this way, despite all the other demands on his time, the Wood Dragon will enjoy some treasured moments. Similarly, Wood Dragons with children will find that by supporting and guiding them, they can often encourage them to make pleasing progress. With input and consideration, home life for the Wood Dragon in 2003 really will be rewarding.

His social life is also favourably aspected and he will not only appreciate meeting friends but also enjoy the various social functions he attends over the year. For any Wood Dragon who may be looking to brighten his social life or is perhaps seeking new friendships and romance, the Goat year holds wonderful prospects, but it does require the Wood Dragon to make the effort to go out and immerse himself in new activities. By doing so he can move his personal life forward (and perhaps away from disappointments) and enjoy some newfound happiness. April, May, August, September and December are particularly favoured for personal and social matters.

Travel too is well aspected and all Wood Dragons should try and go away for a holiday over the year. For some, a break arranged at short notice could turn out to be especially memorable.

In many respects, the Wood Dragon will find the Goat year a constructive one. His domestic and social life can bring pleasure, while in his work and interests he will be able to add to his skills, with what he achieves now preparing the way for some of the more substantial successes he is soon to enjoy.

TIP FOR THE YEAR

Plan ahead. By learning, developing your skills and furthering your experience, you can considerably enhance your future prospects.

The *Fire Dragon* possesses a determined and ambitious nature. He knows he is capable of a great deal and has some aspirations he is particularly keen to reach. However, there will be times in the Goat year that he will find frustrating, especially when the results he is hoping for seem a long time in coming. But while his actual progress may at times seem elusive, this can still be a valuable year for him. He will learn a lot about himself and by the year's end will have done much to enhance his prospects as well as gained a clearer understanding of where his future lies. In this respect, the Goat year can prove a constructive and illuminating one.

In his work the Fire Dragon should continue to build on his present position. With his commitment and enthusiasm he will already have made an impression and by continuing to give his best he will find his reputation, standing and prospects all enhanced. Also, with his future in mind, he should take advantage of any training he may be offered, even if it is a case of refreshing certain skills or keeping up to date with developments. The more he can learn about what he does and the more he can improve his skills, the better he will fare. He would also find it helpful to build up contacts in his work, both in the areas in which he is currently involved and in those he is hoping to move to. By getting to know (and impress) others he will not only find himself benefiting from some useful advice but also being advised of possibilities he had not considered before. By putting himself forward and getting himself known, he can do his prospects much good. He should remember that while in the Goat year his actual progress may – to him – be modest, what he accomplishes now will play a major part in the more substantial advances he is soon to make, particularly in 2004.

For those Fire Dragons who are anxious to move from their present position or who are seeking work, the Goat year will certainly have its opportunities, but the Fire Dragon should keep his expectations realistic rather than be over-ambitious. Again, the positions that these Fire Dragons obtain this year can be a useful springboard to future successes. March, April, July and November will bring some interesting opportunities.

The Fire Dragon will, though, need to be careful in money matters. In 2003 he will have many outgoings and will also want to do and acquire a great deal. As a result he would do well to keep an account of both his income and outgoings and manage his resources carefully. He would find it helpful to keep a tight control over his purse strings, even though this may mean forsaking a few indulgences, and should be wary of taking risks, particularly with money he can ill afford to lose. Financially, this is a year that requires both discipline *and* restraint.

More positively aspected is the Fire Dragon's domestic life. It will be a busy year and many Fire Dragons will decide to tackle projects in their home, with some even moving altogether. Although some of the more practical undertakings will be more involved and time-consuming than the Fire Dragon initially envisaged, everyone in the household will be satisfied with the improvements made. The Fire Dragon will also enjoy mutual interests with his partner or others close to him and, if a parent, will encourage his children in their activities. However, there will inevitably be occasions when the Fire Dragon will feel tired or under pressure. At such times, rather than drive himself relentlessly, it is essential he gives himself the chance to rest, even if this means certain household tasks do have to be put back. He may wish to do a great deal, but this must not be at the expense of his well-being or of feeling constantly under pressure. In some cases, spending time on interests unrelated to his usual daily concerns could be useful, including those that take him out of doors and provide him with some additional exercise.

The Fire Dragon's social life can bring him much pleasure over the year and he will find that meeting up with friends and going out to various social events will bring balance to his life as well as give rise to some agreeable occasions. With affairs of the heart so well aspected, those Fire Dragons who start the year alone may see a substantial upturn in their fortunes in 2003, with the prospects of a wonderful new romance occurring over the year.

In so many respects, this can be a constructive and rewarding year and on a personal level it will certainly contain some happy times.

TIP FOR THE YEAR

Be active and be prepared to learn and to meet those who can advise you or who could be helpful in the future. This is very much a year of preparation for the successes soon to come.

This will be an important year for the *Earth Dragon* and while it will not be without its challenging moments, he will be generally pleased with what he accomplishes.

For the many Earth Dragons in education, there will be much material to be covered and the pressures will sometimes be great. However, if the Earth Dragon works steadily and carefully organizes what he has to do (and he *is* a good organizer), he will be building up a useful foundation as well as preparing himself for the examinations he will soon have to take. Also, although he may have certain strengths and favoured subject areas, he should not close his mind to those which he finds more difficult or less attractive. By persisting and mastering some of his weaker areas he will often find this can have a positive bearing on other parts of his education as well as increase his eventual number of exam passes. The Earth Dragon will be well supported by those around him and if he has problems or uncertainties, he should not hesitate to raise these with his tutors or other people who could help.

In addition to the progress he will make academically, the young Earth Dragon will get much satisfaction from his various interests, both those he can pursue by himself and those he can carry out with friends, including sport and outdoor activities. He should aim to extend his interests over the year, perhaps by learning new skills or trying something different. Whatever he does, with his keen approach and inquisitive nature, he will find his interests bringing him a great deal of pleasure. The Goat year favours cultural pursuits and for those Earth Dragons who enjoy the arts or are able to draw on creative talents, 2003 can be an encouraging year. Those Earth Dragons born in 1928 could also find that doing some form of research, possibly into their family history, could be an absorbing use of their time.

The Earth Dragon will also enjoy the travel he undertakes over the year and for the more senior Earth Dragon this could include visiting friends or relations living some distance away or revisiting areas of which he is particularly fond. Whether born in 1988 or 1928, the Earth Dragon will find the change of scene will do him good and the places he visits will often be interesting.

The Earth Dragon does, though, need to be careful in money matters. For those born in 1988 there will be many temptations to spend but it would be worth thinking seriously before proceeding. Too much impulse buying could quickly deplete the Earth Dragon's resources and he could find his money could have been saved or put towards something of greater value or use. Some of these Earth Dragons may, though, be able to help their financial situation by taking on a small job or assisting others in some way, and the rewards of their enterprise will not only be helpful now but will also provide valuable lessons for later on. Over the year the Earth Dragon does need to look after his belongings, as there is a risk of a loss or theft which, with more care, could have been avoided. The more senior Earth Dragon also needs to exercise care when dealing with bureaucracy, particularly with forms relating to tax, benefits or other money matters. Should he have any uncertainties, he would do well to seek advice rather than jump to conclusions.

More positively, the Earth Dragon's personal life will generally go well, with those around being encouraging and supportive, and if at any time over the year the Earth Dragon feels under pressure or is worried over any matter, he should raise it with others rather than keep it to himself. As he will find, a worry shared *is* a worry halved. The young Earth Dragon will also find that any help he can give others in his family, such as assisting with jobs around the house, will be warmly appreciated and he should try not to remain closeted in his room, as is so tempting for many teenagers. By contributing more to family life, he will find that the rapport he has with those around him is much improved and that some of the tasks he can help with turn out to be more satisfying than he thought.

Generally, the Earth Dragon will fare well in 2003 and while the younger Earth Dragon will need to remain disciplined and focused on his education, what he learns now will stand him in excellent stead for later. The time the Earth Dragon spends on his interests will bring him much satisfaction and, whether born in 1928 or 1988, he will be grateful for the support he receives over the year. Overall, this will be a pleasant time.

TIP FOR THE YEAR
Spend time on developing your personal interests and skills. These will be satisfying and rewarding and can often have hidden benefits.

FAMOUS DRAGONS

Clive Anderson, Maya Angelou, Jeffrey Archer, Joan Armatrading, Joan Baez, Roseanne Barr, Michael Barrymore, Count Basie, Maeve Binchy, James Brown, Sandra Bullock, Julie Christie, James Coburn, Courteney Cox, Bing Crosby, Roald Dahl, Salvador Dali, Charles Darwin, Lindsay Davenport, Neil Diamond, Bo Diddley, Matt Dillon, Christian Dior, Placido Domingo, Fats Domino, Kirk Douglas, Faye Dunaway, Bruce Forsyth, Sigmund Freud, James Garner, Graham Greene, Che Guevara, Herbie Hancock, David Hasselhoff, Sir Edward Heath, James Herriot, Paul Hogan, Joan of Arc, Tom Jones, Martin Luther King, Eartha Kitt, John Lennon, Abraham Lincoln, Elle MacPherson, Queen Margrethe II of Denmark, Yehudi Menuhin, François Mitterrand, Bob Monkhouse, Andrew Motion, Hosni Mubarak, Florence Nightingale, Nick Nolte, Al Pacino, Gregory Peck, Pele, Edgar Allan Poe, Vladimir Putin, Christopher Reeve, Keanu Reeves, Sir Cliff Richard, Harold Robbins, George Bernard Shaw, Alicia Silverstone, Ringo Starr, Princess Stephanie of Monaco, Dave Stewart, Karlheinz Stockhausen, Shirley Temple, Maria von Trapp, Andy Warhol, Johnny Weissmuller, Raquel Welch, the Earl of Wessex, Mae West, Frank Zappa.

4 FEBRUARY 1905 ⌇ 24 JANUARY 1906	*Wood Snake*
23 JANUARY 1917 ⌇ 10 FEBRUARY 1918	*Fire Snake*
10 FEBRUARY 1929 ⌇ 29 JANUARY 1930	*Earth Snake*
27 JANUARY 1941 ⌇ 14 FEBRUARY 1942	*Metal Snake*
14 FEBRUARY 1953 ⌇ 2 FEBRUARY 1954	*Water Snake*
2 FEBRUARY 1965 ⌇ 20 JANUARY 1966	*Wood Snake*
18 FEBRUARY 1977 ⌇ 6 FEBRUARY 1978	*Fire Snake*
6 FEBRUARY 1989 ⌇ 26 JANUARY 1990	*Earth Snake*
24 JANUARY 2001 ⌇ 11 FEBRUARY 2002	*Metal Snake*

THE
SNAKE

THE PERSONALITY OF THE SNAKE

Knowing is not enough; we must apply. Willing is not
enough; we must do.

Johann Wolfgang von Goethe, a Snake

The Snake is born under the sign of wisdom. He is highly
intelligent and his mind is forever active. He is always
planning and always looking for ways in which he can use
his considerable skills. He is a deep thinker and likes to
meditate and reflect.

Many times during his life he will shed one of his
famous Snake skins and take up new interests or start a
completely different job. The Snake enjoys a challenge and
he rarely makes mistakes. He is a skilful organizer, has
considerable business acumen and is usually lucky in
money matters. Most Snakes are financially secure in their
later years, provided they do not gamble – the Snake has
the distinction of being the worst gambler in the whole of
the Chinese zodiac!

The Snake generally has a calm and placid nature and
prefers the quieter things in life. He does not like to be in a
frenzied atmosphere and hates being hurried into making a
quick decision. He also does not like interference in his
affairs and tends to rely on his own judgement rather than
listen to advice.

The Snake can at times appear solitary. He is quiet,
reserved and sometimes has difficulty in communicating
with others. He has little time for idle gossip and will

certainly not suffer fools gladly. He does, however, have a good sense of humour and this is particularly appreciated in times of crisis.

The Snake is certainly not afraid of hard work and is thorough in all that he does. He is very determined and can occasionally be ruthless in order to achieve his aims. His confidence, will-power and quick thinking usually ensure his success, but should he fail it will often take a long time for him to recover. He cannot bear failure and is a very bad loser.

The Snake can also be evasive and does not willingly let people into his confidence. This secrecy and distrust can sometimes work against him and it is a trait which all Snakes should try to overcome.

Another characteristic of the Snake is his tendency to rest after any sudden or prolonged bout of activity. He burns up so much nervous energy that without proper care he can, if he is not careful, be susceptible to high blood pressure and nervous disorders.

It has sometimes been said that the Snake is a late starter in life and this is mainly because it often takes him a while to find a job in which he is genuinely happy. However, the Snake will usually do well in any position which involves research and writing and where he is given sufficient freedom to develop his own ideas and plans. He makes a good teacher, politician, personnel manager and social adviser.

The Snake chooses his friends carefully and while he keeps a tight control over his finances, he can be particularly generous to those he likes. He will think nothing of buying expensive gifts or treating his friends or loved ones to the best theatre seats in town. In return he demands loyalty. The Snake is very possessive and he can become extremely jealous and hurt if he finds his trust has been abused.

The Snake is also renowned for his good looks and is never short of admirers. The female Snake in particular is most alluring. She has style, grace and excellent (and usually expensive) taste in clothes. A keen socializer, she is likely to have a wide range of friends and has the happy knack of impressing those who matter. She has numerous interests and her advice and opinions are often highly valued. She is generally a calm-natured person and while she involves herself in many activities, she likes to retain a certain amount of privacy in her undertakings.

Affairs of the heart are very important to the Snake and he will often have many romances before he finally settles down. He will find that he is particularly well suited to those born under the signs of the Ox, Dragon, Rabbit and Rooster. Provided he is allowed sufficient freedom to pursue his own interests, he can also build up a very satis-factory relationship with the Rat, Horse, Goat, Monkey and Dog, but he should try to steer clear of another Snake as they could very easily become jealous of each other. The Snake will also have difficulty in getting on with the honest and down-to-earth Pig, and will find the Tiger far too much of a disruptive influence on his quiet and peace-loving ways.

The Snake certainly appreciates the finer things in life. He enjoys good food and often takes a keen interest in the arts. He also enjoys reading and is invariably drawn to subjects such as philosophy, political thought, religion or the occult. He is fascinated by the unknown and his enquiring mind is always looking for answers. Some of the world's most original thinkers have been Snakes, and – although he may not readily admit it – the Snake is often psychic and relies a lot on intuition.

The Snake is certainly not the most energetic member of the Chinese zodiac. He prefers to proceed at his own pace and to do what he wants. He is very much his own master and throughout his life he will try his hand at many things. He is something of a dabbler, but at some time – usually when he least expects it – his hard work and efforts will be recognized and he will invariably meet with the success and financial security he so much desires.

THE FIVE DIFFERENT TYPES OF SNAKE

In addition to the 12 signs of the Chinese zodiac, there are five elements and these have a strengthening or moderating influence on the sign. The effects of the five elements on the Snake are described below, together with the years in which the elements were exercising their influence. Therefore all Snakes born in 1941 and 2001 are Metal Snakes, those born in 1953 are Water Snakes, and so on.

Metal Snake: 1941, 2001

This Snake is quiet, confident and fiercely independent. He often prefers to work on his own and will only let a privileged few into his confidence. He is quick to spot opportunities and will set about achieving his objectives with an awesome determination. He is astute in financial matters and will often invest his money well. He also has a liking for the finer things in life and has a good appreciation of the arts, literature, music and good food. He usually has a small group of extremely good friends and can be generous to his loved ones.

Water Snake: 1953

This Snake has a wide variety of interests. He enjoys studying all manner of subjects and is capable of undertaking quite detailed research and becoming a specialist in his chosen area. He is highly intelligent, has a good memory and is particularly astute when dealing with business and financial matters. He tends to be quietly spoken and a little reserved, but he does have sufficient strength of character to make his views known and attain his ambitions. He is very loyal to his family and friends.

Wood Snake: 1905, 1965

The Wood Snake has a friendly temperament and a good understanding of human nature. He is able to communicate well with others and often has many friends and admirers. He is witty, intelligent and ambitious. He has numerous interests and prefers to live in a quiet, stable environment where he can work without too much interference. He enjoys the arts and usually derives much pleasure from collecting paintings and antiques. His advice is often very highly valued, particularly on social and domestic matters.

Fire Snake: 1917, 1977

The Fire Snake tends to be more forceful, outgoing and energetic than some of the other types of Snake. He is ambitious, confident and never slow in voicing his opinions – and he can be very abrasive to those he does not like. He does, however, have many leadership qualities and can win the respect and support of many with his firm and resolute manner. He usually has a good sense of humour, a wide circle of friends and a very active social life. The Fire Snake is also a keen traveller.

Earth Snake: 1929, 1989

The Earth Snake is charming, amusing and has a very amiable manner. He is conscientious and reliable in his work and approaches everything he does in a level-headed and sensible way. He can, however, tend to err on the cautious side and never likes to be hassled into making a decision. He is extremely adept at dealing with financial matters and is a shrewd investor. He has many friends and is very supportive towards the members of his family.

PROSPECTS FOR THE SNAKE IN 2003

The Chinese New Year starts on 1 February 2003. Until then, the old year, the Year of the Horse, is still making its presence felt.

The Horse year (12 February 2002 to 31 January 2003) will have been a variable one for the Snake and while it will not have been without its successes or happier moments, during its final months the Snake will still need to exercise care in all his activities. Fortunately, by nature the Snake is both cautious and thorough, but he must not let his vigilance slip at this time.

In his work the Snake will find the attention he gives to presentation and detail will serve him well and for those Snakes looking to progress or seeking a change, October and November could both hold some fine possibilities. The Horse year is also an excellent time for the Snake to add to his skills and he should take full advantage of any training opportunities. What he accomplishes at this time can prove very helpful in the forthcoming Goat year, but while the Horse year still reigns supreme, the Snake should be wary of taking risks or shortcuts or being less than thorough.

The cautionary aspects also extend to the Snake's personal life. He should make sure he gives adequate attention to those who matter and does not become over-preoccupied with his own concerns. Usually the Snake is most considerate in this respect, but failure to consult, listen or be fully involved in domestic activities could give rise to some ill feeling. If he is careful to make an input into family life, however, it will be appreciated and can, as the year draws to a close, lead to some meaningful occasions.

On a social level, too, the Snake must make sure he listens to the views of his friends and bears them in mind, otherwise differences of opinion could emerge and, in the case of new and budding romances, sometimes relationships could be affected. Once again, the key for the Snake is to avoid acting in any way that could be resented by others.

More favourably aspected, however, are the Snake's own personal interests and he will not only find developing them a satisfying use of his time but also that they can lead to some interesting consequences.

Although the Snake may not always be at ease with the events of the Horse year, it can leave a powerful legacy which he will be able to profit from in the much more favourable Goat year.

The Year of the Goat starts on 1 February and holds interesting prospects for the Snake. However, while he is capable of making good progress, the year does require some discipline and dedication. This is a time when the Snake should stick to what he knows best rather than strike out into less familiar areas. On a personal level, however, the Snake can really enjoy himself, with many unattached Snakes finding new romance in the Goat year.

In his work the Snake will have every chance to improve on his present position and by using his training and ideas to good effect, he will both impress and make headway. The Snake is very much an original thinker and some of his proposals could receive a pleasing response. However, as he will find, his main successes in 2003 will come from the areas in which he has most experience rather than from more fanciful notions. Also, throughout the year, although the Snake can be reserved, he should make the most of the chances he gets to meet others in his line of work and build up contacts. Some of those he meets will be particularly taken with his manner and abilities and can be of help to him as he develops his career further. Similarly, when he does have ideas, the Snake will find it helpful to run these past those who can give him informed feedback. During the Goat year he can really benefit from the support and input of others, but he does need to be forthcoming.

April, June, September and November could all see positive developments concerning the Snake's work and for those looking to progress, these months could contain some interesting openings.

The Goat year also favours culture and creativity and those Snakes who work in the arts, design, fashion, the media or in a way which allows them to express and promote themselves can enjoy some pleasing successes. Again, these Snakes should listen carefully to any constructive advice they receive and should hold faith with what they are aiming to do. As they will find, persistence *will* be rewarded.

As far as financial matters are concerned, however, the Snake will need to remain his careful and vigilant self. He should keep a watchful eye over his situation and monitor both his outgoings and income. Without such attention he could find his outgoings far greater than allowed for. Also, he should be wary of committing his money to possibly risky ventures. This is a year for caution. The Snake could find it helpful to carry out a review of his financial situation and by doing so may discover ways of getting a better return on his money. By controlling his assets, he may find he is able to improve his situation as well as his level of security.

The Snake will obtain much pleasure from his personal interests during the Goat year and those that allow him to tap into his imagination and creativity could go particularly well. By getting to know others who share his interests, the Snake could make some new friends as well. Some Snakes could also find that their knowledge and skills give rise to freelance work and those interested in this area would do well to explore further.

As far as far as the Snake's personal life is concerned, this will be a busy and sometimes demanding year. For the most part his family life will bring him much contentment and he will encourage his loved ones in their various activities as well as enjoy times spent on mutual interests and household projects. The Snake's contribution to family life will be much appreciated. However, while much will go well, the year could be tinged with some sadness or challenging moments. At such times the supportive and considerate nature of the Snake will be greatly valued and by being willing to assist others, he can do much to help the situation. At more difficult times the one thing the Snake should avoid doing is withdrawing into himself. If he has any anxieties, he should be open about them, as that way he will be able to benefit from the advice and support of those around him. Family life is an important part of the Snake's life and although there will, as in all years, be some difficult moments, there will also be much pleasure as well as pride.

This will also be an eventful year socially and Snakes who are unattached or enjoying romance could see some major developments. Some will choose to marry or settle down with their loved one, while for others, a chance meeting will develop into a serious and often passionate romance. Being of a quiet and reserved nature the Snake does not enter into such commitments lightly, but in 2003 his passion could reach new heights. Any Snake who may be feeling in low spirits will find that going out and meeting others can bring a definite sparkle to the year and sometimes long-overdue happiness as well. For romance, March, June, July and September could be significant.

Overall, the Goat year is a generally promising one for the Snake and by using his strengths and skills, he can make good progress. Personally, the year holds good prospects, but the Snake does need to be forthcoming and in some cases overcome his more reticent and inhibited side. However, the prospects are excellent for meeting others and for love.

As far as the different types of Snake are concerned, this will be an interesting year for the *Metal Snake*. Keen and determined, he will set about his various activities with relish and in every sphere of his life he can look forward to some heartening results.

One area which will see considerable activity will be his family life and over the year the Metal Snake will do much to help and support his loved ones. There will be some personal and family successes to celebrate and these will mean a great deal to him. If at any time a difficult domestic matter should arise, the Metal Snake would find it helpful to encourage dialogue rather than keep his thoughts to himself. Family bonds are very close to the Metal Snake's heart and his input into family life will be highly valued in 2003. In addition to the support the Metal Snake will give, he will also enjoy sharing interests with his loved ones and undertaking practical projects, particularly adding features to his home and garden.

Travel, too, is well aspected and a family holiday or just days out could lead to some enjoyable occasions. Some spontaneous trips could turn out to be especially memorable.

This will also be a favourable year for social matters. Although the Metal Snake will already have a close band of good friends – and he does choose his friends carefully – his social circle is set to grow over the year. This may come about through his personal interests, his acquaintances or someone he meets while away. For any Metal Snake who has had some recent sadness to bear, the Goat year can bring a major transformation, with good prospects of meeting someone who will quickly become special. As all Metal Snakes will find, the Goat year does have a supportive element to it. All Metal Snakes should take advantage of opportunities to go out over the year, perhaps to local events or to places which might be of interest. The months from April to July and September and November are particularly favoured for social matters.

With the Goat year favouring creativity and innovation, the Metal Snake could find it a good time to enrol on a course, either to study a subject new to him or to develop his existing interests. If he is able to do something which furthers his own development in some way, he will find this adds another fulfilling element to the year. Those Metal Snakes with creative talents could find interests such as photography, art, writing, craft or design work especially pleasing.

Similarly, for those in work there will often be the chance to take on new duties, which will be a refreshing change and a greater incentive.

As far as financial matters are concerned, the Metal Snake will need to proceed carefully, however. This is not a year to take unnecessary risks or enter into wild speculations. To prevent mistakes, the Metal Snake should keep watch over his resources. If he enters into any major transaction or has important forms to complete, he needs to make sure he understands the implications. Usually he is careful in such matters, but an oversight or even error could have awkward consequences. However, while caution is necessary, the Metal Snake could be fortunate in some of his purchases over the year, particularly items for his home and his personal interests. For the collector or those who like more aesthetic items, a chance find could bring a great deal of pleasure as well as be something of a bargain.

Generally, the Goat year will be a positive one for the Metal Snake, allowing him to further his interests and make good use of his time and talents. His relations with others will also mean a great deal to him and he can look forward to some pleasing times in the company of family and friends and to adding to his social circle.

TIP FOR THE YEAR
Extend yourself and your skills in some way – and reap the benefits this will bring.

This will be a year of considerable change for the *Water Snake*. It marks his fiftieth year and many Water Snakes will feel the time has come to reassess their position and to usher in some of the changes they have been considering for some time.

One area which will be particularly affected will be the Water Snake's work. For those who have been in the same position for some time and are feeling in need of a change, the Goat year will bring some interesting opportunities. However to uncover these, the Water Snake will need to take action. By seizing the initiative and investigating new possibilities, he will find positive results will follow. In many cases the Water Snake will be able to advance to a position which makes effective use of his skills but in a different capacity from what he has recently been doing. He will relish the change and find his new work that much more fulfilling. The months from April to July and September and November could all see some interesting developments workwise.

There will of course be some Water Snakes who are content to remain in their present role, but even these are likely to experience changes. Some, because of their experience and in-house knowledge, could be asked to take on a new role or additional duties and significant promotion could beckon.

All Water Snakes, regardless of their present position, should make the most of their ideas over the year. The Water Snake is an innovative thinker and some of his proposals could bring forth a winning response.

Another favourably aspected area is the Water Snake's own personal interests and over the year these could develop in a new and exciting way. Some Water Snakes could become totally absorbed in an interest they discover almost by chance. This could be artistic, academic, recreational, a discipline such as yoga or *tai chi* or something very different, but whatever it is, it will intrigue the Water

Snake as well as do him much good. Those Water Snakes with interests of a creative nature will continue to gain satisfaction from them and some could even find their talents bringing in additional income. In 2003 the Water Snake's personal interests will give him great pleasure and despite other pressures, he should always set aside time for them.

As far as financial matters are concerned, this will be a reasonable year. However, as with all of his sign, the Water Snake should not take risks or commit money to schemes he has not properly investigated. The year calls for prudence and careful management. The Water Snake should, though, consider setting some funds aside for travel. Some Water Snakes may be tempted to go on a special holiday or visit somewhere they have long wanted to see and by planning and saving for this in advance, they could make their trip that much more special.

This will also be an eventful year in the Water Snake's domestic life. Some Water Snakes will see a relation leave home, perhaps for the purpose of further education, marriage or work. In addition, some could find themselves supporting a loved one who may be under some strain. Although this may affect the Water Snake deeply, his calm, considerate and kind-hearted ways will be appreciated by those dear to him, perhaps more than he may realize. While the Water Snake's domestic life may see some difficult moments, for much of the year his home life will bring a great deal of contentment as well as some truly joyous occasions, including for some a possible wedding or the birth of a grandchild. In addition, the Water Snake will enjoy the projects and interests he can carry out with those around him, particularly any that lead to practical improvements that everyone can appreciate.

The Water Snake's social life, too, is favourably aspected and while Water Snakes may not be the most active of socializers, there will be quite a few social occasions for them to enjoy over the year, especially when meeting up with others with similar interests and outlooks. Water Snakes who may feel that their social life has suffered recently because of work pressures will find that if they make the effort and go out more there will be a vast improvement in their situation. Unattached Water Snakes may even find happiness in an exciting new romance. For socializing, the months of March, April, June and September are well aspected.

In most respects the Goat year will be supportive of the Water Snake, but to benefit he does need to take action. By following through his ideas and making the most of the opportunities that arise, however, he can make his fiftieth year a significant one.

TIP FOR THE YEAR
Be enterprising and hold faith with your ideas, talents and aims. Positive action and persistence will be well rewarded.

This will be a satisfying year for the *Wood Snake*, particularly as it will allow him to make good use of his skills and experience as well as develop both himself and his ideas.

Many Wood Snakes will have seen considerable changes in their work over the last 12 months and the Goat year will give them the chance to build on these and consolidate their position. The Wood Snake would find it helpful to add to his contacts over the year and get to know others in his line of work. Some of those he meets will prove helpful as the year progresses and with his positive and friendly manner, the Wood Snake will impress many. He should also take advantage of any training offered. Although he may feel he already knows a great deal about his work, by refreshing and adding to his skills, he will not only help his performance but also enhance his prospects. He should advance his ideas and even if not all of them develop along the lines he intended, his initiative and contribution will be noted.

Although many Wood Snakes will be content to consolidate their present position this year, some interesting opportunities will arise. These could include promotion or the chance to take on different responsibilities. Sometimes these opportunities will appear with little warning and to benefit the Wood Snake will need to take some quick decisions.

The Goat year also contains some excellent opportunities for those Wood Snakes currently seeking a position or wanting to move to a different line of work. They could find it helpful to talk to those who may be able to assist them as well as consider other ways in which they could use their expertise. By drawing on their experience as well as following up openings that interest them, many will be successful in gaining a new position which will be a welcome contrast to their previous role but will still make good use of their strengths. April, June and the months from September to November could see some interesting developments workwise, but the whole of 2003 does hold good prospects for the Wood Snake.

The progress he makes in his work will also lead to an improvement in his financial situation and as a result many Wood Snakes will decide to spend money on both their home and themselves over the year. What the Wood Snake acquires will, in many cases, bring him much pleasure, with his fine taste often being admired by others. However, he should still keep tabs over his outgoings, otherwise he could find that his spending does mount up and could turn out to be greater than he anticipated. In addition, he should be wary of taking financial risks over the year.

Personal interests will, however, bring the Wood Snake much satisfaction, particularly those which allow him to tap into his creative talents as well as bring him into contact with others. He can gain a great deal by developing his interests, perhaps by learning about a new aspect or starting a new project. Whatever he chooses, by doing something purposeful and enjoyable, the Wood Snake can make his interests that much more fulfilling and they can also provide a useful balance to his other activities.

Domestically, this will be an active year. The Wood Snake's home life will often be busy, particularly as he may have to juggle his own activities with supporting others in his family, including more senior relations. At demanding times, the Wood Snake should not hesitate to ask others for assistance with certain household tasks rather than try to complete everything on his own. Similarly, if he has any concerns, he would find it helpful to talk them over rather than dwell on them by himself. Busy though his home life may be, it will still be rewarding and he will not only take much pride in the successes of his loved ones, but will also enjoy undertaking joint projects, including improving certain areas of his home and spending time on mutual interests. His contribution and input will, as ever, be appreciated.

The Wood Snake's social life will also see much activity and in addition to meeting friends, he can look forward to going to some fine social occasions and to adding to his social circle. The Wood Snake will impress many over the year. Those Wood Snakes who have had some recent difficulty in their personal life will find the Goat year can do much to heal this, with many seeing the start of a significant new relationship.

Overall, the Goat year is a promising one for the Wood Snake and by making the most of his abilities and the situations which arise, he will be pleased with how the year works out.

TIP FOR THE YEAR
Build on your existing skills, strengths and interests. By using your talents and time to good advantage, you can make this a rewarding and significant year.

This will be a busy year for the *Fire Snake* with a great deal happening in many areas of his life. He can look forward to some great personal successes and important progress, but the year will not be free from more difficult and challenging moments.

In particular, the Fire Snake's personal life will sometimes be quite demanding, with many calls upon his time both from younger and more senior relations. As a result, there will be occasions when the Fire Snake will despair of all that is being asked of him and his patience will be sorely tested. However, when the pressures are great, the Fire Snake should make allowance for the time he is giving to others and, whenever possible, keep his other commitments to realistic levels. It is better to defer certain household projects or tasks, for example, than to put himself under too much strain. In addition, he would find it helpful to prioritize all he has to do and manage his time sensibly. With good organization he will often be surprised at the considerable amount he is able to do. And although the year will be busy, it will nevertheless contain some happy times, especially when the Fire Snake joins with his family in carrying out activities that can be enjoyed and appreciated by everyone. Fire Snakes with young children will also derive much pleasure from guiding them and following their progress. If possible, the Fire Snake should make sure he takes a holiday or break with his loved ones over the year as well as occasionally suggest outings or treats that everyone can enjoy. His input, ideas and the time he sets aside for more pleasurable pursuits will be greatly appreciated.

On a social level, too, the Goat year will be active for the Fire Snake. Not only will he find himself much in demand with his friends but he will be invited to a wide range of social gatherings, both for pleasure and also connected with his work. The middle parts of the Goat year, from May to September, could be particularly busy and the Fire Snake could find his social circle increasing quite considerably at this time. For those who are unattached, a new romance could quickly become significant. Personally, this will be an important and active year.

The Fire Snake's work will also see activity and change. Over the year many Fire Snakes will decide to switch to a new position or be offered different responsibilities. For many this will represent promotion and will allow them to add to their experience and skills. Admittedly, some of the tasks they take on will be challenging, but by remaining focused and using his skills and initiative the Fire Snake will accomplish a great deal. He knows he has it in him to do well and the progress he makes this year will be a step towards achieving his greater ambitions.

This also applies to those Fire Snakes seeking work. By following up openings that interest them, many will be successful in gaining a position which will not only add to their experience but also be helpful to their longer-term prospects.

With the Goat year's emphasis on creativity, those Fire Snakes whose work or personal interests allow them to use their creative talents in any way should aim to further what they do. In many cases, their originality and often distinctive style will make quite an impression.

The Goat year will see a modest improvement in the Fire Snake's income, although with his many commitments, he does still need to manage his finances carefully. In addition, he should keep control of his purse strings and ignore temptation! Too many indulgences or spur of the moment purchases could soon mount up and in some cases prevent him from carrying out other plans later in the year. Spending levels do need to be watched in 2003 and ideally funds should be set aside for specific purposes.

Overall, this will be a busy and demanding year for the Fire Snake, but despite its pressures it will still contain some enjoyable times. In particular the Fire Snake's relations with those close to him will mean a great deal and what he accomplishes in his work will often have long-term value. However, throughout the Goat year, he does need to manage his time well and balance his various activities and commitments.

TIP FOR THE YEAR

The road to success can be a long one. Resolve to make further progress this year. The experience you gain can prove significant in the long term.

This will be a favourable year for the *Earth Snake* and by using his time well, he can look forward to some rewarding results.

Particularly well aspected are the Earth Snake's own personal interests and over the year he should aim to develop these in some way, perhaps by adding to his knowledge, tackling more ambitious projects or, if appropriate, obtaining guidance and tuition. Whatever he chooses to do, by devoting time to his interests the Earth Snake will find them taking on added meaning and bringing him a great deal of satisfaction. This is especially true for those Earth Snakes who enjoy more creative pursuits or have interests that allow them to express themselves in some way. One area which could particularly appeal is music. For those Earth Snakes who play an instrument or would like to learn one, this would be an excellent year to take this further. Some Earth Snakes will get additional pleasure from composing and playing their own music. The Goat year certainly does favour artistic and creative pursuits. Outdoor activities can also go well, with the year producing some memorable moments, and those Earth Snakes who enjoy sport should aim to improve on their skills.

There will also be some good opportunities for the Earth Snake to travel in 2003 and his journeys can lead to some rewarding experiences as well as be a lot of fun. If there is a particular destination those Earth Snakes born in 1929 have longed to see or want to revisit, they should make enquiries and discuss their ideas with others. Sometimes they will find that if they just express an interest, events will start to move in curious ways and will allow them to travel quite considerably.

The Earth Snake will also be grateful for the support of those around him and throughout the year he should be forthcoming about any concerns he has as well as his hopes and ideas. By being forthcoming, he will find others better able to advise and support him. While those Earth Snakes born in 1989 may feel that a gap of years may prevent proper understanding with others in their household, by being open as well as prepared to listen, they will find that others can be particularly helpful as well as more tolerant towards some of their ideas than they may have thought. However, this does require dialogue!

Over the year the Earth Snake will value his social life and those born in 1989 will particularly enjoy the time spent with friends and the range of social activities they engage in, especially in the months from June to September. Also, by joining in with activities outside school, perhaps at a local group or club, the young Earth Snake will give himself the opportunity of forging some new and good friendships. Similarly, the more senior Earth Snake will not only value his close band of long-standing friends but by getting involved in different activities over the year he too could build up some new friends. For social matters, the Goat year is favourably aspected.

As far as finance is concerned, however, the Earth Snake needs to remain prudent and avoid risks. When considering any major purchase, he should take the time to compare the prices and ranges available, otherwise he could find some of his more impulsive buys will cost him dear. Earth Snakes, take note!

For the many Earth Snakes in education, this will be an important time and these Earth Snakes should aim to work steadily and consistently. Although, for some, major exams will still be a few years away, what they learn now will give them a solid foundation for their future studies. Also, by being involved in their schoolwork, rather than remaining passive, they will find that many subjects do become more interesting as a result. The Earth Snake does, after all, possess an enquiring mind and the Goat year will provide him with ample chance to learn.

Overall, this will be a valuable and constructive year for the Earth Snake and one he can enjoy.

TIP FOR THE YEAR
Be willing to learn and extend your present skills. The greater your input, the greater the rewards.

FAMOUS SNAKES

Muhammad Ali, Ann-Margret, Yasser Arafat, Lord Baden-Powell, Ronnie Barker, Kim Basinger, Bjork, Tony Blair, Michael Bloomberg, Heinrich Böll, Michael Bolton, Brahms, Pierce Brosnan, Casanova, Chubby Checker, Dick Cheney, Jackie Collins, Tom Conti, Jim Davidson, Cecil B. de Mille, Bob Dylan, Elgar, Sir Alex Ferguson, Sir Alexander Fleming, Henry Fonda, Mahatma Gandhi, Greta Garbo, Art Garfunkel, J. Paul Getty, Dizzy Gillespie, W. E. Gladstone, Goethe, Princess Grace of Monaco, Stephen Hawking, Audrey Hepburn, Jack Higgins, Howard Hughes, Tom Hulce, Liz Hurley, James Joyce, Stacy Keach, Ronan Keating, Howard Keel, J. F. Kennedy, Carole King, Cindi Lauper, Lennox Lewis, Courtney Love, Dame Vera Lynn, Mao Tse-tung, Henri Matisse, Robert Mitchum, Nasser, Bob Newhart, Alfred Nobel, Mike Oldfield, Aristotle Onassis, Jacqueline Onassis, Pablo Picasso, Mary Pickford, Brad Pitt, André Previn, Franklin D. Roosevelt, Mickey Rourke, Jean-Paul Sartre, Franz Schubert, Brooke Shields, Paul Simon, Delia Smith, Paul Theroux, Madame Tussaud, Shania Twain, Dionne Warwick, Charlie Watts, Ruby Wax, Oprah Winfrey, Victoria Wood, Virginia Woolf, Susannah York.

25 JANUARY 1906 ∿ 12 FEBRUARY 1907	*Fire Horse*
11 FEBRUARY 1918 ∿ 31 JANUARY 1919	*Earth Horse*
30 JANUARY 1930 ∿ 16 FEBRUARY 1931	*Metal Horse*
15 FEBRUARY 1942 ∿ 4 FEBRUARY 1943	*Water Horse*
3 FEBRUARY 1954 ∿ 23 JANUARY 1955	*Wood Horse*
21 JANUARY 1966 ∿ 8 FEBRUARY 1967	*Fire Horse*
7 FEBRUARY 1978 ∿ 27 JANUARY 1979	*Earth Horse*
27 JANUARY 1990 ∿ 14 FEBRUARY 1991	*Metal Horse*
12 FEBRUARY 2002 ∿ 31 JANUARY 2003	*Water Horse*

THE
HORSE

THE PERSONALITY OF THE HORSE

If you do things well, do them better. Be daring, be
different, be just.

Anita Roddick, a Horse

The Horse is born under the signs of elegance and ardour.
He has a most engaging and charming manner and is
usually very popular. He loves meeting people and likes
attending parties and other large social gatherings.

The Horse is a lively character and enjoys being the
centre of attention. He has considerable leadership qualities
and is much admired for his honest and straightforward
manner. He is an eloquent and persuasive speaker and has
a great love of discussion and debate. He also has a particularly agile mind and can assimilate facts remarkably
quickly.

He does, however, have a fiery temper and although his
outbursts are usually short-lived, he can often say things
which he will later regret. He is also not particularly good
at keeping secrets.

The Horse has many interests and involves himself in a
wide variety of activities. He can, however, get involved in
so much that he can often waste his energies on projects
which he never has time to complete. He also has a
tendency to change his interests rather frequently and will
often get caught up with the latest craze or 'in thing' until
something better or more exciting turns up.

The Horse also likes to have a certain amount of
freedom and independence. He hates being bound by petty

rules and regulations and as far as possible likes to feel that he is answerable to no one but himself. But despite this spirit of freedom, he still likes to have the support and encouragement of others in his various enterprises.

Due to his many talents and likeable nature, the Horse will often go far in life. He enjoys challenges and is a methodical and tireless worker. However, should things work against him and he fail in any of his enterprises, it will take a long time for him to recover and pick up the pieces again. Success to the Horse means everything. To fail is a disaster and a humiliation.

The Horse likes to have variety in his life and he will try his hand at many different things before he settles down to one particular job. Even then, he will probably remain alert to see whether there are any better opportunities for him to take up. The Horse has a restless nature and can easily get bored. He does, however, excel in any position which allows him sufficient freedom to act on his own initiative or which brings him into contact with a lot of people.

Although the Horse is not particularly bothered about accumulating great wealth, he handles his finances with care and will rarely experience any serious financial problems.

The Horse also enjoys travel and he loves visiting new and far-away places. At some stage during his life he will be tempted to live abroad for a short period of time and due to his adaptable nature he will find that he will fit in well wherever he goes.

The Horse pays a great deal of attention to his appearance and usually likes to wear smart, colourful and rather distinctive clothes. He is very attractive to the opposite sex and will often have many romances before he settles down. He is loyal and protective to his partner, but despite his family commitments, still likes to retain a certain measure of independence and have the freedom to carry on with his own interests and hobbies. He will find that he is especially well suited to those born under the signs of the Tiger, Goat, Rooster and Dog. The Horse can also get on well with the Rabbit, Dragon, Snake, Pig and another Horse, but he will find the Ox too serious and intolerant for his liking. The Horse will also have difficulty in getting on with the Monkey and the Rat – the Monkey is very inquisitive and the Rat seeks security, and both will resent the Horse's rather independent ways.

The female Horse is usually most attractive and has a friendly, outgoing personality. She is highly intelligent, has many interests and is alert to everything that is going on around her. She particularly enjoys outdoor pursuits and often likes to take part in sport and keep-fit activities. She also enjoys travel, literature and the arts, and is a very good conversationalist.

Although the Horse can be stubborn and rather self-centred, he does have a considerate nature and is often willing to help others. He has a good sense of humour and will usually make a favourable impression wherever he goes. Provided he can curb his slightly restless nature and keep a tight control over his temper, he will go through life making friends, taking part in a multitude of different activities and generally achieving many of his objectives. His life will rarely be dull.

THE FIVE DIFFERENT TYPES OF HORSE

In addition to the 12 signs of the Chinese zodiac, there are five elements, and these have a strengthening or moderating influence on the sign. The effects of the five elements on the Horse are described below, together with the years in which the elements were exercising their influence. Therefore all Horses born in 1930 and 1990 are Metal Horses, those born in 1942 and 2002 are Water Horses, and so on.

Metal Horse: 1930, 1990
This Horse is bold, confident and forthright. He is ambitious and a great innovator. He loves challenges and takes great delight in sorting out complicated problems. He likes to have a certain amount of independence and resents any outside interference in his affairs. The Metal Horse has charm and a certain charisma, but he can also be very stubborn and rather impulsive. He usually has many friends and enjoys an active social life.

Water Horse: 1942, 2002
The Water Horse has a friendly nature, a good sense of humour, and is able to talk intelligently on a wide range of topics. He is astute in business matters and quick to take advantage of any opportunities that arise. He does, however, have a tendency to get easily distracted and can

change his interests – and indeed his mind – rather frequently, and this can sometimes work to his detriment. He is nevertheless very talented and can often go far in life. He pays a great deal of attention to his appearance and is usually smart and well turned out. He loves to travel and also enjoys sport and other outdoor activities.

Wood Horse: 1954

The Wood Horse has a most agreeable and amiable nature. He communicates well with others and, like the Water Horse, is able to talk intelligently on many different subjects. He is a hard and conscientious worker and is held in high esteem by his friends and colleagues. His opinions are often sought and given his imaginative nature, he can quite often come up with some very original and practical ideas. He is usually widely read and likes to lead a busy social life. He can also be most generous and often holds high moral views.

Fire Horse: 1906, 1966

The element of Fire combined with the temperament of the Horse creates one of the most powerful forces in the Chinese zodiac. The Fire Horse is destined to lead an exciting and eventful life and to make his mark in his chosen profession. He has a forceful personality and his intelligence and resolute manner bring him the support and admiration of many. He loves action and excitement and his life will rarely be quiet. He can, however, be rather blunt and forthright in his views and does not take kindly to interference in his own affairs or to obeying orders. He is a flamboyant character, has a good sense of humour and will lead a very active social life.

Earth Horse: 1918, 1978

This Horse is considerate and caring. He is more cautious than some of the other types of Horse, but he is wise, perceptive and extremely capable. Although he can be rather indecisive at times, he has considerable business acumen and is very astute in financial matters. He has a quiet, friendly nature and is well thought of by his family and friends.

PROSPECTS FOR THE HORSE IN 2003

The Chinese New Year starts on 1 February 2003. Until then, the old year, the Year of the Horse, is still making its presence felt.

The Horse year (12 February 2002 to 31 January 2003) holds considerable potential for its own sign, although to benefit the Horse will need to make the most of changing situations.

In what remains of his year the Horse can make good headway in his work, although he should keep a close eye on any new proposals and be accommodating if asked to take on new duties or responsibilities. He also needs to be mindful of the views of his colleagues. In the closing months of the year he can make progress – some Horses will be promoted at this time – but he will need to show himself to be adaptable and a good team member rather than appear too independent. September and October could, in particular, offer some fine opportunities to progress.

This will also be a positive year for money matters, although the Horse should take his time over any major purchases he is considering and could find it helpful to spread out his more seasonal spending. Without some control, he could find his outgoings much greater than he anticipated.

As always, the Horse will value his relations with those around him and in the remaining months of the year both his domestic and social life will be busy and generally pleasurable. However, with so many activities to fit in, the Horse will need to consult closely with others as well as be flexible over some of his own arrangements. Again, to appear too single-minded could cause some tensions and sometimes sour what could otherwise be a pleasant time.

With so much activity going on, the Horse should also give some consideration to his own well-being in the closing months of the year and ensure that he has sufficient exercise and a balanced diet. To be at his best and able to lead the full and busy life he so enjoys, he does need to look after himself.

Overall, the Horse year does hold good prospects for its sign and by adapting to the situations that arise and paying careful attention to the views of those around him, the Horse will find his own year generally agreeable and productive.

The Year of the Goat starts on 1 February and will be a rewarding one for the Horse. In particular it will give him more opportunity to use his ideas and strengths to good effect. It is also favourably aspected for personal matters.

As the Goat year starts, the Horse would do well to take stock of his current position and give some thought to what he would like to accomplish over the next 12 months. By having some idea of what he wants to do, he will find himself becoming more focused as well as taking the action necessary to achieve his aims. In this respect, the Goat year will be a satisfying one, with the Horse feeling much more in control of his destiny.

For work matters, this can be a particularly constructive year, especially with regard to long-term benefits. Aware of his strengths and expertise, the Horse's employers will often single him out for specific tasks or give him new responsibilities. By rising to what is asked of him, the Horse can look forward to a good level of achievement. Furthermore, he will find that others will look favourably on ideas he puts forward. For those Horses whose work involves an element of creativity or allows them to express themselves in some way, this can be an especially rewarding time. However, rather than look to make big career jumps this year, the Horse will obtain greater success by concentrating on what he does best. By adding to his experience he can prepare the way for the significant progress that awaits in the auspicious Monkey year.

The Goat year will offer interesting prospects for those Horses who are seeking work or a change from their present role. However, rather than pursue every vacancy on offer, these Horses should consider what it is they want to do and, if appropriate, take advantage of any training or retraining opportunities as well as talk to those who are able to offer career advice. By investigating the type of work they want, many Horses will start a chain of events which will have far-reaching consequences. Even if initial applications do not go their way, they should persist. By preparing for interviews and remaining determined (and the Horse does possess a determined streak!), many will make the breakthrough that will give their career a new lease of life. And although the positions some Horses obtain will be modest, often they will hold the key to significant advances later. April and May and the last quarter of the year could see some positive career developments.

As far as financial matters are concerned, this will be quite an expensive year for the Horse, particularly concerning his accommodation. In view of this the Horse does need to manage his finances carefully and if he takes on any loan or enters into a financial agreement, he should ensure he is fully aware of the obligations he is taking on and makes allowance for them in his budgeting. He would also find it helpful to keep an account of his income and expenditure. The more control he exercises, the better he will fare.

Accommodation matters will, though, draw heavily on the Horse's resources during the Goat year, particularly as quite a few Horses will decide to move or make improvements to their home. Moving could turn out to be a protracted process, particularly in finding suitable accommodation. However, after some searching, many Horses will discover an ideal place which will become their home for many years to come. Although moving or carrying out home improvements will be time-consuming and involve considerable outlay, if the Horse sets his ideas in motion, the Goat year will reward him.

While the Horse will face some heavy expenses in 2003, he should, if possible, still aim to take a holiday over the year. Even if this is simply visiting relations or friends he has not seen for some time, the break from his usual routine will do him good.

As far as the Horse's domestic life is concerned, this will be a busy but pleasing year. Others are keen to offer support to the Horse, but to benefit from it he does need to be prepared to talk through his ideas as well as any concerns he might have. Similarly, he needs to plan major projects carefully with all concerned rather than go ahead without adequate consultation. Horses, take note and do be prepared to discuss matters fully.

In spite of all the domestic activity, the Horse can, however, look forward to some rewarding times with his loved ones, particularly some of the more spontaneous occasions, for example an outing taken on the spur of the moment. Domestically, there will be much to enjoy in the Goat year.

The Horse's social life will also be rewarding as well as often busy. Over the year he can look forward to attending a wide range of sometimes unusual social gatherings as well as socializing with friends. Horses who would like to widen their social circle will find that by going out more they will soon get to meet others and form what can become good friendships. April, May, September and December will be especially favourable times socially.

For those Horses newly in love or seeking romance, the Goat year is wonderfully aspected and many unattached Horses will meet someone who will quickly become special. Love, passion and marriage will certainly figure prominently for many Horses in the Goat year.

In many respects this will be an enjoyable and constructive year and by deciding what he wants to accomplish, the Horse will find many of his plans will work out well and often have far-reaching results. The aspects are encouraging and the Horse, with his talents, enterprise and outgoing personality, can make much of them and reap some fine rewards as a result.

As far as the different types of Horse are concerned, this will be a positive as well as interesting year for the *Metal Horse*. However to benefit from the generally favourable aspects, he will need to make the most of available opportunities as well as show a certain flexibility in attitude. Some Metal Horses can be particularly self-willed and to remain too set in their ways or be unwilling to consider new possibilities could prevent them from making as much of the year as they might. The Goat year has a pioneering spirit to it and for the adventurous and willing, it holds much promise.

For those Metal Horses born in 1990 there will certainly be many opportunities to learn as well as to discover new strengths and talents. However, for these to unfold, the young Metal Horses need to show willing and be prepared to make the most of the opportunities available to them. By taking part in after-school activities, joining a youth group or taking up a new interest, they will be able to extend their skills and make new friends as well as have fun, but to benefit they do need to take advantage of such opportunities. Also, in their schoolwork, while they will have their strong areas, they should not close their minds to subjects with which they feel they have little affinity. By giving them a try they could find their doubts misplaced and enjoy the satisfaction when their extra effort pays off with better marks or they master something that had previously given some difficulty.

The young Metal Horse should also extend his existing interests over the year. Whether these are of a sporting nature (and the Metal Horse often excels in such areas) or musical, artistic or in some other sphere, by doing something he enjoys and developing his skills, he will find that his interests bring him a great deal of pleasure. This also applies to those Metal Horses born in 1930. Activities which they enjoy and which allow them to tap into their ideas and creative talents can bring them considerable benefit.

On a domestic level this will be an active year. For those Metal Horses born in 1990, others will be willing to support, encourage and advise them, but to benefit from this the Metal Horse does need to be prepared to talk over any matters that may be giving him concern. Also, if there are interests, activities or ideas that he would like to try, he should be open about these rather than keep his thoughts to himself. That way he will give others more chance to consider and possibly help with what he wants rather than, in some cases, letting his hopes come to nothing.

The more senior Metal Horse will also have good reason to be thankful for the support given by family members and if he has any concerns or requires more practical assistance, he should not hesitate to ask. In addition, quite a few Metal Horses will decide to move to accommodation more suitable to their needs and again they will be grateful for the assistance given by family and close friends, particularly with the considerable sorting and packing that will have to be done. Similarly, many of those who do not move will decide to tidy up certain areas of their home and rid themselves of accumulated paperwork or items they no longer require. Although this process may take longer than anticipated, they will be pleased with how much better organized certain parts of their home have become.

In matters of finance the year is reasonably aspected. However, the Metal Horse does need to be careful with his outgoings as well as with any sizeable agreements he enters into, especially those related to moving or accommodation costs. Should he have any questions or uncertainties, he must check and, if appropriate, seek professional guidance. This is not a year in which he can take financial risks or jump to conclusions. The younger Metal Horse also needs to be careful with his outgoings, in particular to avoid succumbing to too many immediate temptations. Sometimes he could find money that he has spent on impulse purchases could have been put towards something of more use. It would be in the young Metal Horse's interest to have greater control over his purse strings, difficult though this sometimes might be.

Socially, the year will see the young Metal Horses in fine spirits and particularly enjoying the company of their best friends. And with the chance to go to special interest groups, parties and other social occasions, there will be ample opportunity to extend their social circle. The more senior Metal Horses will also welcome the opportunities they get to go out. Should any Metal Horse be feeling lonely, perhaps after moving to a new area, he will find that by joining in with local activities, clubs or special interest groups, he will soon befriend others with similar interests.

Overall, the Goat year is favourably aspected for all Metal Horses, whether born in 1930 or 1990, but to benefit they do need to make the most of the opportunities available to them.

TIP FOR THE YEAR
This is an active year. Follow through your ideas and plans and be willing to learn and discover.

The Year of the Goat holds interesting prospects for the *Water Horse* with much happening in the different areas of his life.

Many Water Horses will have recently moved or will decide to do so in 2003 and as a result they will devote much time and attention to their home, sorting through and clearing out belongings and arranging their home as they would like. With the Water Horse's practical nature, he may also set himself some projects to tackle, redesigning certain areas, changing the décor or adding new comforts and features to his home. Although some of what the Water Horse has in mind is ambitious and will require considerable time and energy to carry out, he will be pleased with what he achieves. Those Water Horses with gardens may similarly decide to add new features, alter the layout in some way or experiment with new stock. Again, the Water Horse will derive much pleasure from seeing his ideas unfold. In his more practical activities he does, though, need to liaise closely with everyone around him and be mindful of any suggestions and ideas raised. By fully involving others, he will also find their assistance will make the projects that much easier and quicker to complete.

In addition to the practical activities that take place in his home life, the Water Horse can look forward to some pleasing family news. This includes the possible birth of a grandchild or great-grandchild as well as the progress of someone who means a great deal to him. The Water Horse will also enjoy meeting up with various family members, including some he does not see as often as he would like. However, while much will go well, there could be some family issues which require more delicate handling. At such times, the Water Horse will need to think carefully of the effect his words will have and be tactful and discreet as well as listen closely to what others are saying. Overall, though, his domestic life will be pleasant and rewarding.

The Water Horse's social life, too, is favourably aspected and likely to become busier as the year develops. In addition to the activities he is already involved with, he can look forward to a variety of social occasions and these will allow him to add to his social circle. The months from March to May and the last quarter of the year will be active and promising times.

Another area which is well favoured is self-development and if there is an interest or skill the Water Horse feels it would be useful to learn, he should aim to find out more.

Something worthwhile and of potential benefit will appeal to his practical nature as well as often be pleasurable to do.

The Water Horse will enjoy the travelling he undertakes over the year and some Water Horses will decide to visit an area they have not been to before and will see some interesting and sometimes awe-inspiring sights.

The Goat year will also contain some important developments workwise. Although many Water Horses will be content to remain in their present position, change is in the offing. For some, promotion or increased responsibilities will beckon, while others may be tempted to retire or seek a position which involves fewer hours. Whatever the Water Horse chooses, the Goat year will offer him more chance to determine what he does and often obtain a greater degree of satisfaction as a result.

As far as financial matters are concerned, the Water Horse can look forward to receiving some additional sums of money over the year, either as a bonus or some form of gift. While this will be welcome, he will still have many expenses to meet, especially accommodation-wise, and will need to manage his finances with care. When entering into any major transaction or handling important paperwork, he needs to be thorough and check all the implications. Water Horses, do take note.

Overall, though, the year of the Goat will be a pleasing one for the Water Horse and by following through his ideas, he will accomplish a great deal.

TIP FOR THE YEAR
Be organized and use your time well.

This will be a successful year for the *Wood Horse*, allowing him to build on his present position as well as enjoy a pleasing and often active personal life. In addition, the Goat year will give him more chance to develop some of his ideas and see them through to fruition.

Workwise, the Goat year offers much promise. Many Wood Horses will be content to build on the changes of the last 12 months, learn more about the various aspects of their job and use their skills to often telling effect. Those whose work contains an element of creativity, or allows them to communicate with others, could find the Goat year bringing them some notable successes. The Wood Horse will, though, find his greatest gains will come from concentrating on his areas of expertise rather than looking to switch to completely new activities.

While many Wood Horses will choose to make the most of their present role, for those who are eager to move on or who are seeking a position, the Goat year holds some interesting prospects. However, to benefit, these Wood Horses should consider the different ways in which they can draw on their experience as well as the type of role they are seeking. With some imaginative thinking as well as discussion with those able to offer informed advice, some interesting possibilities could emerge. Again, the Wood Horse's strengths, interests and experience will hold the key to his future success and, for some, now is the time to consider other ways in which these could be used and the long-term implications. For many Wood Horses, their ideas and achievements in 2003 can have far-reaching consequences.

The Wood Horse can look forward to a modest improvement in his income over the year, although many Wood

Horses will spend a lot on their accommodation, buying equipment, furnishings, redecorating certain areas and perhaps moving altogether. To carry out his plans and make the most of his resources, the Wood Horse will need to manage his money carefully and he could find it helpful to set a certain amount aside for specific items as well as make allowance for his various obligations. Despite his often considerable expenditure, he should still make sure he enjoys the fruits of his labours and, if possible, makes provision for a holiday as well as for recreational pursuits, including hobbies, family occasions and general socializing.

The Wood Horse will derive much satisfaction from his personal interests over the year and should make sure he devotes time to these. Practical and creative pursuits are particularly favoured, especially those which allow the Wood Horse to act upon some of his ideas or express himself in some way. Many Wood Horses will also enjoy the times they spend out of doors, whether gardening, following or taking part in sport or visiting places of interest in their area.

As always, the Wood Horse will value his relations with others over the year. Domestically, he will do much to support family members, particularly those much younger and also considerably senior to himself. While sometimes this will lead to moments of pressure and demand a great deal from the Wood Horse, his efforts will be appreciated. The Wood Horse will also enjoy some of the interests and projects he can carry out with his loved ones and should always make sure there is time to be together, to talk and to spend on activities that can be shared.

The Wood Horse's social life will also benefit him by allowing him to go out, unwind and just enjoy himself. Some of the year will be pleasantly busy and rewarding, with a variety of social occasions to attend. For those Wood Horses who are unattached and would like more company, the Goat year is superbly aspected, with a chance encounter in the early months of 2003 quickly becoming significant.

In many respects this will be an important year for the Wood Horse and by using his strengths and following through his ideas, he will be satisfied with much of what he does and content in the knowledge that the experience he is gaining will be to his future good.

TIP FOR THE YEAR
Be sure to balance your commitments and activities. Too much attention in one area could cause problems or conflicts in another.

After the challenges and some of the tribulations of recent times, the *Fire Horse* can look forward to a much improved year which will give him more chance to follow through some of his ideas as well as use his skills to good effect.

At work in particular the Goat year holds interesting prospects and as the year starts, the Fire Horse should give some thought to what he would like to accomplish over the next 12 months. Although his initial ideas may have to be modified to fit in with prevailing situations, at least forming some idea of his aims will give him a clearer sense of direction as well as increase his resolve. The way his career develops in 2003 is very much in his own hands.

Some Fire Horses will decide to remain with the company they currently work for, concentrating on duties they do so well and drawing on their experience. However, with their contacts and in-house knowledge, many will find themselves excellently placed for promotion should they wish to make further advances. Also, if offered the chance of further training or taking on different responsibilities, they will find this will improve their prospects and, in some cases, widen the scope of positions available to them in the future.

For those Fire Horses who are eager for a change or seeking employment, the Goat year will also bring some interesting developments and by actively following up openings that appeal to them, they will be given what can turn out to be an important opportunity. Admittedly, this may be slightly different from what the Fire Horse may have envisaged, but it will allow him to broaden his experience and in many cases be an excellent stepping-stone to something better in the near future. Indeed, one of the benefits of the Goat year is that it will allow many Fire Horses to set their career on an often more suitable and exciting track.

The Fire Horse should also aim to extend his personal interests over the year, either by adding to his knowledge, setting himself some new challenges or taking up a different interest. Whatever he chooses, by doing something purposeful as well as enjoyable, he will find his interests can turn out to be a rewarding aspect of the year. In some cases, an interest or special skill could even become another source of income.

The Goat year will be a positive one for financial matters, with many Fire Horses not only seeing an increase in their income but also receiving an unexpected gift or bonus. With this financial upturn, many Fire Horses will decide to add some improvements to their accommodation as well as spend money on themselves, perhaps adding to their wardrobe or engaging in recreational pursuits. By planning his purchases carefully, rather than proceeding in too much haste, the Fire Horse will be pleased with what he acquires. In addition, he should also aim to set some funds aside for his future, perhaps starting or adding to a savings scheme or pension policy. The one area that does require especial care is paperwork, particularly forms relating to finance, tax and longer-term commitments. The Fire Horse does need to be thorough and check the small print, and should he have any doubts, he should seek guidance. Without increased vigilance he could find himself at some disadvantage as well as involved in some awkward and protracted correspondence.

The Fire Horse will, though, take much pleasure from his family life over the year. He will do much to support and encourage those around him and those Fire Horses with children in education will find the effective way they are able to help build their confidence and to guide them – even if subtly – really will count for a great deal. Similarly, the help and support the Fire Horse gives to more senior relations will be valued. While certain developments within his family may concern him (and indeed, almost every year does have its awkward moments), his judgement and assistance will be appreciated. The Fire Horse will take great pleasure in the activities he can share with others and will value the gestures of love and affection he receives from those important to him. Any Fire Horse who may have been experiencing some strains in his relations with others will find that being prepared to talk more and giving time and attention rather than being so preoccupied can do much to help, particularly in healing any rifts that may have occurred.

The year is also favourably aspected for social matters, with the Fire Horse again enjoying many of the social functions he attends as well as the chances to meet up with friends and extend his social circle. For those who may start the year alone, the first few months of the Goat year can bring the gift of an important friendship.

In many respects the Goat year will bring the Fire Horse a greater degree of contentment and by making the most of his talents and ideas, he will fare well and often reap some important rewards.

TIP FOR THE YEAR
Think, plan and then act.

This will be a good year for the *Earth Horse* with some positive developments in many areas of his life.

On a personal level the Goat year holds some fine prospects for the Earth Horse, with the chance of an addition to his family as well as many meaningful times with his partner and others who mean a lot to him. In particular, the Earth Horse will delight in the activities he can share with others and whether these involve developing mutual interests, carrying out projects or just spending time talking, there will be some special moments. In addition, there will be many Earth Horses who decide to change their accommodation over the year and although this will give rise to some hectic weeks, the Earth Horse will enjoy settling into his new home and getting it as he wants. He will also do much to help more senior relations in 2003 and although with his own commitments and activities he already has much to occupy his time, the assistance he can give will be appreciated.

Socially, too, this is a well aspected year. In addition to enjoying the company of his existing friends, the Earth Horse will find himself going to a wide range of social occasions and having many agreeable times. With his amiable manner and wide interests, he will also find his social circle widening quite considerably. Some new acquaintances and work contacts will become important and helpful as the year develops.

For those Earth Horses who have had some problems in their personal life of late and may be feeling dispirited, the Goat year offers excellent prospects. Rather than dwell too much on the past, these Earth Horses should draw a line under it and move forward. In the process, they will not only find themselves establishing a new and more rewarding social life but also meeting someone early in the year who will quickly become important. Personally, the Goat year offers much promise and, in some cases, a new start.

The Earth Horse should also devote time to his personal interests. Whether these are purely of a recreational nature or involve developing some skill, they can help provide an important balance to his life as well as often prove most satisfying.

Travel, too, is favoured and the Earth Horse should try to go away at some time during 2003. In some cases his adventurous nature will get the better of him and he will visit places off the usual tourist map. Some of these will leave a strong and lasting impression.

As far as the Earth Horse's work is concerned, this will be an interesting although demanding year. He will be given an excellent chance to further his experience and may take on new responsibilities. While these new duties will often be exacting, by rising to the challenge, the Earth Horse will not only acquire new skills but also do much to further his prospects. He should take advantage of any training opportunities as well as any chances to promote his ideas. The Earth Horse has a practical and enterprising streak, and his input and earnestness will be both recognized and appreciated.

For those Earth Horses seeking work, the Goat year offers excellent prospects and by following up vacancies that interest them, many will be given a position which holds considerable scope for the future. The Earth Horse certainly has many fine skills, some of which have yet to be discovered or fully explored, and the developments of the year will help to unlock some of his potential.

In matters of finance the Earth Horse will, though, need to manage his resources with care. With his many obligations and commitments, he does need to budget carefully as well as make provision for forthcoming expenses and for any new agreements he may be considering. Although sometimes his finances will be tricky to balance, with care and resourcefulness he will be pleased with how he manages and with all that he is able to do.

Overall, this will be a positive year for the Earth Horse and it will not only allow him to develop himself and his strengths, but also be a time of considerable personal happiness.

TIP FOR THE YEAR
Widen your horizons. The future holds much promise and this is a time to look forward and consider future possibilities and ambitions.

FAMOUS HORSES

Neil Armstrong, Rowan Atkinson, Samuel Beckett, Ingmar Bergman, Leonard Bernstein, Karen Black, Cherie Blair, Helena Bonham Carter, James Cameron, Ray Charles, Chopin, Sir Sean Connery, Billy Connolly, Catherine Cookson, Ronnie Corbett, Elvis Costello, Kevin Costner, Cindy Crawford, Michael Crichton, James Dean, Iain Duncan Smith, Clint Eastwood, Thomas Alva Edison, Britt Ekland, Chris Evans, Harrison Ford, Aretha Franklin, Sir Bob Geldof, Samuel Goldwyn, Billy Graham, Gene Hackman, Rolf Harris, Rita Hayworth, Jimi Hendrix, J. Edgar Hoover, Bob Hoskins, Janet Jackson, Neil Kinnock, Calvin Klein, Lenin, Annie Lennox, Desmond Lynam, Sir Paul McCartney, Nelson Mandela, Princess Margaret, Ben Murphy, Sir Isaac Newton, Louis Pasteur, Harold Pinter, J. B. Priestley, Puccini, Lou Reed, Rembrandt, Ruth Rendell, Jean Renoir, Anita Roddick, Theodore Roosevelt, Helena Rubenstein, Peter Sissons, Lord Snowdon, Alexander Solzhenitsyn, Barbra Streisand, Kiefer Sutherland, Patrick Swayze, John Travolta, Kathleen Turner, Mike Tyson, Vivaldi, Robert Wagner, Denzil Washington, Billy Wilder,

Andy Williams, the Duke of Windsor, Boris Yeltsin, Michael York, Will Young.

13 FEBRUARY 1907 〜 1 FEBRUARY 1908	*Fire Goat*
1 FEBRUARY 1919 〜 19 FEBRUARY 1920	*Earth Goat*
17 FEBRUARY 1931 〜 5 FEBRUARY 1932	*Metal Goat*
5 FEBRUARY 1943 〜 24 JANUARY 1944	*Water Goat*
24 JANUARY 1955 〜 11 FEBRUARY 1956	*Wood Goat*
9 FEBRUARY 1967 〜 29 JANUARY 1968	*Fire Goat*
28 JANUARY 1979 〜 15 FEBRUARY 1980	*Earth Goat*
15 FEBRUARY 1991 〜 3 FEBRUARY 1992	*Metal Goat*
1 FEBRUARY 2003 〜 21 JANUARY 2004	*Water Goat*

THE
GOAT

THE PERSONALITY OF THE GOAT

Let a man who has to make his fortune in life remember this maxim: Attacking is the only secret. Dare and the world yields, or if it beats you sometimes, dare it again and you will succeed.

William M. Thackeray, a Goat

The Goat is born under the sign of art. He is imaginative, creative and has a good appreciation of the finer things in life. He has an easy-going nature and prefers to live in a relaxed and pressure-free environment. He hates any sort of discord or unpleasantness and does not like to be bound by a strict routine or rigid timetable. The Goat is not one to be hurried against his will, but despite his seemingly relaxed approach to life, he is something of a perfectionist and when he starts work on a project he is certain to give of his best.

The Goat usually prefers to work in a team rather than on his own. He likes to have the support and encouragement of others and if left to deal with matters on his own he can get very worried and tends to view things rather pessimistically. Wherever possible he will leave major decision-making to others while he concentrates on his own pursuits. If, however, he feels particularly strongly about a certain matter or has to defend his position in any way, he will act with great fortitude and precision.

The Goat has a very persuasive nature and often uses his considerable charm to get his own way. He can, however, be rather hesitant about letting his true feelings be known and if he were prepared to be more forthright he would do much better as a result.

The Goat tends to have a quiet, somewhat reserved nature but when he is in company he likes he can often become the centre of attention. He can be highly amusing, a marvellous host at parties and a superb entertainer. Whenever the spotlight falls on him, his adrenalin starts to flow and he can be assured of giving a sparkling performance, particularly if he is allowed to use his creative skills in any way.

Of all the signs in the Chinese zodiac, the Goat is probably the most gifted artistically. Whether in the theatre, literature, music or art, he is certain to make a lasting impression. He is a born creator and is rarely happier than when occupied in some artistic pursuit. But even in this the Goat does well to work with others rather than on his own. He needs inspiration and a guiding influence, but when he has found his true *métier*, he can often receive widespread acclaim and recognition.

In addition to his liking for the arts, the Goat is usually quite religious and often has a deep interest in nature, animals and the countryside. He is also fairly athletic and there are many Goats who have excelled in some form of sporting activity or who have a great interest in sport.

Although the Goat is not particularly materialistic or concerned about finance, he will find that he will usually be lucky in financial matters and will rarely be short of the necessary funds to tide himself over. He is, however, rather indulgent and tends to spend his money as soon as he receives it rather than make provision for the future.

The Goat usually leaves home when he is young but he will always maintain strong links with his parents and the other members of his family. He is also rather nostalgic and is well known for keeping mementos of his childhood and souvenirs of places that he has visited. His home will not be particularly tidy but he knows where everything is and it will also be scrupulously clean.

Affairs of the heart are particularly important to the Goat and he will often have many romances before he finally settles down. Although he is fairly adaptable, he prefers to live in a secure and stable environment and will find that he is best suited to those born under the signs of the Tiger, Horse, Monkey, Pig and Rabbit. He can also establish a good relationship with the Dragon, Snake, Rooster and another Goat, but he may find the Ox and Dog a little too serious for his liking. Neither will he care particularly for the Rat's rather thrifty ways.

The female Goat devotes all her time and energy to the needs of her family. She has excellent taste in home furnishings and often uses her considerable artistic skills to make clothes for herself and her children. She takes great care over her appearance and can be most attractive to the opposite sex. Although she is not the best organized of people, her engaging manner and delightful sense of humour create a favourable impression wherever she goes. She is also a good cook and usually derives much pleasure from gardening and outdoor pursuits.

The Goat can win friends easily and people generally feel relaxed in his company. He has a kind and understanding nature and although he can occasionally be stubborn, with the right support and encouragement he can live a happy and very satisfying life. The more he can use his creative skills, the happier he will be.

THE FIVE DIFFERENT TYPES OF GOAT

In addition to the 12 signs of the Chinese zodiac, there are five elements, and these have a strengthening or moderating influence on the sign. The effects of the five elements on the Goat are described below, together with the years in which the elements were exercising their influence. Therefore all Goats born in 1931 and 1991 are Metal Goats, those born in 1943 and in this year are Water Goats, and so on.

Metal Goat: 1931, 1991

This Goat is thorough and conscientious in all that he does and is capable of doing very well in his chosen profession. Despite his confident manner, he can be a great worrier and he would find it helpful to discuss his concerns with others rather than keep them to himself. He is loyal to his family and employers and will have a small group of extremely good friends. He has good artistic taste and is usually highly skilled in some aspect of the arts. He is often a collector of antiques and his home will be very tastefully furnished.

Water Goat: 1943, 2003

The Water Goat is very popular and makes friends with remarkable ease. He is good at spotting opportunities but does not always have the necessary confidence to follow them through. He likes to have security both in his home life and at work and does not take kindly to change. He is articulate, has a good sense of humour and is usually very good with children.

Wood Goat: 1955

This Goat is generous, kind-hearted and always eager to please. He usually has a large circle of friends and involves himself in a wide variety of different activities. He has a very trusting nature but he can sometimes give in to the demands of others a little too easily and it would be in his own interests if he were to stand his ground more often. He is usually lucky in financial matters and, like the Water Goat, is very good with children.

Fire Goat: 1907, 1967

This Goat usually knows what he wants in life and he often uses his considerable charm and persuasive personality in order to achieve his aims. He can sometimes let his imagination run away with him, however, and has a tendency to ignore matters which are not to his liking. He is rather extravagant in his spending and would do well to exercise a little more care when dealing with financial matters. He has a lively personality, many friends and loves attending parties and social occasions.

Earth Goat: 1919, 1979

This Goat has a very considerate and caring nature. He is particularly loyal to his family and friends and invariably creates a favourable impression wherever he goes. He is reliable and conscientious in his work but he finds it difficult to save and never likes to deprive himself of any little luxury which he might fancy. He has numerous interests and is often very well read. He usually derives much pleasure from following the activities of various members of his family.

PROSPECTS FOR THE GOAT IN 2003

The Chinese New Year starts on 1 February 2003. Until then, the old year, the Year of the Horse, is still making its presence felt.

The Year of the Horse (12 February 2002 to 31 January 2003) will have been a reasonable one for the Goat, with the closing months being both interesting and active. One of the key features of the Horse year is that it is a time for action and provided the Goat is prepared to follow through his ideas and make the most of the opportunities that arise, he can make headway.

As far as his work is concerned, September and October 2002 could hold some particularly fine opportunities and for those Goats who are eager for a change or who are looking for work, these two months could see some openings which would be well worth pursuing. Also, by using their skills to good effect and maintaining their high standards, all Goats can considerably enhance their reputation and this will serve them well in their own year.

The closing months of the Horse year will, though, be an expensive time. The Goat will spend a lot on both his domestic and social life and will also want to make many seasonal purchases. Although he will not begrudge much of this expense – and some of it is unavoidable – it would be in his interest to keep an eye on his purse strings and perhaps think twice about some of his more expensive indulgences, especially when he has other commitments to meet.

The Goat's domestic and social life is well aspected in the Horse year and the Goat will take heart from the support he receives from those close to him. The closing months will be active, with the Goat much in demand. There will be a lot to arrange and fit in as well as a variety of social occasions to attend and enjoy. September and December will be two especially busy months, with chances for the Goat to extend his social circle as well as meet up with those he has not seen for some time.

With so much happening and an often considerable amount on his mind, the Goat does need to take care of himself at this time and ensure he has a good diet as well as sufficient rest. Pushing himself too hard could leave him lacking his usual energy and sparkle. Goats, take note!

Overall, the Horse year will be a favourable one for the Goat, but it does call for him to make the most of the situations that arise.

The Year of the Goat starts on 1 February and holds considerable potential for the Goat. Almost all areas of his life are favourably aspected, but to make the most of this he will need to be organized and focus upon what he wants. This is the year to move forward and to reap some well-deserved rewards.

The Goat year will certainly offer some excellent opportunities at work and will allow the Goat to develop his ideas and strengths. With the year favouring creativity and innovation, the inventive Goat can be a major beneficiary of the prevailing aspects. However, as the year begins, he would do well to consider what he would like to achieve over the next 12 months. In particular those Goats who feel in a rut or are uninspired in their present role should make it their resolution to look for something more in line with what *they* want to do. The destiny of the Goat is very much in his own hands in 2003, but it does rest with him to take the initiative and go after what he wants.

For any Goat who has been thinking of a career change, some form of training or even personal study which would demonstrate his commitment and add to his knowledge would certainly be to his advantage. Also, if he is able to talk through his ideas with those able to offer informed guidance or to approach professional bodies for further information, he could receive useful advice and, in some cases, learn of possible openings. By taking positive action, many of these Goats will be able to move to a more suitable position over the year. Similarly, those seeking work should follow up any positions which they feel could be a good outlet for their talents, even though the experience they have in those areas may be limited. In many cases, their determination, enthusiasm and earnestness will show through and many will be successful in obtaining what will turn out to be an interesting position and one which offers the chance of development in the future.

Some Goats will of course be content to put their skills and training to good use where they are. However, for quite a few of these Goats, their contribution will lead to the offer of new responsibilities or promotion during the year. As the Goat will find, this is a year of positive and sometimes far-reaching change.

This will also be a successful year for those Goats whose work is in any way creative. The aspiring Goat writer, artist, musician, designer or inventor really should make the most of his ideas and promote his work. Those in the early stages of their career could benefit by contacting someone qualified to give an expert opinion. So many Goats have, in the past, enjoyed success after finding a mentor and this year many more could meet that all-important figure.

Although the whole year is generally favourable for work matters, the months from February to April and mid-September to November could see some key developments.

The Goat should also take advantage of the encouraging aspects by furthering his personal interests over the year. Whether he chooses to develop a current interest or take up a new one, he will find his interests will not only be a source of pleasure but will also provide an important balance to his life.

The progress that the Goat makes in his work will lead to an increase in his income. However, with all his obligations and all that he wants to do, he does need to handle his finances with care. Where large purchases are concerned, he should allow himself plenty of time to consider the options, terms and ranges available. To act too impulsively could result in some unnecessary expense. However, while caution and some restraint may be advisable, the year will certainly not be without its lucky streaks and if there is a competition or contest which particularly interests the Goat, he would do well to enter. A competition win is certainly a possibility in 2003!

The Goat always sets much store by his relations with others and these will go well this year and can bring him much happiness. The Goat can look forward to some splendid occasions with his loved ones, including a family celebration. This could be a wedding, an addition to his family or some pleasing news concerning either his own progress or that of someone close to him. In addition, the support he receives from those around him will give him the necessary encouragement to follow through some of his ideas. And when decisions need to be made, the backing and advice he receives will be both constructive and welcome. In addition to benefiting from the assistance of others, the Goat will often be able to reciprocate the kindnesses shown him by taking a caring interest in those close to him and offering advice when needed. His loved ones will value his input and his understanding yet perceptive manner.

The Goat will also enjoy an active and fulfilling social life in his own year. In addition to meeting up with friends, he will find himself invited to various parties and social gatherings. At these he will not only enjoy himself but the prospects are excellent for widening his social circle and, for the unattached, finding serious romance. April, May, August and September are particularly favourable for social matters, but throughout this will be a promising and often happy year. The aspects are so favourable that quite a few unattached Goats will marry in 2003 or settle down with their partner.

Overall, the Goat year offers considerable promise to its own sign and with a willingness to make the most of himself, the Goat can look forward to some pleasing personal successes as well as a greater fulfilment. The key factors are decisiveness and action, however, and this means that the Goat does need to come to terms with his capriciousness and be bold. This is his year and he should make the most of his talents and the chances that come his way.

As far as the different types of Goat are concerned, this will be an active and rewarding year for the *Metal Goat.*

For those born in 1991, there will be much material to be covered at school and sometimes they may despair of all that is being expected of them. However, the young Metal Goat should take heart. As he will find, by making an effort to master what is expected of him, he will not only make impressive headway but also learn much about persistence and self-discipline, qualities which will serve him so well as he progresses through life.

In addition, the young Metal Goat will be well supported by those around him and should he have problems or particular difficulties he should not hesitate to raise them rather than keep them to himself. By being forthcoming, he will gain so much more.

The two areas in which the Metal Goat could particularly excel in over the year are those which allow him to demonstrate and extend his creative abilities and those of an outdoor and/or sporting nature. In both cases, the Metal Goat should further his skills and knowledge and take full advantage of the opportunities available. These could include after-school clubs, youth groups or some personal pursuit, but whatever he chooses to do, the Metal Goat will find that if he extends himself in some way, his activities will bring him great satisfaction over the year.

In addition, he will enjoy the company of his close band of friends as well as some of the lively occasions that will take place. The two words of warning that should be sounded are that the young Metal Goat should avoid getting involved in any situations about which he has misgivings and he should not let his exuberant nature get the better of him. His instinct should be his guide. If he does have concerns at any time, he could save himself a considerable amount of anguish by discussing them with others and thereby gaining valuable advice.

Travel is favourably aspected and if the Metal Goat has the opportunity to go on any trips or activity breaks, he will find these will be enjoyable and will do him a lot of good. Travel could also bring a great deal of pleasure to those Metal Goats born in 1931 and if they are able to visit destinations which are of special interest to them, they will find their time away that much more fascinating and enjoyable. Some Metal Goats will also take delight in more local excursions, perhaps visiting places of interest which they may have heard about but not had the chance to visit properly. By making the most of their time and possibly adding a purpose to some of their trips, they will find this will become another enjoyable aspect of the year.

Metal Goats will also derive much pleasure from their personal interests, particularly those that allow them to draw on their creative talents or take them out of doors, with gardening being another pleasurable activity for many.

The Metal Goat sets much store by his relations with others and both domestically and socially the Goat year is well aspected. The more senior Metal Goat will greatly appreciate the support given him by family members as well as enjoy following the successes of those who mean a lot to him. While he may not wish to be seen as interfering, if he feels able to assist or advise a younger relation who may be under pressure, his attention will be appreciated.

These Metal Goats can also look forward to a pleasant social life and will not only enjoy meeting up with existing friends but will also make some new acquaintances, perhaps by joining local groups or meeting people when travelling. Some of these new acquaintances will, in time, become firm friends.

Financial matters will go well, with many Metal Goats receiving an additional sum over the year, perhaps in the form of a maturing policy, a gift or some stroke of good fortune. However, rather than be tempted to spend this too readily, the Metal Goat should give some thought to what he wants to do and plan his purchases carefully. The more consideration he gives to his spending, the more satisfying the results will be.

Overall, this will be a favourable year for the Metal Goat and whether born in 1931 or 1991, if he is able to make the most of himself, his talents and the support, love and friendship of those around him, he will be pleased with how the year develops.

TIP FOR THE YEAR
Develop your interests and skills. They will not only be satisfying now but could also be helpful in the future.

This marks the sixtieth year of the *Water Goat* and it promises to be a significant one. As the year starts, many Water Goats will find themselves in reflective mood, thinking back over all that has happened – both successes and regrets – as well as considering their future. As a result, many will decide that now is the time to start a new chapter in their life.

Some Water Goats will retire completely from work while others will be tempted to switch to different duties, in some cases working fewer hours a week. By considering what he wants to do and then taking action, the Water Goat will be satisfied with how many of his plans do work out. In addition, the Goat year is capable of springing some surprises and an interesting opportunity will often open up for the Water Goat to use his talents in a new way. As he will find, his experience and skills will be in demand.

The Water Goat should also set a regular time aside for his personal interests and by giving himself an interesting project or challenge, he will find his interests – especially those that allow him to draw on his creativity – will become a particularly enjoyable element of the year. Water Goats who do retire and have more time available could find enrolling on a course a good use of their time. Whether to develop themselves, their interests or improve fitness levels, what they do or learn will often be beneficial as well as fun.

Travel is also favoured, with some Water Goats choosing to mark their sixtieth year with a special trip. By planning this carefully, they can make it something that they will enjoy and remember.

As far as domestic matters are concerned this will be a year of change, with quite a few Water Goats deciding to move to accommodation more suitable to their present needs. While these Water Goats will feel the decision is the right one, the whole moving process will be demanding both in terms of time and effort. However, many Water Goats will eventually find an ideal home.

All Water Goats, whether they move or not, should not hesitate to ask for assistance should they feel under pressure at any time or have any particularly strenuous tasks to do. The help others can give can make a considerable difference. Despite the often busy nature of the year, it will still give rise to many happy and meaningful occasions. In addition to celebrating his sixtieth birthday, the Water Goat will follow the progress of loved ones with much interest as well as help with some of the other family activities that take place.

On a social level, too, the year is favourably aspected, with the Water Goat again enjoying meeting friends and attending a variety of events. For those who may have had some recent personal sadness or difficulty, the Goat year can mark the start of a new chapter, with the dawning of an important friendship or romance, perhaps arising from an interest or activity the Water Goat takes up.

However, while the year is generally well aspected for the Water Goat, the one word of caution that does need to be sounded concerns money matters. While many Water Goats will enjoy a financial bonus, a gift or even stroke of luck, they do still need to be careful when taking on new agreements or commitments as well as when completing financial forms. A slip or mistake could be to their detriment. Water Goats, take note.

Overall, though, the Goat year does hold good prospects

for the Water Goat. However, to benefit fully, he does need to follow through his ideas and plans.

TIP FOR THE YEAR
Decide what you want to do and venture forth. The action you take will often have pleasing and far-reaching consequences.

This has the potential for being a positive and exciting year for the *Wood Goat*, although just how he fares will depend on his attitude. In 2003 some interesting opportunities will arise and although this may entail the Wood Goat venturing into unfamiliar territory, it is those who are prepared to move forward who stand to gain the most.

In particular, the Wood Goat will see some significant changes in his work over the year, with the effects often being far-reaching. Because of the expertise they have built up, some Wood Goats will decide the time has come to try for promotion or positions which offer more scope and potential. By putting themselves forward, many will be given the chance to set their career off on a new and more fulfilling path. While their new duties may initially be daunting, by making the most of the opportunities given them, these Wood Goats will not only quickly impress but also do much to enhance their longer-term prospects.

For those Wood Goats seeking work, either at the start of the year or later on, the Goat year can again be a time of change and sometimes new starts. Sometimes it is all too tempting to remain in the 'comfort zone', but the Goat year does offer the Wood Goat the chance to develop both personally and professionally and to move ahead.

He can also look forward to a noticeable increase in his income over the year, although money matters will still need careful handling. In addition to his own expenses the Wood Goat could help certain family members, particularly with education, wedding or accommodation costs, and as a result he does need to keep a close watch over his financial situation. With care and prudence, he can put his money to good use, maybe even being able to add to his savings, but the year does call for careful financial management.

This is, though, a favourably aspected year for personal matters and one which will also bring change. The Wood Goat could see a family member moving out for the purpose of education, work or marriage, and with change in the air, a few Wood Goats could decide to move house themselves. For those that do, some parts of the year will be demanding, but they will be generally pleased with how their plans work out and, come the end of the year, will be satisfied (and sometimes surprised) by the very great deal that has taken place. Throughout the year, the Wood Goat will also be grateful for the support he receives from his loved ones and, by being willing to help each other and pool ideas and talents, he will find his home life reward-ing and meaningful. Amid all the activity, there will also be some good causes for personal and family celebra-tions. The Goat year will not be without its memorable moments!

With the many demands upon his time the Wood Goat should, though, make sure that neither his personal inter-ests nor his social life gets squeezed out. Both provide an important and necessary balance to his life and help him to relax and unwind. By making the effort to go out, the

Wood Goat can look forward to some particularly enjoyable social occasions. For those who may have been experiencing some personal problems or are feeling alone, the Goat year will mark a considerable improvement in their fortunes and, for many, bring an important person into their lives.

In many respects, 2003 is a year for moving forward, although just how the Wood Goat fares does rest with him. The opportunities will be there and by making the most of them, the Wood Goat can make substantial progress and reap some fine and well-deserved rewards.

TIP FOR THE YEAR
Take on new challenges and make the most of your talents and potential.

This will be a rewarding year for the *Fire Goat*, with both his personal and professional life well aspected.

In his work the Fire Goat will be able to build on his current position and those who have been working towards a particular objective or developing certain skills will see their efforts producing some fine results. As has so often been demonstrated, persistence does pay off and in 2003 the Fire Goat will not only be pleased with what he achieves but also find himself excellently placed to make further advances.

This also applies to those Fire Goats who are seeking work or who feel they are in a rut. By drawing on their skills and past experience and looking for a position which offers a new challenge, they can give their career a new lease of life and set themselves off on what can prove a very successful path. The Goat year really does hold excellent prospects for the Fire Goat and will allow him to use his own special talents to good effect. This is a particularly favourable year for creative endeavours and for those Fire Goats whose work involves some form of expression or allows them to draw on their ideas, it can be a most successful time. February and March and the months from September to November will see some interesting work developments and, for those who may have been disappointed with their recent progress, 2003 does offer real hope and the chance of a new beginning.

The Fire Goat will also get much pleasure from his personal interests over the year. Despite the many other demands on him, he should set a regular time aside for them, as they will not only help balance his other activities but also be a good way for him to relax and unwind.

Travel, too, is well aspected and the Fire Goat should try to go away at some point over the year. The change of scene and chance to get away from his usual routine will do him good.

As far as the Fire Goat's home life is concerned, this will be a busy year. In addition to his own activities, those around him will also have a great deal to do. Younger relations could be involved in study and exam preparation as well as having to make important decisions about their future, while a partner could be concerned about work pressures. Added to this, more senior relations could look to the Fire Goat for advice and, in some cases, practical assistance. However, while a lot will be asked of the Fire Goat, by helping, advising and giving his time to those who are important to him, he will find his input can make a real difference and be greatly appreciated. As events will show, he does have a special place in the hearts of many. If, though, at any time, the Fire Goat feels under just too much pressure or is worried that some household chores are falling behind, he should not hesitate to ask others for assistance. And while some parts of the year will be busy, there will also be much to enjoy, including the interests and activities that the Fire Goat can share with his loved ones. Domestically, the year will bring many fine occasions.

The Fire Goat will also value his social life and in some cases a long-standing friend will have some advice which he would do well to heed. Those who know the Fire Goat well can prove especially helpful in what is such a favourable year. For Fire Goats who are lonely, unattached, feeling low or disillusioned, the Goat year will offer much brighter prospects. However to benefit, these Fire Goats do need to go out and meet others as well as focus on the present rather than dwell on the past. By making the effort, they will find the Goat year can bring a real transformation, whether in the form of friendship, romance, a new partner or just a general feeling of contentment and worth. For social matters, February, April, May and July are especially well aspected, but 2003 is generally a promising year for socializing and meeting others.

The one area that does require care is finance. While the year will see an increase in the Fire Goat's income, he will have many commitments to meet as well as plans he wants to carry out. To prevent problems he does need to manage his resources well and keep a close eye on his level of spending.

Overall, though, the Goat year does offer considerable promise to the Fire Goat, with almost all areas of his life going well. He should aim to develop his ideas and reveal his considerable potential. The aspects are on his side and he should make the most of them.

TIP FOR THE YEAR
Persist in whatever it is you want to do. The year offers some great rewards, but they do need to be worked for.

This will be an active and often exciting year for the *Earth Goat* with significant developments in many areas of his life.

Personal affairs are especially well aspected, with many Earth Goats marrying, seeing an addition to their family or meeting someone special over the year. The Earth Goat himself will be in excellent form, with his *joie de vivre* and friendly manner making him popular company and leading to some wonderful occasions. He will benefit from the love and affection of those who mean much to him and, with their backing, will grow both in confidence and stature over the year. He can also look forward to sharing some particularly happy times with his loved ones.

Accommodation matters will also figure prominently, with many Earth Goats likely to be involved in a move. Quite a few will spend a good proportion of their free time setting up their new home and getting it the way they want it. With the Earth Goat's good taste and eye for style, his efforts will be both welcomed and appreciated.

For those Earth Goats with children, or who become parents in 2003, these will be interesting times.

Admittedly, the demands of babies or young children will sometimes leave these Earth Goats feeling jaded or despairing when certain household tasks fall behind, but by making allowance for this and drawing on the support of loved ones, they will be able to enjoy these special times. When pressures do mount, the Earth Goat does need to be organized and prioritize his tasks. He should also make sure he gives himself time to relax and unwind. Although it may sometimes be difficult, his life should not always be conducted at such a heady or demanding pace.

With travel well aspected, if he is able the Earth Goat should aim to go away at some time during the year. By choosing his destination carefully he can look forward to some enjoyable times as well as benefit from the rest.

Although his own activities will preoccupy him, the Earth Goat will also have much contact with more senior relations over the year. Not only will he be grateful for the support they are often able to give him, but he will also be able to reciprocate this by offering practical assistance and advice on sometimes complex issues. The Earth Goat's family does mean a great deal to him and his own role will be evident and appreciated as the year progresses.

This will also be an important year for work matters, with many Earth Goats being able to build on their position and take on greater responsibilities. Those who are keen on promotion or wanting a change should actively follow up the opportunities that arise. Admittedly, not all their applications will go their way, but by persisting and showing initiative as well as continually improving on their interview technique and application forms, they will eventually be given a chance and will quickly establish themselves in their new role. This is very much a year for the Earth Goat to advance and widen his experience. He should also make the most of any special skills and talents he has. If he is able to promote these, they will be noticed and can lead to some encouraging developments. Although the Earth Goat is still in the early years of his working life, this can be a significant year with far-reaching consequences.

The Earth Goat's income will improve in 2003, but with all his plans and expenses, particularly connected with his accommodation, he does need to watch his outgoings and avoid succumbing to too many temptations. With careful control, combined with resourcefulness, he will manage to do a lot, but he does need to remain vigilant and prudent.

Overall, though, this is a splendid year for the Earth Goat, with good progress indicated in his work as well as some special times with his loved ones.

TIP FOR THE YEAR
Draw strength from the love and respect of those around you and go forth with confidence. This is a year to use your skills and talents to good effect.

FAMOUS GOATS

Pamela Anderson, Isaac Asimov, W. H. Auden, Jane Austen, Anne Bancroft, Cilla Black, Lord Byron, Leslie Caron, John le Carré, Coco Chanel, Mary Higgins Clark, Nat 'King' Cole, Angus Deayton, Catherine Deneuve, John Denver, Charles Dickens, Ken Dodd, Sir Arthur Conan

Doyle, Daphne Du Maurier, Douglas Fairbanks, Dame Margot Fonteyn, Noel Gallagher, Bill Gates, Mel Gibson, Whoopi Goldberg, Mikhail Gorbachev, John Grisham, Oscar Hammerstein, George Harrison, Sir Edmund Hillary, John Humphrys, Billy Idol, Julio Iglesias, Mick Jagger, Nicole Kidman, Ben Kingsley, Doris Lessing, Franz Liszt, John Major, Michelangelo, Joni Mitchell, Rupert Murdoch, Mussolini, Randy Newman, Robert de Niro, Des O'Connor, Sinead O'Connor, Michael Palin, Eva Peron, Marcel Proust, Keith Richards, Julia Roberts, William Shatner, Gary Sinise, Jerry Springer, Lana Turner, Mark Twain, Rudolph Valentino, Vangelis, Barbara Walters, John Wayne, Fay Weldon, Bruce Willis, Debra Winger.

2 FEBRUARY 1908 ～ 21 JANUARY 1909   *Earth Monkey*

20 FEBRUARY 1920 ～ 7 FEBRUARY 1921   *Metal Monkey*

6 FEBRUARY 1932 ～ 25 JANUARY 1933   *Water Monkey*

25 JANUARY 1944 ～ 12 FEBRUARY 1945   *Wood Monkey*

12 FEBRUARY 1956 ～ 30 JANUARY 1957   *Fire Monkey*

30 JANUARY 1968 ～ 16 FEBRUARY 1969   *Earth Monkey*

16 FEBRUARY 1980 ～ 4 FEBRUARY 1981   *Metal Monkey*

4 FEBRUARY 1992 ～ 22 JANUARY 1993   *Water Monkey*

THE
MONKEY

THE PERSONALITY OF THE MONKEY

'Where there is a will there is a way' is an old true saying. He who resolves upon doing a thing by that very resolution often scales the barriers to it and secures its achievement. To think we are able is almost to be so – to determine upon attainment is frequently attainment itself.

Samuel Smiles, a Monkey

The Monkey is born under the sign of fantasy. He is imaginative, inquisitive and loves to keep an eye on everything that is going on around him. He is never backward in offering advice or trying to sort out the problems of others. He likes to be helpful and his advice is invariably sensible and reliable.

The Monkey is intelligent, well read and always eager to learn. He has an extremely good memory and there are many Monkeys who have made particularly good linguists. The Monkey is also a convincing talker and enjoys taking part in discussions and debates. His friendly, self-assured manner can be very persuasive and he usually has little trouble in winning people round to his way of thinking. It is for this reason that the Monkey often excels in politics and public speaking. He is also particularly adept at PR work, teaching and any job which involves selling.

The Monkey can, however, be crafty, cunning and occasionally dishonest, and he will seize on any opportunity to make a quick gain or outsmart his opponents. He has so much charm and guile that people often don't realize what he is up to until it is too late. But despite his resourceful nature, the Monkey does run the risk of outsmarting even himself. He has so much confidence in his abilities that he rarely listens to advice or is prepared to accept help from anyone. He likes to help others but prefers to rely on his own judgement when dealing with his own affairs.

Another characteristic of the Monkey is that he is extremely good at solving problems and has a happy knack of extricating himself (and others) from the most hopeless of positions. He is the master of self-preservation.

With so many diverse talents the Monkey is able to make considerable sums of money, but he does like to enjoy life and will think nothing of spending his money on some exotic holiday or luxury which he has had his eye on. He can, however, become very envious if someone else has what he wants.

The Monkey is an original thinker and despite his love of company, he cherishes his independence. He has to have the freedom to act as he wants and any Monkey who feels hemmed in or bound by too many restrictions can soon become unhappy. Likewise, if anything becomes too boring or monotonous, the Monkey soon loses interest and turns his attention to something else. He lacks persistence and this can often hamper his progress. He is also easily distracted, a tendency which all Monkeys should try to overcome. The Monkey should concentrate on one thing at a time and by doing so will almost certainly achieve more in the long run.

The Monkey is a good organizer and even though he may behave slightly erratically at times, he will invariably have some plan at the back of his mind. On the odd occasion when his plans do not quite work out, he is usually quite happy to shrug his shoulders and put it down to experience. He will rarely make the same mistake twice and throughout his life he will try his hand at many things.

The Monkey likes to impress and is rarely without followers or admirers. There are many who are attracted by his good looks, his sense of humour or simply because he instils so much confidence.

Monkeys usually marry young and for it to be a success their partner must allow them the time to pursue their many interests and the opportunity to indulge their love of travel. The Monkey has to have variety in his life and is especially well suited to those born under the sociable and outgoing signs of the Rat, Dragon, Pig and Goat. The Ox, Rabbit, Snake and Dog will also be enchanted by the Monkey's resourceful and outgoing nature, but he is likely to exasperate the Rooster and Horse, and the Tiger will have little patience with his tricks. A relationship between two Monkeys will work well – they will understand each other and be able to assist each other in their various enterprises.

The female Monkey is intelligent, extremely observant and a shrewd judge of character. Her opinions are often highly valued and, having such a persuasive nature, she invariably gets her own way. She has many interests and involves herself in a wide variety of activities. She pays great attention to her appearance, is an elegant dresser and likes to take particular care over her hair. She can also be a caring and doting parent and will have many good and loyal friends.

Provided the Monkey can curb his desire to take part in all that is going on around him and can concentrate on one thing at a time, he can usually achieve what he wants in life. Should he suffer any disappointments, he is bound to bounce back. The Monkey is a survivor and his life is usually both colourful and very eventful.

THE FIVE DIFFERENT TYPES OF MONKEY

In addition to the 12 signs of the Chinese zodiac, there are five elements and these have a strengthening or moderating influence on the sign. The effects of the five elements on the Monkey are described below, together with the years in which the elements were exercising their influence. Therefore all Monkeys born in 1920 and 1980 are Metal Monkeys, those born in 1932 and 1992 are Water Monkeys, and so on.

Metal Monkey: 1920, 1980

The Metal Monkey is very strong-willed. He sets about everything he does with a dogged determination and often prefers to work independently rather than with others. He is ambitious, wise and confident, and is certainly not afraid of hard work. He is very astute in financial matters and usually chooses his investments well. Despite his somewhat independent nature, the Metal Monkey enjoys attending parties and social occasions and is particularly warm and caring towards his loved ones.

Water Monkey: 1932, 1992

The Water Monkey is versatile, determined and perceptive. He has more discipline than some of the other Monkeys and is prepared to work towards a certain goal rather than be distracted by something else. He is not always open about his true intentions and when questioned can be particularly evasive. He can be sensitive to criticism but also very persuasive and usually has little trouble in getting others to fall in with his plans. He has a very good understanding of human nature and relates well to others.

Wood Monkey: 1944

This Monkey is efficient, methodical and extremely conscientious. He is also highly imaginative and is always trying to capitalize on new ideas or learn new skills. Occasionally his enthusiasm can get the better of him and he can get very agitated when things do not quite work out as he had hoped. He does, however, have a very adventurous streak and is not afraid of taking risks. He also loves travel. He is usually held in great esteem by his friends and colleagues.

Fire Monkey: 1956

The Fire Monkey is intelligent, full of vitality and has no trouble in commanding the respect of others. He is imaginative and has wide interests, although sometimes these can distract him from more useful and profitable work. He is very competitive and always likes to be involved in everything that is going on. He can be stubborn if he does not get his own way and he sometimes tries to indoctrinate those who are less strong-willed than himself. He is a lively character, popular with the opposite sex and extremely loyal to his partner.

Earth Monkey: 1908, 1968

The Earth Monkey tends to be studious and well read, and can become quite distinguished in his chosen line of work. He is less outgoing than some of the other types of Monkey and prefers quieter and more solid pursuits. He has high principles, a very caring nature and can be most generous to those less fortunate than himself. He is usually successful in handling financial matters and can become very wealthy in old age. He has a calming influence on those around him and is respected and well liked by those he meets. He is, however, especially careful about whom he lets into his confidence.

PROSPECTS FOR THE MONKEY IN 2003

The Chinese New Year starts on 1 February 2003. Until then, the old year, the Year of the Horse, is still making its presence felt.

The Year of the Horse (12 February 2002 to 31 January 2003) holds interesting prospects for the Monkey, although to benefit he needs to be clear about his aims and persistent in his activities. If he lets himself drift, spreads his energies too widely or dabbles in too many different areas, his results will not be as good.

In the Monkey's work the aspects are promising and in what remains of the Horse year, he should use his skills and talents wisely. He possesses some unique gifts and by raising the level of his contribution and putting his ideas and experience to good use, he can look forward to some satisfying results as well as enhance his prospects. For those Monkeys who are keen on moving ahead, there will certainly be opportunities to take on greater responsibilities or move to a better position in the closing months of the year.

The Horse year is also a favourable one for financial matters and many Monkeys will enjoy some strokes of good fortune and an increase in their income. As a result, many will decide to spend money on themselves and their accommodation, improving their wardrobe as well as adding comforts to their home. By considering his options carefully, the Monkey will be pleased with what he acquires. He could also be fortunate in the post-Christmas sales, with his keen eye spotting some excellent bargains.

The Monkey will also enjoy himself on a social level, with the last quarter of the Horse year being an especially active time. As always, the Monkey will welcome the chance to meet up with friends – some of whom he has not seen for some time – as well as enjoy the various events he attends.

His domestic life will also be busy and to prevent too many rushed or pressured moments the Monkey would do well to organize his commitments and be prepared to consult others over any arrangements that need to be made. Despite the often considerable activity, he will value his home life and can look forward to some special occasions with his loved ones.

Generally, the Monkey will fare well in the Horse year, but he does need to stay focused on what he wants. Provided he makes good use of his time and opportunities, he can make some satisfying headway.

The Year of the Goat starts on 1 February and will be a reasonable one for the Monkey. There will certainly be chances for him to further both his position and experience, but he does need to be realistic in his expectations. Sometimes the Monkey can let his eager and resourceful spirit run away with him and if he overreaches himself, takes unnecessary risks or trusts his luck too far, then there could be disappointments in store. In 2003 the Monkey should build on his present position rather than embark on more uncertain ventures.

In his work the Monkey can make good headway, though this will come from him making the most of his experience and concentrating on what he is good at rather than striking out into a new area. If he gives of his best, advances his ideas and uses his personal skills to good advantage, particularly in building up contacts, several excellent openings will become available to him. In some cases, colleagues moving on will open up promotion possibilities or a vacancy will arise for which the Monkey is ideally suited. Many Monkeys will be able to advance within the organization in which they are currently based, while others will decide to seek positions with greater potential elsewhere. By following up such opportunities in the areas they know best, they will be able to make progress. March, May, September and October are particularly favourable for work opportunities.

Those Monkeys seeking work will again fare best by considering the different ways in which they can draw on their previous experience and skills. By emphasizing their past achievements as well as outlining the positive contribution they feel they can make, many will be successful in gaining a position which will give them the chance to use their talents to advantage.

The Monkey is also blessed with an innovative and resourceful mind and could come up with some fine ideas related to his work. By taking these further, he could receive an encouraging response and some of his ideas could develop in a significant manner.

As far as financial matters are concerned, the Monkey will enjoy a relatively good year. Some Monkeys may even be able to supplement their main income with freelance work. However, while money will flow into the Monkey's accounts, it can also flow out all too easily. The Monkey does find it hard to resist living in fine style and too many bouts of extravagant spending could deplete his resources. Also, with an active social life indicated, he could spend quite considerably on entertaining and going out. So, although he will certainly enjoy the fruits of his labours, he would do well to watch his spending levels and manage his resources wisely rather than proceed in too cavalier a fashion.

Another area which will see much activity is travel, with many Monkeys deciding to visit friends and relations living some distance away as well as treating themselves to a special break over the year. Again, the Monkey would find it helpful to budget for this in advance and this will sometimes leave him with something extra to spend and enjoy while away.

With his outgoing and genial manner, the Monkey sets much store by his relations with others, but in the Goat year these do require care. To prevent problems and differences of opinion, the Monkey must be sure to consult others when making plans and arrangements as well as listen carefully to their views. Sometimes, in his enthusiasm, he assumes he has automatic support or that others will fall in readily with his ideas, but to proceed without adequate discussion this year could cause some resentment. Also, with work pressures and all the other activities that he is keen to pursue, there could be times when the Monkey becomes preoccupied and either does not spend as much time as he should with those who matter or, when he is with them, finds his mind wandering off elsewhere. Even though this may be unintentional, important relationships *do* need care and time and the Monkey should remember this. With a little effort on his part, he can certainly avoid some of the trickier aspects of the Goat year and enjoy what can be a fulfilling domestic life.

The Goat year will also be a busy one socially, with many Monkeys keen to build up contacts in their area of work or finding that their personal interests will lead them to meet other enthusiasts. With his warm and outgoing manner, the Monkey will impress many of those he meets and will find his social circle widening quite appreciably. In some parts of the year, especially May, June and the last quarter, his social diary could become quite full. For those Monkeys looking for new friends, the year is favourably aspected, although where affairs of the heart are concerned, the Monkey should allow time for any new relationship to develop rather than rush into a sometimes too hasty commitment. This way each will have more chance to get to know the other better and that will help to put the relationship on a firmer foundation.

In most respects the Goat year is favourably aspected for the Monkey, but he does need to proceed with some care. In his work he should concentrate on the areas in which he has most experience and use his talents to good effect. He also needs to pay attention to his relations with others and should try to ensure that his life has balance and that his different activities and commitments do not encroach too much on each other. With discipline, organization and a sense of personal priorities, many Monkeys will be able to achieve such a balance, however, and will enjoy the opportunities the year will bring.

As far as the different types of Monkey are concerned, 2003 will be an active year for the *Metal Monkey*. He can certainly make good headway as well as enjoy himself, although, as with all Monkeys in the Goat year, he does need to listen to the views of others and to bear them in mind. To be too self-willed or act without adequate consultation could undermine his relationships and bring some difficult moments. Whether personally or professionally, the Metal Monkey must liaise, listen and show understanding. Provided he bears this in mind, then he can certainly overcome some of the more awkward aspects of the year and turn this into a constructive and positive time. His personal life in particular does promise some exciting occasions and many Metal Monkeys will marry, settle down with their partner or see an addition to their family during 2003. The year can certainly bring many much happiness, but it will also call for some adjustments to the Metal Monkey's lifestyle and he must accept this and allow for it. In some cases he will need to be more flexible and accommodating in his attitude and to maintain the rapport and closeness he so values, he will need to be more forthcoming when discussing his ideas. He should also encourage interests that can be shared and, where more practical household projects are concerned, aim to carry these out with others rather than single-handed. However, if the Metal Monkey is mindful of those who are important to him and makes sure he gives them his time, then this can be a domestically happy year.

Socially, this will be a busy year, with the Metal Monkey not only keeping in regular contact with his friends but also going to a variety of social occasions, including several connected with his work. Some of the people he meets over the year will, in time, become part of his close social circle. For those Metal Monkeys who may find themselves alone, perhaps after moving to a new area, or who have had some recent personal problems, the Goat year will often bring the gift of a new friendship as well as, in many cases, true love. The whole year is favourably aspected for meeting and getting to know others, with the months from April to June and last quarter being particularly busy.

This will also be an important year for the Metal Monkey's work, although rather than look to make rapid advances or set his sights too high, he would profit more by adding to his skills and learning about different aspects of his work. By becoming more proficient in what he does, he will be establishing an excellent base from which he can progress later. The Metal Monkey should also make use of any chances he gets to meet others in his line of work. By extending his contacts and impressing those he meets, he will benefit from the advice he is given as well as make himself better known.

For those Metal Monkeys who are seeking work or discontented with their present role, this will be an important year. By deciding what they want to do and looking for suitable openings, many will find a position which, although in some cases modest, will be an important new start. By looking to learn more and become established, the Metal Monkey can make an impact and his achievements over the year can turn out to be far-reaching. March, May and the months from September to November can see interesting developments workwise.

The year is also well aspected for travel and whether taking trips for work or pleasure, the Metal Monkey will get to see some interesting sights as well as benefit from the break from his usual routine.

As far as his finances are concerned, he will enjoy an increase in his income as well as some strokes of fortune, but with his many commitments and so much that he wants to do, he does need to manage his money well and keep control of his purse strings. There will be many temptations to spend in 2003 and too much outlay could result in problems. This is a year for common sense and some restraint.

Also, while the Metal Monkey does generally take good care of himself, he should be careful not to neglect his well-being. With his busy lifestyle, he should ensure he gets sufficient rest and exercise as well as enjoys a balanced diet. With so much happening, he does need to keep in good form.

Overall, this will be a constructive year and provided the Metal Monkey is his considerate self and makes the most of the situations that arise, he will do well and enhance his prospects. On a personal level, the Goat year certainly promises some special times.

TIP FOR THE YEAR
Build and value your relationships. These are priceless treasures.

This will be a year of change for the *Water Monkey* and while it will bring pressures and moments of uncertainty, what takes place will often be to his long-term benefit.

Many of those Water Monkeys born in 1992 will change their school this year and with the new environment will come the prospects of getting used to new routines and making new friends as well as tackling more involved subject matter. Although the initial days may be daunting, with his genial manner and sense of fun, the Water Monkey will quickly form what will become important new friendships. Some of the subjects he has to study will be demanding, but by maintaining an open mind and giving his best, the young Water Monkey will be pleased with his progress. He will find that what he learns will be an important introduction to the more advanced work that follows and that making an effort now will help him in the years ahead. The Water Monkey will also be well supported by those around him and should he find himself struggling in any subject or with a particular piece of work, he should ask for help. Often he will find that just one more explanation or a little time spent going over a certain topic will make something much easier to understand.

The young Water Monkey will get a lot of pleasure from recreational pursuits over the year, especially from a new interest or activity he takes up. For quite a few Water Monkeys this will have an outdoor or sporting element to it and will be fun as well as beneficial. Creative interests are also well favoured and those Water Monkeys who enjoy art, music, drama, dance or some other form of expression will gain a great deal from their interests over the year.

Change is also on the agenda for those Water Monkeys born in 1932, particularly as many will decide to move to more suitable accommodation during the year. The moving process will be demanding, particularly with all the sorting and packing that needs to be done in addition to finding a new home, but once settled, these Water Monkeys will delight in finding out about the amenities their new area offers as well as establishing a new social circle. Any Water Monkey who may start the year feeling lonely can look forward to a real improvement in his social life, but this does call for action on his part, perhaps by joining a local society or study group.

The more senior Water Monkey will also take pleasure in his personal interests over the year, with practical and creative pursuits being especially satisfying. Those Water Monkeys who enjoy craftwork, design and art will find that some projects started this year will keep them absorbed for many an hour.

Travel is also favourably aspected and if possible the Water Monkey should aim to go away at some point over the year and perhaps consider visiting a place he has long wanted to see. By making enquiries and expressing an interest to others, many Water Monkeys will find their trip becoming much more of a possibility than they may have initially thought.

The Water Monkey will also appreciate the support given by family members over the year and, although he may sometimes feel he does not want to bother others with any concerns or requests for practical assistance, he should not hold back. Others will only be too glad to help as well as be pleased to repay the Water Monkey's own many kindnesses. His family is an important part of his life and in 2003 he really will have a good cause to be thankful for the love and assistance he is given as well as be proud of the progress of some of those dear to him.

This will be a reasonable year for financial matters, but throughout the Water Monkey does need to remain aware of his spending levels and check the terms of any new agreement he may enter into. Without sufficient care and attention, problems could arise. Water Monkeys, take note and do be vigilant when dealing with important paperwork.

Overall, though, this will be a generally positive year for the Water Money and while for many it will be a time of disruption and sometimes upheaval, the changes will work out well and usher in many new possibilities. The Water Monkey's relations with others and personal interests will bring him particular satisfaction.

TIP FOR THE YEAR

Make the most of the changes that take place and the opportunities that arise. By taking advantage of these, your life can be made that much more rewarding.

This will be a year of interesting developments for the *Wood Monkey* and in most respects he will be pleased with how the year unfolds.

The Wood Monkey will be particularly grateful for the support he receives from both family and friends over the year and whenever he has any important decisions to make or matters concerning him, he will find it of great value to talk these over and so benefit from the assistance others can give. Similarly, if at any time he finds himself grappling with complex issues, paperwork or forms (especially finance, tax or benefit related) which he does not fully comprehend or agree with, he should contact a helpline or seek professional advice. As he will find, it is better to obtain assistance rather than struggle on unaided and perhaps cause himself unnecessary worry.

One area which will involve considerable decision-making will be the Wood Monkey's work and he will sometimes find himself in a dilemma about what to do for the best. Some Wood Monkeys, by virtue of their experience and strengths, will have the opportunity of taking on greater responsibilities, but, while often representing promotion, these will involve them leaving the role that they know so well. In some cases, the change will be something of a wrench, but by rising to the opportunities now offered, the Wood Monkey could find his career taking on a new lease of life. Other Wood Monkeys, though, may decide to retire or, if they change their accommodation over the year (as some Wood Monkeys will), seek a different job, perhaps with fewer hours. Workwise, 2003 is certainly a year for change, but it is often a positive one too.

Creativity is favoured in the Goat year and the Wood Monkey will derive much satisfaction from developing an existing personal interest or taking up a new one. By learning more as well as possibly contacting fellow enthusiasts, he will find this becoming a rewarding aspect of his life.

Another area which is favoured is travel and the Wood Monkey should aim to go away for a break at some time over the year. By choosing his destination with care, he can make his trip both enjoyable and interesting.

The Wood Monkey will also fare well in financial matters, with many receiving an additional and sometimes unexpected sum over the year, either as a gift, bonus or in some cases, even a competition win. Money-wise, this can be a lucky year and this can prompt many Wood Monkeys to carry out some plans they have been thinking about for some time, especially in relation to their accommodation. A few will decide to move altogether. However, despite the favourable aspects, the Wood Monkey does need to watch his spending. Also, to prevent possible problems, it would be wise for him to keep receipts, guarantees and agreements safely.

As always, the Wood Monkey will value his domestic life and it will be quite active over the year, particularly for those Wood Monkeys who decide to move. However, by being prepared to discuss plans and arrangements, the

Wood Monkey will find that even the most involved activities are much easier to carry out than he thought. Also, he can look forward to some fine occasions in the company of his loved ones.

On a social level, too, this is a promising year, with the Wood Monkey enjoying meeting up with friends and the events and gatherings that he attends. Wood Monkeys who desire more companionship will find that by going out and perhaps joining a special interest group, they will soon make friends. Some Wood Monkeys will also form good friendships on holiday.

In such a busy year, one area that the Wood Monkey cannot afford to ignore is his well-being. To keep himself on good form, he does need to look after himself, making sure he has regular and appropriate exercise and eats a balanced and nutritious diet. If not, he could find that during some parts of the year he is lacking his usual energy and sparkle. Wood Monkeys, do take note.

Generally, though, this is a favourably aspected year for the Wood Monkey and by taking advantage of the opportunities that arise and using his time well, he will be satisfied with how the year works out for him.

TIP FOR THE YEAR
Do let others help with plans and seek advice over any complex matter or when making important decisions. In 2003 you will gain much from the support that is available.

This will be an interesting year for the *Fire Monkey* and while it will not be without its moments of pressure or difficult decisions, he will be able to make some useful advances and find greater fulfilment in much of what he does.

As the Goat year starts, the Fire Monkey should give some thought to his present situation and to what he would like to achieve over the year. His plans might concern his work, his accommodation, personal ambitions, self-development, travel (which is particularly well aspected) or personal interests and recreational pursuits, but by having some idea in mind, the Fire Monkey will find himself becoming more focused. He would also do well to talk his ideas over with those close to him and, where his work is concerned, with colleagues who are able to give informed advice. If he can overcome his tendency to keep his thoughts to himself, he will be given a much greater level of support and encouragement.

In his work the Goat year offers the Fire Monkey considerable promise. He may find himself ideally placed to make progress, perhaps as more senior colleagues move on, or be asked to take on different responsibilities. By taking advantage of such opportunities, he will not only widen his experience but also find a greater range of possibilities opening up for him in the future. He may have his longer-term goal but, as will become apparent to so many in 2003, there are many possible routes to the top.

The Fire Monkey should also take advantage of any training opportunities that are available, particularly those that will keep him up to date with developments in his own line of work. Again, what he accomplishes now can be to his future benefit.

For those Fire Monkeys who are disillusioned with their present job or seeking work, again the year offers excellent prospects. However, the Fire Monkey does need to be clear about the direction he would now like his career to take. The months from March to May and September and October could all see interesting developments, but in general this is a year of progress and one which can have far-reaching significance.

The Fire Monkey should also aim to further his personal interests over the year, especially those that appeal to his creative and enquiring side. Experimenting, learning and creating can bring him considerable satisfaction over the year. For some Fire Monkeys, an interest or skill could even bring in extra income and if they wish to take this further, the Goat year could have some surprises in store.

The Fire Monkey should also give some consideration to his well-being over the year and make sure he has suffi-cient exercise as well as a balanced diet. He should aim to go away for a break at some time, ideally to a destination which will allow him to unwind. He should regard a holiday as a necessary and well-deserved treat.

The Fire Monkey's family life will mean a great deal to him over the year and by spending time on family and household activities, he can look forward to some rewarding occasions. He will delight in some of the successes enjoyed by younger relations and while he may not want to appear interfering, any advice and practical help he feels able to offer will be greatly appreciated.

Amid all the activity the Fire Monkey should make sure his social life does not suffer and by going out to events that appeal to him, whether some form of entertainment, a party, an evening with friends or a local event, he will enjoy some pleasant occasions and do himself a lot of good.

In many respects this will be a favourable year for the Fire Monkey and one which will have considerable bearing on his future, particularly in the auspicious Monkey year that follows.

TIP FOR THE YEAR
Give some thought to your future aims and then work towards them. This is a time to move ahead in the direction that you want.

This will be a year of interesting developments for the *Earth Monkey* with some of the events proving of long-term significance.

At work there will be chances for the Earth Monkey to take on a greater role, and while he may have misgivings about some of his new tasks, by being prepared to rise to the challenge, he will not only widen his experience but also enhance his prospects. Workwise, the Earth Monkey does have a good future ahead of him and what he accomplishes in 2003 will prepare the way for some of the more substantial strides he will make later on. During the year he should take full advantage of any training or retraining he may be offered. By keeping his skills up to date, as well as adding to them wherever possible, he will not only be able to conduct his activities in a more efficient manner but also open up other possibilities.

For those Earth Monkeys who are seeking work or who feel bored or in a rut in their present job, the Goat year will again offer some interesting opportunities. By resolving to seek something more in line with what they want, many Earth Monkeys will be successful in gaining a new position. Even if this is in a lesser capacity than they might have wanted, at least it will give them additional experience which they can use as a basis for future progress, especially in the auspicious Monkey year that follows. For work opportunities, April, May and last quarter of the year are well aspected.

The developments that occur at work will lead to a modest improvement in the Earth Monkey's income over the year. He is usually careful when handling money matters, although to make the most of his resources he does need to plan ahead and ideally set funds aside for specific purposes rather than proceeding in an ad hoc manner. By keeping control of both his income and expenditure, he will find he is able to do a great deal more as well as perhaps build up a surplus which he can use for personal treats and a possible holiday. With travel favourably aspected, all Earth Monkeys would do well to try and go away for a break at some time over the year as well as take up any invitations to visit friends and family living some distance away.

As far as his personal life is concerned, this will be a busy year for the Earth Monkey. His home life will be particularly active and he will help both younger and more senior relations during the year. Although sometimes he may find the demands on his time considerable, his assistance will be greatly appreciated. However, when times are busy, the Earth Monkey should be careful not to overload himself. In some cases he should consider deferring certain household projects and activities and just concentrating on major priorities. Also, rather than feel that certain household tasks are just his preserve, he should ask others to help. With good time management and assistance from others, he will often be surprised by the amount he is able to do. And amid the activity, there will still be a great deal for him to enjoy. By encouraging shared interests, suggesting occasional family treats and spending time in the company of those who matter, the Earth Monkey can enjoy some wonderful moments.

Socially, this will also be an active year. During 2003, the Earth Monkey will not only find himself in demand with his circle of friends but often, due to the nature of his work or personal interests, with invitations to go out and socialize more generally. His circle of friends and acquaintances is set to grow quite considerably and for the unattached, one new friendship could develop into something very special.

Overall, the Goat year holds good prospects for the Earth Monkey, particularly in preparing for the often substantial advances he will make in the years ahead. And although on a personal level the year will be busy, by managing his time well, the Earth Monkey can make it an interesting and often rewarding time.

TIP FOR THE YEAR
Take advantage of the opportunities to learn and to further your skills. What is accomplished now can bear sizeable fruit later.

FAMOUS MONKEYS

Gillian Anderson, Jennifer Aniston, Francesca Annis, Christina Aguilera, Michael Aspel, J. M. Barrie, Julius

Caesar, Johnny Cash, Jacques Chirac, Joe Cocker, Colette, John Constable, Alistair Cooke, David Copperfield, Patricia Cornwell, Joan Crawford, Leonardo da Vinci, Timothy Dalton, Roger Daltrey, Bette Davis, Danny De Vito, Bo Derek, Celine Dion, Michael Douglas, Mia Farrow, Carrie Fisher, F. Scott Fitzgerald, Ian Fleming, Dick Francis, Fiona Fullerton, Paul Gauguin, Jerry Hall, Tom Hanks, Martina Hingis, Harry Houdini, P. D. James, Pope John Paul II, Lyndon B. Johnson, Buster Keaton, Edward Kennedy, Alicia Keys, Don King, Gladys Knight, Bob Marley, Walter Matthau, Kylie Minogue, V. S. Naipaul, Peter O'Toole, Anthony Perkins, Lisa Marie Presley, Debbie Reynolds, Sir Tim Rice, Little Richard, Anne Robinson, Mary Robinson, Mickey Rooney, Diana Ross, Donald Rumsfeld, Boz Scaggs, Gerhard Schröder, Michael Schumacher, Tom Selleck, Omar Sharif, Wilbur Smith, Rod Stewart, Jacques Tati, Elizabeth Taylor, Dame Kiri Te Kanawa, Harry Truman, Venus Williams.

22 JANUARY 1909 ⁓ 9 FEBRUARY 1910   *Earth Rooster*

8 FEBRUARY 1921 ⁓ 27 JANUARY 1922   *Metal Rooster*

26 JANUARY 1933 ⁓ 13 FEBRUARY 1934   *Water Rooster*

13 FEBRUARY 1945 ⁓ 1 FEBRUARY 1946   *Wood Rooster*

31 JANUARY 1957 ⁓ 17 FEBRUARY 1958   *Fire Rooster*

17 FEBRUARY 1969 ⁓ 5 FEBRUARY 1970   *Earth Rooster*

5 FEBRUARY 1981 ⁓ 24 JANUARY 1982   *Metal Rooster*

23 JANUARY 1993 ⁓ 9 FEBRUARY 1994   *Water Rooster*

THE
ROOSTER

THE PERSONALITY OF
THE ROOSTER

When schemes are laid in advance, it is surprising how often the circumstances will fit in with them.

Sir William Osler, a Rooster

The Rooster is born under the sign of candour. He has a flamboyant and colourful personality and is meticulous in all that he does. He is an excellent organizer and wherever possible likes to plan his various activities well in advance.

The Rooster is highly intelligent and usually very well read. He has a good sense of humour and is an effective and persuasive speaker. He loves discussion and enjoys taking part in any sort of debate. He has no hesitation in speaking his mind and is forthright in his views. He does, however, lack tact and can easily damage his reputation or cause offence by some thoughtless remark or action. The Rooster also has a very volatile nature and he should always try to avoid acting on the spur of the moment.

The Rooster is usually very dignified in his manner and conducts himself with an air of confidence and authority. He is adept at handling financial matters and, as with most things, he organizes his financial affairs with considerable skill. He chooses his investments well and is capable of achieving great wealth. Most Roosters save or use their money wisely, but there are a few who are the reverse and are notorious spendthrifts. Fortunately, the Rooster has great earning capacity and is rarely without sufficient funds to tide himself over.

Another characteristic of the Rooster is that he invariably carries a notebook or scraps of paper around with him. He is constantly writing himself reminders or noting down important facts lest he forgets – the Rooster cannot abide inefficiency and conducts all his activities in an orderly, precise and methodical manner.

The Rooster is usually very ambitious, but can be unrealistic in some of what he hopes to achieve. He occasionally lets his imagination run away with him and while he does not like any interference from others, it would be in his own interests if he were to listen to their views a little more often. He also does not like criticism and if he feels anybody is doubting his judgement or prying too closely into his affairs, he is certain to let his feelings be known. He can also be rather self-centred and stubborn over relatively trivial matters, but to compensate for this he is reliable, honest and trustworthy, and this is appreciated by all who come into contact with him.

Roosters born between the hours of five and seven, both at dawn and sundown, tend to be the most extrovert of their sign, but all Roosters like to lead an active social life and enjoy attending parties and big functions. The Rooster usually has a wide circle of friends and is able to build up influential contacts with remarkable ease. He often belongs to several clubs and societies and involves himself in a variety of different activities. He is particularly interested in the environment, humanitarian affairs and anything affecting the welfare of others. The Rooster has a very caring nature and will do much to help those less fortunate than himself.

He also gets much pleasure from gardening and while he may not always spend as much time in the garden as he would like, his garden is invariably well kept and productive.

The Rooster is generally very distinguished in his appearance and if his job permits, he will wear an official uniform with great pride and dignity. He is not averse to publicity and takes great delight in being the centre of attention. He often does well at PR work or any job which brings him into contact with the media. He also makes a very good teacher.

The female Rooster leads a varied and interesting life. She involves herself in many different activities and there are some who wonder how she can achieve so much. She often holds very strong views and, like her male counterpart, has no hesitation in speaking her mind or telling others how she thinks things should be done. She is supremely efficient and well organized and her home is usually very neat and tidy. She has good taste in clothes and usually wears smart but very practical outfits.

The Rooster usually has a large family and takes a particularly active interest in the education of his children. He is very loyal to his partner and will find that he is especially well suited to those born under the signs of the Snake, Horse, Ox and Dragon. Provided they do not interfere too much in the Rooster's various activities, the Rat, Tiger, Goat and Pig can also establish a good relationship with him, but two Roosters together are likely to squabble and irritate each other. The rather sensitive Rabbit will find the Rooster a bit too blunt for his liking, and the Rooster will quickly become exasperated by the ever-inquisitive and artful Monkey. He will also find it difficult to get on with the anxious Dog.

If the Rooster can overcome his volatile nature and exercise more tact, he will go far in life. He is capable and talented and will invariably make a lasting – and usually favourable – impression almost everywhere he goes.

THE FIVE DIFFERENT TYPES OF ROOSTER

In addition to the 12 signs of the Chinese zodiac, there are five elements and these have a strengthening or moderating influence on the sign. The effects of the five elements on the Rooster are described below, together with the years in which the elements were exercising their influence. Therefore all Roosters born in 1921 and 1981 are Metal Roosters, those born in 1933 and 1993 are Water Roosters, and so on.

Metal Rooster: 1921, 1981
The Metal Rooster is a hard and conscientious worker. He knows exactly what he wants in life and sets about everything he does in a positive and determined manner. He can at times appear abrasive and he would almost certainly do better if he were more willing to reach a compromise with others rather than hold so rigidly to his beliefs. He is very articulate and most astute when dealing with financial matters. He is loyal to his friends and often devotes much energy to working for the common good.

Water Rooster: 1933, 1993

This Rooster has a very persuasive manner and can easily gain the co-operation of others. He is intelligent, well read and enjoys taking part in discussions and debates. He has a seemingly inexhaustible amount of energy and is prepared to work long hours in order to secure what he wants. He can, however, waste much valuable time worrying over minor and inconsequential details. He is approachable, has a good sense of humour and is highly regarded by others.

Wood Rooster: 1945

The Wood Rooster is honest, reliable and often sets himself high standards. He is ambitious, but also more prepared to work in a team than some of the other types of Rooster. He usually succeeds in life, but does have a tendency to get caught up in bureaucratic matters or attempt too many things at the same time. He has wide interests, likes to travel and is very considerate and caring towards his family and friends.

Fire Rooster: 1957

This Rooster is extremely strong-willed. He has many leadership qualities, is an excellent organizer and is most efficient in his work. Through sheer force of character he often secures his objectives, but he does have a tendency to be very forthright and not always consider the feelings of others. If the Fire Rooster can learn to be more tactful he can often succeed beyond his wildest dreams.

Earth Rooster: 1909, 1969

This Rooster has a deep and penetrating mind. He is efficient, perceptive and is particularly astute in business and financial matters. He is also persistent and once he has set himself an objective, he will rarely allow himself to be deflected from achieving his aim. The Earth Rooster works hard and is held in great esteem by his friends and colleagues. He usually enjoys the arts and takes a keen interest in the activities of the various members of his family.

PROSPECTS FOR THE ROOSTER IN 2003

The Chinese New Year starts on 1 February 2003. Until then, the old year, the Year of the Horse, is still making its presence felt.

The Horse year (12 February 2002 to 31 January 2003) will have been a variable one for the Rooster and while he will have been able to make progress as well as enjoy some pleasing times, it is still very much a year that calls for care.

In what remains of the Horse year, the Rooster will need to pay close attention to the views of those around him. Although, superb organizer that he is, he likes to play a leading role in making arrangements, he does need to liaise with others and listen to their views if differences of opinion are to be avoided. Also, given the often busy lifestyle that his whole household may lead, there will be times when family members are tired, tense or under strain. Tempers may flare and the Rooster would do well to keep his candid nature in check. He should aim to bring some balance into his domestic life and to ensure that there are times when everyone can relax and unwind together, rather than be continually occupied. Here the Rooster's input can be truly appreciated and by arranging more pleasurable occasions – perhaps an outing somewhere or having friends round or even playing a game – his suggestion can benefit everyone. The holidays at the end of year will be especially appreciated and will lead to some particularly special occasions. In the Horse year the Rooster should make sure that life is not all work and pressure.

At work the Horse year again calls for the Rooster to liaise closely with others and show himself a good team member. By acting in co-operation with those around him, building up contacts and being forthcoming with his ideas, he can do his prospects much good. As the year draws to a close, almost all Roosters will find that their accomplishments and experience will stand them in excellent stead for the more favourable Goat year that follows.

One area which calls for particular care, however, is finance. Horse years can be expensive and the Rooster does need to watch his level of spending and avoid too many spur of the moment purchases. Also, with the last quarter of the year tending to be a more costly time, if the Rooster could spread out some of his purchases or set some money aside for more seasonal expenses, he will find this will help.

Overall, the Horse year can be a reasonable one for the Rooster, but he does need to set about his activities with care and act in close co-operation with others.

The Year of the Goat starts on 1 February and will be a much improved one for the Rooster, although it could take several months for him to get into his stride and start to benefit from its more encouraging aspects.

As the Goat year starts, the Rooster would do well to regard this as a year of opportunity and to draw a line under any recent disappointments. Now is a time to move forward. If there should be any problems still concerning the Rooster, he should use the early months of the year to deal with them rather than letting them hang over him. If talking with others would help, then he should be prepared to do so, or, if he is unhappy in his present situation, he should consider ways in which it can be improved. If the Rooster takes action and addresses problems, results *will* follow and he will feel able to turn his attention to the present rather than be hindered by preoccupations with the past.

One particularly promising area concerns the Rooster's work. For those Roosters looking to advance in their present line of work, some interesting and sometimes unexpected promotion opportunities will become available. The aspects are also encouraging for those Roosters who may feel in a rut, unfulfilled in what they do, or be seeking work. This is a year of real opportunity, but to benefit these Roosters must decide upon the sort of position they want and then seek it out. By making enquiries and persisting in following up opportunities many will find themselves being offered a position which holds good prospects for the future. This is certainly not a year to be fettered by the past – it is a time to make progress. Throughout the year the aspects are on the Rooster's side, but the months of May, June, September and November could see some particularly interesting work developments.

The Rooster should also aim to further his skills over the year, taking advantage of training opportunities, enrolling on courses or reading up on subjects that would be useful to him. Again, this will give him a sense of moving forward.

He will also gain from attending to his well-being, making sure he gets regular exercise and eats a balanced diet. Although many Roosters do keep themselves active by walking, swimming, cycling or some other form of exercise, the Rooster will benefit from the attention he gives to his well-being this year.

As far as financial matters are concerned, this is another year which calls for careful management. With the plans that the Rooster will have for his accommodation, as well as the new equipment and furnishings he will see and want over the year, his outgoings will sometimes be high. To help with this, he should aim to budget in advance and whenever possible set money aside for specific purposes. By keeping control over his financial position he will be able to accomplish a great deal, but he must not to succumb to too many spur of the moment temptations. Without some restraint, spendthrift Roosters could come to regret their more hasty purchases or find their money could have been put to better use.

The Goat year is well aspected for personal matters, with the Rooster's domestic life going well and meaning a great deal to him. Whether initiating and carrying out household tasks, taking on home improvement projects or helping and advising loved ones, the Rooster's often leading role will be appreciated. Also, with his own activities and the often busy lives led by those around him, his ability to organize so many schedules and commitments will be of great value. Should pressures mount at any time, the Rooster would do well to allow a certain flexibility in his plans and, if it would be helpful, consider delaying certain projects. Although he may be eager to get things done, setting an unrealistic pace could put him under strain as well as prevent him from spending time on more pleasurable pursuits. In 2003 his home life can be rich and rewarding, but it must have balance. At some point over the year the Rooster should aim to take a holiday with his loved ones, as the change of scene and rest will do everyone good.

The Rooster's social life will also see much activity and in addition to regularly meeting up with friends, he could find himself being invited to a range of social occasions and having the chance to widen his social circle. For the unattached Rooster or those who would like to make new friends, the Goat year is favourably aspected and by going out and possibly joining in with group activities, these Roosters will soon get to meet others. In some cases, there will be a chance introduction to someone who will quickly become special and for quite a few Roosters, affairs of the heart will figure strongly over the year and bring much happiness. On a personal level, the Goat year can be a significant one for the Rooster, with March and the months from June to September being favoured for social and personal activities.

In many respects, the Rooster will enjoy the Goat year and will do well. Some parts of the year will be busy and demanding, but the Rooster will be moving forward, widening his experience and using his strengths to good effect. And on a personal level, the year will contain many fine times.

As far as the different types of Rooster are concerned, this will be a significant year for the *Metal Rooster* with positive developments occurring in many areas of his life.

Particularly well aspected is the Metal Rooster's personal life. Many Metal Roosters will find themselves enjoying the love and support of a special person, spending time with their partner on shared interests and carrying out projects on their home. These improvements will not only be satisfying but will also appeal to the Metal Rooster's tidy and organized mind. He is, after all, creating his own domain, and he will be at great pains to stamp it with his own personality and taste.

Those Metal Roosters who have children or who do so over the year will spend much time tending to their needs and here the Metal Rooster's loving and conscientious nature will prove an asset and establish a wonderful bond. True, there may be times when the Metal Rooster will feel tired and occasionally despair of the pressures that the year will bring, but these will be days that he will treasure.

For unattached Metal Roosters, the Goat year holds exciting promise. Often by chance they will meet someone who will quickly become important, with many meeting their future partner and soul mate.

The Metal Rooster will also value his social life and though with work and his other commitments he may feel he is not able to go out as often as he used to, he should still keep in regular contact with friends as well as go to any social events that appeal to him. His social life will often act as a tonic, allowing him to unwind and enjoy himself. All Metal Roosters will be able to add to their social circle over the year and will make contacts who could be useful to their career. The Metal Rooster will certainly be on good form throughout much of 2003.

The year will also bring significant developments at work. Metal Roosters who are seeking work or feeling unfulfilled in their present role should take steps to investigate other possibilities and by following up their ideas, they will discover some ideal openings to pursue. Also, if it would help their quest to undertake some additional training or carry out some background research, this too could strengthen their applications and enhance their prospects. This is a year to move forward, but it rests with the Metal Rooster to choose the direction and manner of his advance.

There will of course be many Metal Roosters who will be content to remain in their present role. These Metal Roosters should take advantage of the learning opportunities that the year will bring as well as be willing to take on further responsibilities. By showing initiative and keenness as well as setting about their activities in their usual conscientious way, these Metal Roosters will greatly impress and enhance their prospects, with many earning some well-deserved promotion in the second half of the year.

The progress that the Metal Rooster makes in his work will also lead to an increase in his income. While this will be welcome, he does have many commitments and would do well to manage his resources with care. With sensible control of his purse strings, he can improve his financial position and ease some of the pressures he may be under, but the year does call for vigilance.

Although the Metal Rooster will have much to keep him occupied, he should also allow time for his own personal interests. These will not only provide a break from his usual activities but can sometimes give him welcome exercise or allow him to use his talents in a different and satisfying way.

Overall, this will be an important year for the Metal Rooster, with the progress he makes in his work having far-reaching implications, while personally there will be some wonderful times. This is a year to enjoy, savour and move forward.

TIP FOR THE YEAR

This is a time to take charge and make the most of your strengths and ideas. The year will smile on you and give you good cause to smile back!

This will be a pleasing and often memorable year for the *Water Rooster*. For those born in 1933, the year will mark their seventieth birthday and it will be a time when they will not only reflect on the fascinating course of their lives but also give some thought to the future. And with the Water Rooster's delight in giving himself interesting things to do, this already promising year could become even more rewarding. Indeed, over the year, the Water Rooster will often amuse (and sometimes exasperate) those around him as he puts forward a variety of suggestions and schemes.

One area which will feature prominently will be his home. Many Water Roosters will mount an efficiency drive, tidying up storage areas and installing new comforts. A few will even decide to move altogether. Home improvements, of whatever kind, will bring great satisfaction. And those Water Roosters who have gardens will spend many a happy hour tending their land, experimenting with stock and adding a new feature or two.

In addition, the Water Rooster's inquisitive mind will often get the better of him and many Water Roosters will spend the year pursuing an interest or subject that has intrigued them for some time. By delving, reading, researching and experimenting, again the Water Rooster will enjoy some satisfying times. Many Water Roosters are also interested in the creative arts and will be tempted to go to shows, exhibitions or places of entertainment or use their own creative skills in some way. Again, the way the Water Rooster fills his days will bring him pleasure.

Travel too is favourably aspected and if the Water Rooster wants to mark his seventieth year with a visit to a place he has long wanted to see, he should make enquiries and see what is possible. Over the year he could get to see some interesting sights and would do well to take advantage of any travel opportunities or bargain breaks.

As always, the Water Rooster will value his home life over the year, with those around him being supportive and often sharing in his interests and pursuits. Any Water Rooster who may be lonely or have had some recent sadness to bear will find that by going out and involving himself in group and community activities, he will soon be able to make new friends. With his wide interests and engaging manner, the Water Rooster has a rich personality and by making the effort, difficult though it may perhaps be, he can inject some new happiness into his life. Also if, at any time, any matter is concerning him, he should talk it over with others and, if appropriate, seek professional guidance. To keep worries to himself could sometimes make matters worse and others may be able to solve the problem.

For Water Roosters born in 1993 this will again be a promising year. The young Water Rooster will cover a great deal in his schoolwork and in the process discover new strengths. His earnest and inquisitive nature will serve him well. He will also enjoy outdoor activities over the year and those with sporting interests will often be thrilled with the pleasure that comes from developing their skills. When opportunities are there and the Water Rooster is interested, he can make it a rewarding time. And this does sum up the nature of the year.

Overall, by setting about his activities with enthusiasm and making the most of his talents, the Water Rooster will greatly enjoy the year and will value the love and support of those around him.

TIP FOR THE YEAR
Make the most of the opportunities that arise. By using your time well, you can make this an enjoyable and fulfilling year.

This will be an interesting year for the *Wood Rooster* and one which will bring him much personal satisfaction. His work, family life and interests can offer some particularly pleasing times and the year will also spring a few surprises.

Many Wood Roosters will have seen considerable changes in their work over recent years and the more settled times of the Goat year will allow them to build on their position and put their skills and expertise to good use. Those whose work is in any way creative can enjoy an especially encouraging response. The Goat year will certainly give the Wood Rooster every chance to benefit from his strengths and will bring him a greater level of fulfilment and, in some cases, some long-overdue rewards.

Many Wood Roosters will be content to remain in their existing role, but for those who are seeking work or are interested in transferring to a different position or making progress, the Goat year can bring some interesting developments. By drawing on their experience and pursuing openings that they feel well suited for, many Wood Roosters will succeed in gaining an opening from which they can benefit. Even if initial applications do not go their way, they should persist. Workwise, the Goat year is an encouraging and positive time.

The Wood Rooster will also enjoy developing his personal interests over the year. Whether these involve extending his knowledge or giving himself some satisfying projects to do, they can bring him a great deal of pleasure. Any Wood Rooster who may have let his interests lapse should make it his resolution to take up something over the year. For some, this could be a creative activity such as photography, music, art or craftwork, while others could find pleasure in following up a particular subject, enrolling on a course or even just going out more and perhaps visiting places of interest in their area. Many Wood Roosters are keen gardeners and time spent in the garden will again bring them a great deal of pleasure this year. Whatever he chooses to do, the Wood Rooster will find that by setting himself something interesting and worthwhile, his interest will become another rewarding aspect of the year.

The year is also well aspected for travel and all Wood Roosters should aim to go away at some time during 2003 as well as follow up any invitations to visit family and friends who live some distance away and who they might not see as regularly as they would like. Again, it is a case of taking advantage of the opportunities that arise.

The one area that could give the Wood Rooster some concern relates to finance and paperwork. In 2003 he must be careful when entering into new agreements or making major purchases and should check the terms carefully, making sure he understands the obligations he is taking on and keeps all the paperwork carefully. If he has any doubts, it really would be worth seeking advice. Similarly, with any important forms he has to complete, the Wood Rooster needs to be thorough and vigilant. Without such care, he could find himself having to deal with some unwelcome correspondence. Wood Roosters, take note.

The Wood Rooster will, however, enjoy his home life and in addition to appreciating the support shown for his undertakings, he will follow the progress of his loved ones with much interest. Several times over the year he will be pleased to help those dear to him, whether this is by looking after younger children, passing on advice or helping in some other way. The role he plays in domestic matters will mean a great deal and some of the family events – including a celebration that will occur mid-year – will fill him with pride. Even if on some days, because of the nature of his work, he comes home tired or feels under pressure, he will welcome the comfort and love his home provides.

The Wood Rooster's social life is also favourably aspected and whether he decides to keep this low-key or prefers to go out more regularly, the Goat year will certainly bring him some pleasurable occasions. In some cases, by joining a local group, enrolling on a course or meeting people through one of his interests, the Wood Rooster will get to know some interesting and like-minded people over the year, some of whom will become firm friends.

Overall, 2003 holds some good prospects for the Wood Rooster and by using his time and skills well, he will find this a satisfying and fulfilling year.

TIP FOR THE YEAR
Make the most of your skills, strengths and interests. Many benefits will flow from them.

The steadier nature of the Goat year will come at the right time for the *Fire Rooster*, giving him the chance to follow through some of his ideas as well as concentrate on what he does best rather than be distracted by other matters.

Many Fire Roosters will be content to remain in their existing role at work and with their experience, insight, output, ideas and methodical approach, they will impress many. The Fire Rooster's reputation is set to increase and his prospects to be enhanced. Those Fire Roosters who may in recent years have felt discouraged by a lack of acknowledgement for their efforts will certainly find this changing in 2003. Now the Fire Rooster is very much in the ascendancy. The Goat year is an excellent time for him to move ahead, seek promotion or build on his present position, should he wish to do so.

Similarly, for those Fire Roosters who are unhappy with what they are doing or who are seeking work, the Goat year offers an excellent chance to move their career forward. However, rather than going after every vacancy, they should give serious thought to the type of position they are seeking. With focus and a clearer idea of what *they* want to do, and preparing for this both mentally and physically, many will succeed in gaining the opportunity they seek. Once in a position, they will soon be able to prove themselves and set their career off on a more suitable track. This will require persistence and will-power, but the Fire Rooster certainly possesses these, and what he achieves in the Goat year can often be the first step towards some significant successes later on.

The whole year is favourably aspected for work matters, but the period from mid-April to June and the month of September could see some interesting developments.

The progress that the Fire Rooster makes in his work will lead to an increase in his income, which will be especially welcome as some parts of the year will be expensive. In addition to his existing obligations, the Fire Rooster could spend quite heavily on socializing. Some Fire Roosters could also have large family expenses, including a possible wedding. In view of the high levels of activity, the Fire Rooster should keep a record of his outgoings and, wherever possible, budget in advance for forthcoming expenses. The better he is able to manage his finances, the better he will fare.

Another important aspect of the year concerns the Fire Rooster's own personal development and interests. While he may feel he has enough to occupy him already, it is important he sets time aside for recreational pursuits as well as aims to develop himself in some way, perhaps through a fitness programme, a new hobby or learning about a subject that has been intriguing him. Whatever it is, by doing something new and positive the Fire Rooster will reinforce the spirit of the year – that of moving forward.

The Fire Rooster's personal life will again see much activity, with those around him often looking to him for help, advice and sometimes practical support. There will be activities to arrange, including, for some, a wedding, and being the keen organizer that he is, the Fire Rooster will play a pivotal role. He will also be keen to add some improvements to his home and while this will sometimes be disruptive, the results will be appreciated. Family life in the Goat year will sometimes be busy, but it will be important to the Fire Rooster and the love and support he is shown by those important to him will be especially valued.

The Fire Rooster will also keep himself active on a social level and will want to attend a variety of social events over the year. Sometimes these will be connected with his work or personal interests. The year will certainly contain a great many enjoyable occasions as well as the chance for the Fire Rooster to add to his circle of friends. On a personal level, he will feel on top form for much of the year, with his style, manner and genuine interest in others often making a highly favourable impression. For those Fire Roosters who are unattached and may desire more companionship, the Goat year holds some wonderful prospects, including, for some, the gift of an exciting romance. The months from May to September are particularly well aspected for social matters.

Overall, the Goat year is a favourable one for the Fire Rooster and it will allow him to develop his talents in a satisfying way as well as enjoy good relations with a great many people.

TIP FOR THE YEAR
Make the most of your personal strengths, ideas and skills. The Goat year holds real promise and you should aim to make the most of your potential.

This will be an important year for the *Earth Rooster*, allowing him to build on his more recent achievements as well as enjoy an active personal life. In addition, he will be given the chance to further his own personal development and this too will be something he will find satisfying.

Many Earth Roosters will have seen considerable changes in their work over the last 12 months and often had to learn new duties as well as adapt to different work practices. At times the pressures will have been great. However, the Goat year will give the Earth Rooster the chance to profit from his recent experience and to use his strengths to good effect. Some of the projects and tasks he is set or the ideas he now concentrates on will not only be more fulfilling but also give him the chance to extend his capabilities and reputation. In addition, he will find his colleagues supportive and by working closely with them and being forthcoming with his thoughts and plans, he will often find himself benefiting from their advice. The Goat year will certainly offer the Earth Rooster the chance to demonstrate his best qualities and, as a result, he will greatly impress. For those Earth Roosters desiring promotion, the months from May to September will hold some interesting possibilities.

Similarly, Earth Roosters who are seeking work should draw on their experience and consider the different ways in which this can be used. By mulling over various possibilities, these Earth Roosters could widen the scope of the positions they could apply for. Over the year many will be successful in securing a position which offers the potential for future development.

The Earth Rooster should also take advantage of any training available to him. If he keeps his skills up to date, he will find this will not only help his performance but also strengthen his prospects.

In addition, if there is a personal interest or subject that he wishes to develop, he should set some time aside for this. The Goat year is well aspected for personal development and by furthering himself and his knowledge, the Earth Rooster can make this a personally rewarding time. In many cases, what he learns now will be to his long-term benefit. He is also blessed with a practical nature and many Earth Roosters will set about various projects in their home and garden with great enthusiasm. Although these will often go well, with the Earth Rooster carefully planning what he wants to do, he should allow ample time to complete his projects. Sometimes delays, interruptions or hidden problems can disrupt the best-laid plans. Also, the Earth Rooster would do well to involve others in his various schemes. Not only will he benefit from the pooling of ideas but also from the practical assistance that others can give.

In addition to the projects he carries out, the Earth Rooster will take much pleasure in his home life over the year, particularly in helping those dear to him and watching over their progress. By encouraging mutual interests and activities, he will not only enjoy some rewarding occasions but also help to preserve the rapport he so values. Should any part of the year become particularly busy or pressured, the Earth Rooster will find that if everyone helps out, especially with some of the household chores, this will ease some of the pressure. His ability to organize and prioritize will often prove a great asset, particularly when a lot is happening all at once.

The Earth Rooster's social life will also be active during the year, particularly in the second half. As well as keeping in regular contact with his friends, he will attend a variety of events, and for the unattached Earth Rooster, there could be the added prospect of an exciting new romance or a firm friendship.

In most respects this will be a positive year for the Earth Rooster and if he makes the most of his strengths, he can enjoy some well-deserved success.

TIP FOR THE YEAR

Make the most of your experience and strengths. They are, after all, the keys to your future success.

FAMOUS ROOSTERS

Francis Bacon, Dame Janet Baker, Enid Blyton, Barbara Taylor Bradford, Michael Caine, Enrico Caruso, Christopher Cazenove, Jean Chrétien, Eric Clapton, Joan Collins, Rita Coolidge, Craig David, Daniel Day Lewis, Sacha Distel, the Duke of Edinburgh, Gloria Estefan, Mohamed al Fayed, Bryan Ferry, Errol Flynn, Benjamin Franklin, Dawn French, Stephen Fry, Steffi Graf, Melanie Griffith, Richard Harris, Deborah Harry, Goldie Hawn, Katherine Hepburn, Quincy Jones, Diane Keaton, D. H. Lawrence, David Livingstone, Ken Livingstone, Jayne Mansfield, Steve Martin, James Mason, W. Somerset Maugham, Paul Merton, Bette Midler, Van Morrison, Willie Nelson, Kim Novak, Yoko Ono, Sir William Osler, Dolly Parton, Michelle Pfeiffer, Priscilla Presley, Mary Quant, Nancy Reagan, Joan Rivers, Paul Scofield, Jenny Seagrove, George Segal, Carly Simon, Britney Spears, Johann Strauss, Sir Peter Ustinov, Richard Wagner, Serena Williams, Neil Young, Catherine Zeta-Jones.

10 FEBRUARY 1910 ⌒ 29 JANUARY 1911   *Metal Dog*

28 JANUARY 1922 ⌒ 15 FEBRUARY 1923   *Water Dog*

14 FEBRUARY 1934 ⌒ 3 FEBRUARY 1935   *Wood Dog*

2 FEBRUARY 1946 ⌒ 21 JANUARY 1947   *Fire Dog*

18 FEBRUARY 1958 ⌒ 7 FEBRUARY 1959   *Earth Dog*

6 FEBRUARY 1970 ⌒ 26 JANUARY 1971   *Metal Dog*

25 JANUARY 1982 ⌒ 12 FEBRUARY 1983   *Water Dog*

10 FEBRUARY 1994 ⌒ 30 JANUARY 1995   *Wood Dog*

THE
DOG

THE PERSONALITY OF THE DOG

To be what we are, and to become what we are capable of
becoming, is the only end of life.

Robert Louis Stevenson, a Dog

The Dog is born under the signs of loyalty and anxiety. He
usually holds very firm views and beliefs and is the cham-
pion of good causes. He hates any sort of injustice or unfair
treatment and will do all in his power to help those less
fortunate than himself. He has a strong sense of fair play
and will be honourable and open in all his dealings.

The Dog is very direct and straightforward. He is never
one to skirt round issues and speaks frankly and to the
point. He can also be stubborn, but he is more than
prepared to listen to the views of others and will try to be
as fair as possible in coming to his decisions. He will
readily give advice where it is needed and will be the first
to offer assistance when things go wrong.

The Dog instils confidence wherever he goes and there
are many who admire him for his integrity and resolute
manner. He is a very good judge of character and can often
form an accurate impression of someone very shortly after
meeting them. He is also very intuitive and can frequently
sense how things are going to work out long in advance.

Despite his friendly and amiable manner, the Dog is not
a big socializer. He dislikes having to attend large social
functions or parties and much prefers a quiet meal with
friends or a chat by the fire. He is an excellent conversationalist and is often a marvellous raconteur of amusing

stories and anecdotes. He is also quick-witted and his mind is always alert.

The Dog can keep calm in a crisis and although he does have a temper, his outbursts tend to be short-lived. He is loyal and trustworthy, but if he ever feels badly let down or rejected by someone, he will rarely forgive or forget.

The Dog usually has very set interests. He prefers to specialize and become an expert in a chosen area rather than dabble in a variety of different activities. He usually does well in jobs where he feels that he is being of service to others and is often suited to careers in the social services, the medical and legal professions and teaching. The Dog does, however, need to feel motivated in his work. He has to have a sense of purpose and if ever this is lacking he can quite often drift through life without ever achieving very much. Once he has the motivation, however, very little can prevent him from securing his objective.

Another characteristic of the Dog is his tendency to worry and to view things rather pessimistically. Quite often his worries are totally unnecessary and are of his own making. Although it may be difficult, worrying is a habit which the Dog should try to overcome.

The Dog is not materialistic or particularly bothered about accumulating great wealth. As long as he has the necessary money to support his family and to spend on the occasional luxury, he is more than happy. However, when he does have any spare money he tends to be rather a spendthrift and does not always put his money to its best use. He is also not a very good speculator and would be advised to seek professional advice before entering into any major long-term investment.

The Dog will rarely be short of admirers, but he is not an easy person to live with. His moods are changeable and his standards high, but he will be loyal and protective to his partner and will do all in his power to provide a good and comfortable home. He can get on extremely well with those born under the signs of the Horse, Pig, Tiger and Monkey, and can also establish a sound and stable relationship with the Rat, Ox, Rabbit, Snake and another Dog, but will find the Dragon a bit too flamboyant for his liking. He will also find it difficult to understand the creative and imaginative Goat and is likely to be highly irritated by the candid Rooster.

The female Dog is renowned for her beauty. She has a warm and caring nature, although until she knows someone well she can be both secretive and very guarded. She is highly intelligent and despite her calm and tranquil appearance she can be extremely ambitious. She enjoys sport and other outdoor activities and has a happy knack of finding bargains in the most unlikely of places. She can also get rather impatient when things do not work out as she would like.

The Dog usually has a very good way with children and can be a loving and doting parent. He will rarely be happier than when he is helping someone or doing something that will benefit others. Providing he can cure himself of his tendency to worry, he will lead a very full and active life – and in that life he will make many friends and do a tremendous amount of good.

THE FIVE DIFFERENT TYPES OF DOG

In addition to the 12 signs of the Chinese zodiac, there are five elements and these have a strengthening or moderating influence on the sign. The effects of the five elements on the Dog are described below, together with the years in which the elements were exercising their influence. Therefore all Dogs born in 1910 and 1970 are Metal Dogs, those born in 1922 and 1982 are Water Dogs, and so on.

Metal Dog: 1910, 1970

The Metal Dog is bold, confident and forthright and sets about everything he does in a resolute and determined manner. He has a great belief in his abilities and has no hesitation about speaking his mind or devoting himself to some just cause. He can be rather serious at times and can become anxious and irritable when things are not going according to plan. He tends to have very specific interests and it would certainly help him to broaden his outlook and become more involved in group activities. He is extremely loyal and faithful to his friends.

Water Dog: 1922, 1982

The Water Dog has a very direct and outgoing personality. He is an excellent communicator and has little trouble in persuading others to fall in with his plans. He does, however, have a somewhat carefree nature and is not as disciplined or as thorough as he should be in certain matters. Neither does he keep as much control over his finances as he should, but he can be most generous to his family and friends and will make sure that they want for nothing. The Water Dog is usually very good with children and has a wide circle of friends.

Wood Dog: 1934, 1994

This Dog is a hard and conscientious worker and will usually make a favourable impression wherever he goes. He is less independent than some of the other types of Dog and prefers to work in a group rather than on his own. He is popular, has a good sense of humour and takes a very keen interest in the activities of the various members of his family. He is often attracted to the finer things in life and can obtain much pleasure from collecting stamps, coins, pictures or antiques. He prefers to live in the country rather than the town.

Fire Dog: 1946

This Dog has a lively, outgoing personality and is able to establish friendships with remarkable ease. He is an honest and conscientious worker and likes to take an active part in all that is going on around him. He also likes to explore new ideas and providing he can get the necessary support and advice, he can often succeed where others have failed. He does, however, have a tendency to be stubborn. Providing he can overcome this, the Fire Dog can often achieve considerable fame and fortune.

Earth Dog: 1958

The Earth Dog is very talented and astute. He is methodical and efficient and is capable of going far in his chosen profession. He tends to be rather quiet and reserved, but has a very persuasive manner and usually secures his objectives without too much opposition. He is generous and kind and is always ready to lend a helping hand when it is needed. He is held in very high esteem by his friends and colleagues and he is usually most dignified in his appearance.

PROSPECTS FOR THE DOG IN 2003

The Chinese New Year starts on 1 February 2003. Until then, the old year, the Year of the Horse, is still making its presence felt.

The Horse year (12 February 2002 to 31 January 2003) holds considerable potential for the Dog, with the later months being a favoured period. This is a time when the Dog can move forward, use his skills and experience to good effect and enjoy a rich personal life.

At work there will be opportunities to progress and for those Dogs who are keen to further their career, currently seeking a position or wanting to move elsewhere, the months of September and November could hold some interesting developments. However, to benefit, these Dogs should follow up any openings that they see as well as investigate some of the career possibilities they may have thought about. By making the decision to advance and then taking action, many will find the closing months of the Horse year a positive and exciting time. Also, any Dogs who may have an interest or skill which they could use on a freelance basis or one day turn into a possible vocation should promote what they do. The Horse year *does* reward the industrious and enterprising, and with the right support and drive, the Dog can be a major beneficiary.

This will also be an active time for personal matters, with much happening in the Dog's home and social life. However, to prevent this becoming so busy that he has no time for himself, the Dog would do well to space out his commitments and keep a check on his diary. If he can spread out some of the preparation leading up to the festivities at the end of the year he will find this helpful as well. The closing months of the Horse year can be enjoyable but do call for careful planning and good management of time.

Overall, the Horse year is favourably aspected for the Dog and by making the most of his considerable abilities and personality, he can make some useful advances as well as enjoy himself.

The Year of the Goat starts on 1 February and will be a demanding one for the Dog. The year will contain some particularly busy periods and sometimes the Dog's progress may not be all that he would like, but to compensate, the long-term effects will often be to his benefit. Despite the varying aspects, provided the Dog remains aware of possible problem areas and exercises care, he can do much to ease some of the difficulties the year could bring.

In his work the Dog should look on the Goat year as a time to consolidate his position and add to his experience rather than seek to make major advances. For the many Dogs who will have seen changes in their work in the Horse year and are still relatively new to their duties, the early months of the year will be an excellent time to become more proficient in the different aspects of the job. All Dogs, whether new to their role or well established, should also take full advantage of any training they may be offered. By showing willing and being prepared to further himself, the Dog will find that what he learns will not only help him now but also be an asset when further openings do arise.

Through the year the Dog also needs to work closely with his colleagues and remain aware of prevailing attitudes and policies. Although he does like to be his own master and holds strong opinions, if he shows himself too independent or too set in his ways he could undermine his position. This is very much a year which calls for teamwork and, should any difficult situation arise, the Dog should be guarded in his comments. Without care, he could come to regret words spoken in heated moments. Dogs, take heed.

Also, if at any time the Dog feels under undue pressure or that unreasonable demands are being placed upon him, rather than keep his worries to himself, he should mention them to others and put forward possible solutions. Although this is a year to tread carefully, the Dog should still be forthcoming in a constructive way. And while this may not be the smoothest of years for him, if he completes his duties to his usual high standards, his efforts will be noticed and the experience he gains will be to his future advantage.

Dogs who are seeking work or particularly anxious to move from their present role would do well to consider ways in which they can draw on their existing experience. In the Goat year making headway *will* require persistence and tenaciousness. Fortunately these are qualities most Dogs possess! By following up possibilities, many Dogs will obtain an interesting new position over the year and April, June, October and November could all hold interesting opportunities.

As with the preceding Horse year, the Dog should also devote time to furthering his personal interests. Not only will these bring him pleasure but they will often provide a useful contrast to his usual activities. Interests that are both practical and creative could be especially satisfying. Any Dog who may be intrigued by a particular subject or skill should take steps to follow it up, as his personal interests can be an important and beneficial part of his life during the Goat year.

As far as financial matters are concerned, this will be an expensive year, especially as quite a few Dogs will decide to move or make major modifications to their home. When involved in any heavy outlay the Dog needs to check the terms and implications carefully and, where applicable, obtain several estimates before proceeding. Large financial transactions do call for careful attention and should he have any uncertainties or questions, the Dog should seek clarification rather than make assumptions. With vigilance and control of his spending, he will be generally satisfied with how he copes, but the year will be expensive and does call for careful management.

Accommodation matters are likely to take up the Dog's time over the year. For those who move, there will be the upheaval caused by the sorting and packing as well as the time spent looking for a new home. And for those who remain where they are, some of the home improvements they embark upon could entail more disruption than envisaged. Domestically, some of the Goat year will be demanding, but once any move has taken place or the disturbance caused by domestic projects finally comes to an end, the Dog and his household will derive much satisfaction from the great deal that has been accomplished and will enjoy the benefits that result.

In view of the domestic pressures and activity of the year, the Dog does need to liaise closely with those around him, discussing plans and arrangements and encouraging a spirit of co-operation. In this way he will benefit from the input of others as well as appreciate the affection and consideration shown him. Domestically, some parts of the Goat year will be busy, but it will certainly not be without its more agreeable side.

With so much happening during the year, the Dog may decide to cut back on his social life and in some cases just restrict this to meeting up with particularly close friends. However, despite the pressures on his time, the Dog should not cut himself off completely from other activities but give himself the chance to go out and enjoy occasions and activities that appeal to him, perhaps small social gatherings (which the Dog generally prefers to larger ones) or some form of entertainment. This will not only do him good but also bring an important balance and variety to his life. In 2003, the Dog should make sure his social life and personal interests do not suffer amid the activity of the year. These can, after all, be a source of much pleasure.

Although the Goat year will contain times of pressure and upheaval, the Dog will be well supported and what he achieves will bring him many benefits as well as be to his long-term good.

As far as the different types of Dog are concerned, the Goat year will be a variable one for the *Metal Dog*. Some aspects of his life are well favoured and will bring much pleasure, but in others, he will face some pressure and uncertainty and, given his tendency to worry, some parts of the Goat year will be tricky for him. However in spite of the varying aspects, the Metal Dog will draw much strength from the love and support of those around him as well as benefit from the learning experiences that the year will bring.

One area which will be challenging will be the Metal Dog's work. Though he is always well intentioned and keen to make the most of his skills, the Metal Dog will nevertheless feel despondent at times. He knows deep down that he is capable of much, but he could also feel that he is not making the most of his strengths or the progress he would like. However, despite his doubts, this can still be a constructive year for him and by setting about his activities in his usual conscientious way, he will increase his reputation and have the chance to try out or take on different duties and so widen his experience. In the process he may discover new strengths as well as increase the range of possibilities available for when he does decide to move on. Also, all Metal Dogs should take advantage of any training opportunities that are available to them. By adding to their skills, they can find new doors opening for them. The experience gained during the Goat year can have positive long-term implications.

As with all Dogs, the Metal Dog's home life will be busy during the year and quite a few Metal Dogs will decide to move. With all the buying and selling and packing that needs to be done, on top of the usual commitments, the Metal Dog may sometimes despair of what he has embarked on, but by keeping the end result in mind and drawing on the help of those around him, he will eventually be pleased with how everything falls into place. Once settled in his new home, the Metal Dogs will often feel excited by the change and the opportunities that now lie ahead.

Many of those Metal Dogs who remain where they are this year will also be busy with home improvement projects, perhaps redecorating and rearranging certain rooms. Again, they will find some weeks of the Goat year disruptive and pressured, but their plans will generally work out and leave them content. That is the nature of the Goat year.

However, even though the year will have its busy periods, the Metal Dog's home life will certainly bring him a great deal of pleasure, especially involving successes enjoyed by younger relations and time spent planning and carrying out activities with his family. The Metal Dog will especially value some of the more spontaneous occasions, perhaps a trip or break arranged at short notice. These can lead to some treasured moments.

Although, with the other demands on his time, the Metal Dog may not feel able to lead such an active social life as in some years, he will nevertheless value meeting up with friends and going out socializing. Any Metal Dog who may feel lonely or have experienced some recent personal sadness will find that by immersing himself in different activities and perhaps joining a special interest group, he can bring a little brightness back into his life and even strike up an important new friendship. For these Metal Dogs, April and May will be particularly promising months.

As far as financial matters are concerned, the Metal Dog will need to proceed with care and remain aware of the terms and costs of any major obligations that he takes on. Money matters do need careful and prudent management. With vigilance and control, however, the Metal Dog will find he is able to cope admirably and by taking his time will often be able to benefit from special deals or make some purchases at advantageous prices.

Overall, the Goat year will be a busy and challenging one for the Metal Dog. However, while there will be times when he will feel under pressure, if he keeps faith with himself and his skills, what he sets in motion can lead to considerable benefits in the near future.

TIP FOR THE YEAR
Make the most of the opportunities that become available. Although not always ideal, they can often be stepping-stones to something greater.

This will be an active year for the *Water Dog* and one which will see important developments in many areas of his life.

As with all Dogs, accommodation matters will figure prominently for the Water Dog. Many Water Dogs could move to a totally new locality over the year, perhaps due to education opportunities, job changes or changes in personal circumstances, including marriage or settling down with a partner. While the move will give rise to some hectic and yet sometimes exciting weeks, once settled, the Water Dog will feel determined to enjoy his new base and, given his practical nature, he will soon stamp his personality on his new home. Accommodation-wise, this will be an interesting and pleasing year for many Water Dogs.

However, with all the costs involved, the Water Dog does need to take careful note of the financial obligations he is taking on and allow for them in his budget. Also, despite the increased income many Water Dogs will receive over the year, spending does need to be watched. Although the Water Dog will enjoy the fruits of his labours, it would be best if he did this in moderation rather than to excess. Too much spending on non-essentials could quickly eat into his resources and sometimes prevent him from making more useful acquisitions later in the year or from taking a holiday. Finances *do* need careful control.

The Water Dog will also see changes in his work over the year. Many Water Dogs will have the chance to move to different duties or will decide to try a different type of job. Change is in the air, but rather than aiming to make major advances, the Water Dog should be looking to extend his skills and experience. He is still in the early stages of his career and what he learns now will shape his further progress. This is a year to explore and learn. The Water Dog would also find it helpful to meet those in the type of work he is in as well as those in areas he would like to progress to. By displaying an interest and commitment, he will impress quite a few and this too can help his subsequent progress. With his future in mind, he should also take advantage of any available training opportunities. By furthering his skills, he can do much to enhance his prospects.

As far as personal matters are concerned, this will be a splendid year, with friendship and love meaning a great deal to the Water Dog. Being encouraged by the support of someone special will inspire the Water Dog to set about his activities with a greater zeal and enthusiasm. For the unattached and also for those who move and may not know many in their new area, the Goat year holds excellent prospects. A chance meeting or introduction could quickly transform the year and sometimes the Water Dog's entire life. For meeting others and for socializing, April, May, August and September will be significant.

Generally, this will be a busy year for the Water Dog, but it will bring a greater happiness in his personal life and will allow him to extend his work experience and skills. Although sometimes he may feel his progress is not all that he would like it to be, what he learns now will often prove of immense value in the years ahead.

TIP FOR THE YEAR
Regard this as a time for learning and building up your experience, skills and knowledge.

This will be a reasonable year for the *Wood Dog*, although some months will be marked by considerable activity and pressure.

In common with many others of his sign, the Wood Dog will find accommodation matters featuring prominently.

Quite a few Wood Dogs will decide to move to somewhere more suitable for their present needs and the process will be a demanding and sometimes emotional one, as they sort through belongings and leave an area they know so well. However, during the move these Wood Dogs will be particularly grateful for the practical help and support they are given by family and friends, and once settled into their new home, they will soon delight in finding out about the attractions their new area offers and in making new friends.

Wood Dogs who do not move over the year will content themselves carrying out plans for their home and in some cases garden. The Goat year is certainly a practical one and the Wood Dog will be pleased with the results of his often considerable efforts. With all this strenuous activity, a warning does, though, need to be sounded. If the Wood Dog has to lift or move any heavy or cumbersome objects, it is important that he seeks help. Without care, a strain could cause him some discomfort as well as take a while to heal. Wood Dogs, take note.

Also, while in a cautionary vein, if the Wood Dog has any uncertainty over any important paperwork or forms he has to complete, he must seek clarification rather than take risks. He would also be wise to keep important paperwork safe, including guarantees and receipts, as it may be needed later.

As always, the Wood Dog will value his home life and appreciate all the support he is given. Though some months will be busy, there will be a great deal for him to enjoy. Holidays or trips out will often be very pleasant and the Wood Dog will also enjoy carrying out some of the activities he can share with his loved ones. In some cases, a new interest which can be taken up jointly will be a source of fun and satisfaction.

The Wood Dog's social life will also mean a lot to him over the year and in addition to the camaraderie of his friends, he will enjoy going to social events that appeal or to which he has been especially invited. Wood Dogs who would welcome more company will find that by going out and meeting others they can bring some joy back into their lives. They may be hesitant, but it really would be worth the effort.

For Wood Dogs born in 1994 this again will be a positive year and one in which they will get much satisfaction from extending their interests and capabilities. Whether the young Wood Dog's interests are sporting or he prefers more creative pursuits, by furthering his skills he will be pleased with the progress he makes as well as enjoy the chance to try new activities. Similarly, in his schoolwork, by showing willing and being open to guidance, the Wood Dog will make this a most constructive year academically.

For a great proportion of the year the young Wood Dog will be content with his situation, but if he does have any problems or feels under pressure, he *must* tell others and seek advice. Help is available should he need it and also, with the Dog sign's tendency to worry, by dealing with worries when they first appear, the young Wood Dog will learn a valuable lesson which will serve him well for a long time to come.

Overall, the Goat year will be a positive one for the Wood Dog and while some months will be challenging, especially for those who move, all Wood Dogs will be very satisfied with what they are able to achieve.

Remain aware of the advice and practical assistance that is available to you and take advantage of it when under any pressure.

This will be a year of interesting possibilities for the *Fire Dog*. As the Goat year starts, he would do well to take stock of his present position and consider how he would like his life to develop. Although many Fire Dogs will have achieved a good deal in recent years, they will certainly have new areas they want to explore. The Fire Dog is an ideas person and by clarifying these in the early stages of the year and then exploring the possibilities, he could set an interesting chain of events in motion.

Some of the Fire Dog's thoughts will relate to his work and whether well established in his present role, seeking a position or feeling in a rut and desiring a change, he should follow his ideas through. In many cases his initiative will lead to him being given new duties or, for those wanting a change, a position which will be a useful platform from which to develop. Although the advances the Fire Dog makes may not be major and may require considerable effort and persistence on his part – the Goat year is not one in which progress is easy – what he does achieve can have positive and far-reaching implications.

This is also an excellent year for the Fire Dog to spend time furthering his existing interests or to taking up a new one. By doing something purposeful, he can make this a fulfilling and rewarding time.

Another area that the Fire Dog would do well to consider is his well-being and if he does not get much regular exercise or feels out of condition, he should seek medical advice on the most appropriate form of exercise to take and then make an effort to improve his levels of fitness.

The Fire Dog will see considerable activity in his home life over the year and this may involve moving or carrying out extensive home improvements. Either way, there will be several weeks of disruption and upheaval, although the Fire Dog will be pleased with the end result. However, with all the activity that takes place and all the plans that he has, the Fire Dog should make a point of fully involving those around him in his schemes. Throughout this often busy year, he will be grateful for the practical assistance, encouragement and advice he is given. He will also follow the progress of a younger relation with much pride and while he may not wish to be seen as interfering, any advice and practical support he feels able to pass on will be appreciated. Overall, the Fire Dog's family life will be busy, but will certainly mean a great deal to him.

On a social level, the Fire Dog will find himself in demand, with invitations to a variety of social gatherings, and will be able to widen his social circle. In some cases his own interests will lead to meetings with fellow enthusiasts and to some pleasing – and sometimes lively – occasions.

As far as financial matters are concerned, the Fire Dog will fare reasonably well, although when considering any major transaction or purchase, he does need to check the details and terms carefully rather than proceed in too much haste. He could also find it helpful to set funds aside for some of the ideas he has in mind for his accommodation. By planning and saving over a period of time he can do much to ease a potentially large bill.

Overall, the Fire Dog can fare well in the Goat year, although in view of the prevailing aspects, he does need to take action and follow through his ideas. However, by remaining determined and persistent, he can look forward to some good results.

TIP FOR THE YEAR
Take action if there is an idea you would like to follow through or something you want. Despite some of the pressures that may result, it could ultimately be worth a great deal.

This will be an interesting year for the *Earth Dog* with often far-reaching results.

In particular, many Earth Dogs will be able to build on the progress they have made in recent years and use their strengths to good effect. Admittedly, the Earth Dog's progress might not be all that he could wish – the Goat year is not one in which the Earth Dog can expect to make major strides – but he will feel that what he does achieve and the experience that he gains will be to his advantage. Certainly his reputation will increase considerably over the year and even though he may feel competent in his work, by being willing to further his skills and take advantage of training opportunities, he will often learn new techniques which will not only help him now but also enhance his prospects later. Also, throughout the year, the Earth Dog should make the most of his ideas and special talents. By using these well, he can ensure his contribution will be valued and this may lead to interesting results.

For those Earth Dogs who are particularly keen to move away from their present role or are seeking work, this can be a significant year. By deciding upon the type of position they would now like and making enquiries, these Earth Dogs will often be able to secure an opening which, although sometimes modest, does offer scope for future development. For work opportunities, March, June and the last quarter of the year could be significant.

The Earth Dog can look forward to a modest improvement in his income, although the Goat year will be an expensive one for him. As with all Dogs, accommodation costs will figure prominently, with some Earth Dogs moving or having maintenance work or improvements carried out on their property. When embarking on any major undertaking, the Earth Dog does need to proceed with care, comparing prices as well as making allowance for any obligations he may be taking on. The Goat year does call for thoroughness and vigilance. In addition, the Earth Dog could have some family expenses to meet, perhaps helping a younger relation with education costs or in some other way. This will often be a demanding year financially and the Earth Dog should keep an eye on his commitments and expenditure.

The year will also be active for family matters and in addition to the possibility of moving, there will some months which will be especially busy. With his own activities, those of his loved ones and some of the projects he wants to carry out, the Earth Dog will find the demands on his time considerable. He would find it helpful to prioritize all that he has to do and manage his time carefully, even if this means some projects have to be deferred. To try to do too much too quickly or to spread his attention too widely will only add to the pressure as well as lead to less satisfactory results. In 2003 the Earth Dog's activities do need careful organization and control. However, while the year will be busy, the Earth Dog should make a point of encouraging some recreational pursuits that everyone can enjoy rather than allowing his home life to be dominated by work and continual activity. Time spent having friends round or going out will be appreciated as well as help maintain the rapport the Earth Dog so values.

He should also make sure that his social life does not suffer because of other demands on his time. This will not only help him unwind and forget some of his other preoccupations, but also lead to some pleasurable occasions. In addition to meeting existing friends, there will also be the opportunity for the Earth Dog to strike up new friendships as the year develops, particularly in connection with his interests. Any Earth Dog who may feel lonely, perhaps after moving to a new area or through other circumstances, will find that by going out and getting involved in different activities, they will soon meet others and often add a brighter aspect to their life. For some, there will also be the gift of a special new friendship.

Overall, the Goat year will be a constructive one for the Earth Dog with what he achieves as well as gains in experience serving him well in the future. However, with so many demands upon his time, he does need to make sure the various aspects of his life are in balance and that he gives himself the chance to appreciate his achievements, interests and the love and companionship of those who mean so much to him.

TIP FOR THE YEAR

Develop your skills and strengths and make the most of them. Experience gained now will often prove of value later.

FAMOUS DOGS

André Agassi, King Albert II of Belgium, Elizabeth Arden, Jane Asher, Brigitte Bardot, Gary Barlow, Candice Bergen, David Bowie, Bertolt Brecht, Michael Buerk, George W. Bush, Kate Bush, Laura Bush, Max Bygraves, Naomi Campbell, Mariah Carey, King Carl Gustaf XVI of Sweden, José Carreras, Paul Cézanne, Cher, Sir Winston Churchill, Petula Clark, Bill Clinton, Leonard Cohen, Jamie Lee Curtis, Charles Dance, Claude Debussy, Dame Judi Dench, Frankie Dettori, Blake Edwards, Sally Field, Joseph Fiennes, Robert Frost, Ava Gardner, Judy Garland, George Gershwin, Barry Gibb, Lenny Henry, O. Henry, Victor Hugo, Barry Humphries, Holly Hunter, Michael Jackson, Al Jolson, Felicity Kendal, Jennifer Lopez, Sophia Loren, Joanna Lumley, Shirley MacLaine, Madonna, Norman Mailer, Barry Manilow, Rik Mayall, Golda Meir, Freddie Mercury, Liza Minnelli, David Niven, Gary Numan, Sydney Pollack, Elvis Presley, Lord George Robertson, Paul Robeson, Linda Ronstadt, Gabriela Sabatini, Susan Sarandon, Jennifer Saunders, Claudia Schiffer, Dr Albert Schweitzer, Sylvester Stallone, Robert Louis Stevenson, Sharon Stone, Jack Straw, David Suchet, Donald Sutherland, Chris Tarrant, Mother Teresa, Uma Thurman, Donald Trump, Voltaire, Prince William, Shelley Winters.

30 JANUARY 1911 〜 17 FEBRUARY 1912   *Metal Pig*

16 FEBRUARY 1923 〜 4 FEBRUARY 1924   *Water Pig*

4 FEBRUARY 1935 〜 23 JANUARY 1936   *Wood Pig*

22 JANUARY 1947 〜 9 FEBRUARY 1948   *Fire Pig*

8 FEBRUARY 1959 〜 27 JANUARY 1960   *Earth Pig*

27 JANUARY 1971 〜 14 FEBRUARY 1972   *Metal Pig*

13 FEBRUARY 1983 〜 1 FEBRUARY 1984   *Water Pig*

31 JANUARY 1995 〜 18 FEBRUARY 1996   *Wood Pig*

THE
PIG

THE PERSONALITY OF THE PIG

Life is a series of experiences, each one of which makes us bigger, even though sometimes it is hard to realize this.

Henry Ford, a Pig

The Pig is born under the sign of honesty. He has a kind and understanding nature and is well known for his abilities as a peacemaker. He hates any sort of discord or unpleasantness and will do all in his power to sort out differences of opinion or bring opposing factions together.

He is also an excellent conversationalist and speaks truthfully and to the point. He dislikes any form of falsehood or hypocrisy and is a firm believer in justice and the maintenance of law and order. In spite of these beliefs, however, the Pig is reasonably tolerant and often prepared to forgive others for their wrongs. He rarely harbours grudges and is never vindictive.

The Pig is usually very popular. He enjoys other people's company and likes to be involved in joint or group activities. He will be a loyal member of any club or society and can be relied upon to lend a helping hand at functions. He is also an excellent fund-raiser for charities and often a great supporter of humanitarian causes.

The Pig is a hard and conscientious worker and is particularly respected for his reliability and integrity. In his early years he will try his hand at several different jobs, but he is usually happiest where he feels that he is being of service to others. He will unselfishly give up his time for the common good and is highly valued by his colleagues and employers.

The Pig has a good sense of humour and invariably has a smile, joke or whimsical remark at the ready. He loves to entertain and to please others, and there are many Pigs who have been attracted to careers in show business or who enjoy following the careers of famous stars and personalities.

There are, unfortunately, some who take advantage of the Pig's good nature and impose upon his generosity. The Pig has great difficulty in saying 'No' and, although he may dislike being firm, it would be in his own interests to say occasionally, 'Enough is enough.' The Pig can also be rather naïve and gullible; however, if at any stage in his life he feels that he has been badly let down, he will make sure that it will never happen again and will try to become self-reliant. There are many Pigs who have become entrepreneurs or forged a successful career on their own after some early disappointment in life. Although the Pig tends to spend his money quite freely, he is usually very astute in financial matters and there are many Pigs who have become wealthy.

Another characteristic of the Pig is his ability to recover from setbacks reasonably quickly. His faith and his strength of character keep him going. If he thinks that there is a job he can do or he has something that he wants to achieve, he will pursue it with a dogged determination. He can also be stubborn and no matter how many may plead with him, once he has made his mind up he will rarely change his views.

Although the Pig may work hard, he also knows how to enjoy himself. He is a great pleasure-seeker and will quite happily spend his hard-earned money on a lavish holiday or an expensive meal – for the Pig is a connoisseur of good food and wine – or taking part in a variety of recreational activities. He also enjoys small social gatherings and if he is in company he likes he can very easily become the life and soul of the party. He does, however, tend to become rather withdrawn at larger functions or among strangers.

The Pig is also a creature of comfort and his home will usually be fitted with all the latest in luxury appliances. Where possible, he will prefer to live in the country rather than the town and will opt to have a big garden, for the Pig is usually a keen and successful gardener.

The Pig is very popular with the opposite sex and will often have numerous romances before he settles down. Once settled, however, he will be loyal to his partner and he will find that he is especially well suited to those born under the signs of the Goat, Rabbit, Dog and Tiger and also to another Pig. Due to his affable and easy-going nature he can also establish a satisfactory relationship with all the remaining signs of the Chinese zodiac, with the exception of the Snake. The Snake tends to be wily, secretive and very guarded, and this can be intensely irritating to the honest and open-hearted Pig.

The female Pig will devote all her energies to the needs of her children and her partner. She will try to ensure that they want for nothing and their pleasure is very much her pleasure. Her home will either be very clean and orderly or hopelessly untidy. Strangely, there seems to be no in between with Pigs – they either love housework or detest it! The female Pig does, however, have considerable talents as an organizer and this, combined with her friendly and open manner, enables her to secure many of her objectives.

She can also be a caring and conscientious parent and has very good taste in clothes.

The Pig is usually lucky in life and will rarely want for anything. Provided he does not let others take advantage of his good nature and is not afraid of asserting himself, he will go through life making friends, helping others and winning the admiration of many.

THE FIVE DIFFERENT TYPES OF PIG

In addition to the 12 signs of the Chinese zodiac, there are five elements and these have a strengthening or moderating influence on the sign. The effects of the five elements on the Pig are described below, together with the years in which the elements were exercising their influence. Therefore all Pigs born in 1911 and 1971 are Metal Pigs, those born in 1923 and 1983 are Water Pigs, and so on.

Metal Pig: 1911, 1971

The Metal Pig is more ambitious and determined than some of the other types of Pig. He is strong, energetic and likes to be involved in a wide variety of different activities. He is very open and forthright in his views, although he can be a little too trusting at times and has a tendency to accept things at face value. He has a good sense of humour and loves to attend parties and other social gatherings. He has a warm, outgoing nature and usually has a large circle of friends.

Water Pig: 1923, 1983

The Water Pig has a heart of gold. He is generous and loyal and tries to remain on good terms with everyone. He will do his utmost to help others, but sadly there are some who will take advantage of his kind nature and he should, in his own interests, be a little more discriminating and be prepared to stand firm against anything that he does not like. Although he prefers the quieter things in life, he has a wide range of interests. He particularly enjoys outdoor pursuits and attending parties and social occasions. He is a hard and conscientious worker and invariably does well in his chosen profession. He is also gifted in the art of communication.

Wood Pig: 1935, 1995

This Pig has a friendly, persuasive manner and is easily able to gain the confidence of others. He likes to be involved in all that is going on around him and can some-times take on more responsibility than he can properly handle. He is loyal to his family and friends and he also derives much pleasure from helping those less fortunate than himself. The Wood Pig is usually an optimist and leads a very full, enjoyable and satisfying life. He also has a good sense of humour.

Fire Pig: 1947

The Fire Pig is both energetic and adventurous and he sets about everything he does in a confident and resolute manner. He is very forthright in his views and does not mind taking risks in order to achieve his objectives. He can, however, get carried away by the excitement of the moment and ought to exercise more caution in some of the enterprises with which he gets involved. The Fire Pig is usually lucky in money matters and is well known for his generosity. He is also very caring towards the members of his family.

Earth Pig: 1959

This Pig has a kindly nature. He is sensible and realistic and will go to great lengths to please his employers and secure his aims and ambitions. He is an excellent organizer and is particularly astute in business and financial matters. He has a good sense of humour and a wide circle of friends. He also likes to lead an active social life, although he does sometimes have a tendency to eat and drink more than is good for him.

PROSPECTS FOR THE PIG IN 2003

The Chinese New Year starts on 1 February 2003. Until then, the old year, the Year of the Horse, is still making its presence felt.

The Horse year (12 February 2002 to 31 January 2003) will have been a constructive one for the Pig and in what remains of it he can accomplish a great deal. As he realizes, to make progress requires both effort and discipline and by setting about his activities with commitment, he will make good headway.

At work the contacts the Pig is building up and experience he is gaining will enhance his standing and his prospects. The Pig possesses an enterprising nature and if he has any ideas he wishes to take further, he should check out the possibilities. Purposeful action could bring some interesting results.

Although the Horse year is reasonably well aspected for financial matters, the Pig could find the last quarter expensive. In addition to activities he wants to carry out and purchases he wants to make, his domestic and social life will be costly and some weeks could see considerable outlay. While the Pig will not begrudge this – especially as his spending will bring so much pleasure – he would do well to watch his outgoings and think twice about more impulsive buys.

On a personal level, the Pig will enjoy himself and be in demand with both his family and friends. His social diary may become quite full as the Horse year draws to a close. As far as possible he should try to spread out his commitments and organize his time, otherwise he could find his life becoming a whirl with little free time left for his own pursuits. Also, he should use some of the more relaxed and informal occasions that take place to heal any rifts or differences of opinion that may have occurred over the year. Great peacemaker that he is, he could find that a few well-chosen words will help.

Overall, the Horse year is a constructive time for the Pig with what he accomplishes often having a bearing on his progress in the next Chinese year.

The Year of the Goat begins on 1 February and will see encouraging developments in many areas of the Pig's life.

His personal life is particularly well aspected and here the Pig will be in sparkling form. In his domestic life he will play a major role, organizing and arranging various family activities, encouraging those in his household and offering advice and support. Those close to him will certainly value his input as well as appreciate his interest. However, while the Pig has such a willing disposition, he should not feel he has to shoulder all the family responsibilities himself. If he needs more help with household projects or other chores, he should ask rather than try to deal with them all single-handed. In 2003 the Pig's home life can be rewarding, but he should make sure that everyone does their fair share.

The Pig will, though, enjoy a variety of pleasurable occasions with his loved ones. These may include having friends round (with the Pig making an attentive host) and any family activities that he arranges. The Pig is a great pleasure-seeker and his knack in putting forward popular suggestions will be appreciated. Also, at busy times, he should make sure that life does not become a continual grind with all work and no play. Again, his input can be of great help in bringing a certain balance and enabling others to enjoy other aspects of life than work.

Although this will be a positive year for the Pig, no year is free from problems. When these do arise, the Pig should be prepared to discuss his concerns rather than keep them to himself. While he will do much to help others in 2003, he must not be reticent in asking for assistance himself, should he need it.

The Pig's social life is well aspected and in addition to meeting up with friends on a regular basis, he will enjoy going out to social events. Working as hard as he does, the Pig certainly feels he deserves to enjoy the fruits of his labours and going out socializing will be one way for him to do this.

For the unattached Pig or for any who may feel that his social life is lacking in some way, the Goat year holds much promise. If it would be helpful to draw a line under any past disappointments or sadnesses, the Pig should be prepared to do so and to regard this as the start of a new chapter in his personal life. The aspects are excellent for meeting others, building new friendships and starting a significant new romance. The months from March to May and August and November are particularly well aspected for meeting others, but as far as personal matters are concerned, the entire year is positive for the Pig.

The Pig will also benefit from his personal interests. Not only will these often bring him into contact with fellow enthusiasts – which in turn can lead to some pleasing social occasions – but they will also be satisfying to carry out. And if his interest allows the Pig to create something that he (and others) can appreciate, this will make it all the more rewarding. As always, the Pig will put his spare time to good use.

Over the year the Pig should also give some consideration to his well-being, ensuring that he eats a healthy and balanced diet as well as takes sufficient exercise. Any medical guidance he can get on ways he can improve his general lifestyle and fitness would be to his benefit.

As far as work is concerned, this will be a constructive year. It will allow the Pig to build on his more recent achievements and put his ideas and often specialist skills to effective use. Although he may sometimes feel that opportunities to progress are limited, those that do occur will turn out to be ideal for him and will be well worth following up. In the Goat year it is a case of 'striking while the iron is hot' and making the most of the openings that do arise.

Similarly, for those Pigs who are seeking work or wanting to switch to a different type of position, opportunities may seem limited, but by being prepared, showing initiative and carrying out background research prior to any interview, often these Pigs will impress sufficiently to be given a position which holds considerable potential. The Pig certainly has many fine abilities and by making the most of these and his personable nature, he can make good headway as well as often find a greater fulfilment in what he does. May, June and November could see some interesting work developments.

The progress that the Pig makes in his work will also lead to an improvement in his income, but his spending levels will remain fairly high as well. Money will flow into his accounts but also out again and it would be prudent for him to monitor his expenditure and ensure he has sufficient funds to cover existing obligations. This is not a year in which the Pig can proceed on too much of an ad hoc basis. Should he find he has dipped too heavily into his resources, however, the Pig is often adept at thinking of ways in which he can replenish his funds. In some cases freelance work, putting a skill to profitable use or taking another job for a few extra hours could help. The Pig's resourcefulness will assist him over the year.

Overall, this is a favourably aspected year for the Pig, particularly on a personal level. His relations with others will mean a great deal to him and the year also holds the promise of new friendships as well as significant romance. Although work-wise there may not be a great many opportunities, those that do arise will offer the Pig a real chance to make good use of his skills and find more fulfilment in what he does. This is a year for him to enjoy.

As far as the different types of Pig concerned, the Goat year holds good prospects for the *Metal Pig*. In his work he will be able to build upon his experience and use his considerable talents well. Also, he will be helped by his rich personality and ability to get on well with others. His colleagues do think highly of him and this will help his general progress. However, just how much the Metal Pig does achieve in 2003 rests with him.

Some Metal Pigs, satisfied with their present role, will decide to continue with it and make good use of their knowledge and skills. Although they may be content with what they do, they could be offered additional responsibilities which will not only add to their experience but also enhance their longer-term prospects. The Metal Pig certainly has the reputation for being a keen and loyal worker and this will be reinforced over the course of the year.

There will, though, be some Metal Pigs who feel the time has come for change and for these, as well as for those seeking work, the Goat year can be significant. Opportunities may not be plentiful, however, and some Metal Pigs may have to reconsider the type of position they are hoping for. There may be disappointments too, but sometimes these can turn out to be blessings in disguise, as the Metal Pig may subsequently gain a position with greater potential. Also, taking on something different from what he originally intended will give him the chance to develop and in some cases discover new skills.

The Goat year rewards creative endeavour and those Metal Pigs whose work allows them to draw on their ideas and creative talents should actively promote what they do. If they write, design, teach, problem solve or are in marketing or PR, some ideas or proposals they put forward could be especially well received. Again, by showing initiative the Metal Pig can advance his reputation.

Although with work and personal commitments the Metal Pig's free time may be limited, he should still set some aside for his interests, especially those that allow him to get additional exercise or are different from his usual activities. His interests can be a real tonic for him and it is important that they are not squeezed out due to other demands on his time.

As far as his finances are concerned, the Metal Pig can look forward to an increase in his income and in many cases an unexpected bonus, possibly a gift. This financial improvement will certainly be welcome, especially in view of his existing commitments and everything else he has in mind. However, if he is able, the Metal Pig would find it to his advantage to put some funds away for the longer term. In years to come these could build into an asset he will be grateful for.

The Metal Pig's domestic life will be both active and meaningful over the year and he will fondly watch over the progress of those around him, particularly younger relations. His encouragement, interest and support will be greatly valued as well as help maintain the often good rapport the Metal Pig enjoys with those close to him. Even though with work and other pressures he has much to think about, the contribution he makes to family life will again count for a lot.

The Metal Pig's social life, too, is positively aspected and in addition to enjoying meeting up with existing friends, he will often go out to a variety of social events. Once more his *joie de vivre* will be to the fore and the Goat year will contain some splendid times for him. For the unattached Metal Pig or those who may have had some recent misfortune, the Goat year offers great promise and, in many cases, the start of an exciting new chapter. A friendship made last year could suddenly blossom into romance or a meeting in the early months of 2003 will quickly become significant. On a personal level, the Goat year can be a blissful time for the Metal Pig.

Generally, 2003 will allow the Metal Pig to use his talents to good effect as well as enjoy a rewarding personal life. This is a year to savour.

TIP FOR THE YEAR

Make the most of your personal strengths. These are a real asset and will be appreciated by family, friends and colleagues.

This will be an exciting year for the *Water Pig* and although it will not be without a few disappointments or pressures, most of the events will work in the Water Pig's favour. Much will have happened over the last 12 months both in the Water Pig's personal and professional life and in the Goat year he will be able to build on the more positive aspects as well as make changes in areas which he feels have not gone so well. With resolve, a good heart and ideas on how he would like the year to develop, he can accomplish a great deal.

One area which will figure prominently will be the Water Pig's relations with others, especially on a romantic level. For those Water Pigs in a serious relationship, this will be a meaningful year. There will be fun, laughter and some great times to be had, although, as with all relationships, there also needs to be some give and take. Such are the favourable aspects, however, that a great many Water Pigs will decide to settle down with their partner or will get engaged or married during the year. And for Water Pigs who start the year feeling unhappy with their personal life, again the aspects are favourable. By going out and pursuing their interests many will meet someone who will quickly become special, perhaps through a chance introduction. Romance is very much in the air and by mid-2003 many of these Water Pigs will have seen a considerable transformation in their personal life. The months from March to early May are well aspected for meeting others, with August to October also seeing some exciting personal developments.

In addition to enjoying the love of another, the Water Pig will also benefit from the support and advice given by family members. Although he may sometimes feel the gap in years prevents more senior relations from appreciating his views or situation, often these same relations have had similar experiences and will be better able to understand than the Water Pig may realize. By being willing to talk and listen, he will not only benefit from their experience but also be reassured by their affection and regard for him.

Another important aspect of the year is that it will allow the Water Pig to add to his qualifications, experience and skills. For those on academic courses, by studying consistently and setting about their often heavy workload in an organized manner, they will find their efforts and disciplined approach rewarded with some fine results which will help their onward progress. For those in work or seeking it, again the Goat year will bring some interesting developments. While some Water Pigs may be content to become more established in their present role, there will be quite a few who may not feel entirely content in what they are doing or who may consider they have not yet found the right career. Rather than become disillusioned, these Water Pigs should take action and pursue openings which they feel could be more suitable. Admittedly, their quest will not be easy and there will be rejections on the way, but by persisting, many will be given an interesting new opportunity. March, June, July and November are well aspected for work matters.

The Water Pig will derive a great deal of satisfaction from his personal interests over the year and those with more creative talents or aspirations should promote their work. The Goat year does favour creativity and for the innovative and imaginative, this can be an encouraging time. The Water Pig also tends to enjoy outdoor pursuits, including travel and sporting activities, and the Goat year will certainly bring some memorable occasions.

On a financial level, however, the Water Pig will need to remain prudent as well as avoid risky undertakings, including any dubious 'get rich quick' schemes he may come across. Some of the year will be difficult financially, especially with all the Water Pig may want to do, but with planning and resourcefulness, he will often be pleased with how well he does manage on often limited means.

In many respects this will be a fine year for the Water Pig. His personal life offers much happiness, while in his work he will be able to add to his skills and experience and prepare for greater advances in the years ahead.

TIP FOR THE YEAR
Take full advantage of the opportunity to learn and widen your experience.

One of the talents of the *Wood Pig* is that he uses his time well and certainly during the Goat year he will find himself pursuing a wide range of often satisfying activities. In addition, his personal life is well aspected and he will not only be grateful for the support he receives but also be glad to help others during the course of the year.

The Wood Pig's home life will, as always, mean a great deal to him and he will delight in some of the activities and projects he undertakes, either on his own or with family members. Some Wood Pigs will use their practical skills in reorganizing and refurnishing a particular room. With his fine taste and eye for colour, the Wood Pig will complete this with style. He will also enjoy interests and activities he can share with those in his household. For some Wood Pigs this could again involve projects on their home and garden, while others might spend time pursuing a joint hobby. Some will also decide to use some of their free time visiting places in their area which they have not seen for some while or have not had the chance to visit properly. These can be enjoyable occasions.

With travel well favoured, the Wood Pig should also aim to go away at some point during 2003 as well as follow up any invitations to visit family and friends who may live some distance away. Some Wood Pigs may be tempted by a bargain break or may travel on the spur of the moment and this spontaneity will often give their time away an added appeal. Again, the Wood Pig's capacity to use his time well and live life to the full will certainly be evident over the year.

The Wood Pig sets great store by his social life and in addition to enjoying meeting up with friends, he will value their support and assistance. Any Wood Pig who may feel lonely or have experienced some personal sadness in recent times really would find it in his interest to go out and meet others, perhaps at a special interest group or social club. By doing something positive, he can bring some brightness back into his life.

This will also be a reasonable year for financial matters, with many Wood Pigs receiving an additional sum of money or gift over the year. While this will be welcome, the Wood Pig does need to remain vigilant when dealing with financial matters as well as when taking on any new commitment. Before completing forms or transactions, he should check the details as well as query anything that is not clear. Without some care, he could find himself involved in some burdensome correspondence as well as sometimes at a financial disadvantage. Important correspondence and financial matters do need care.

For those Wood Pigs born in 1995 this will also be a positive year, as they take up new interests and further their knowledge and skills. Their curiosity and eagerness will be satisfied and by taking advantage of the opportunities available to them as well as enjoying the friendship of others of their own age, they can certainly make this a good and active year.

Overall, the Goat year is a favourable one for the Wood Pig and, whether born in 1935 or 1995, he will enjoy the company and support of others as well as derive much satisfaction from his various activities. The Wood Pig has a great capacity for life and his willingness to try new experiences will lead to many rewarding times.

TIP FOR THE YEAR
Follow through your ideas and make the most of your opportunities.

This will be a pleasant year for the *Fire Pig* and while it may lack the activity of some, the Fire Pig will be content to use his skills and ideas to good effect as well as enjoy a rewarding personal life.

At work the aspects are especially encouraging, with the Fire Pig being given greater opportunity to draw on his expertise as well as further his skills. For those Fire Pigs whose work allows them to put forward ideas or use their creative skills in any way, this will be a particularly fulfilling and successful year. Indeed, many will have lamented in the past that they have not really been doing what they are best suited for and the Goat year will allow them to redress this and enjoy some notable successes.

Although some Fire Pigs will choose to remain in their present position, though often in an expanded capacity, there will be those who want to move and take on fresh challenges or who are seeking work. Their quest may not always be straightforward, but while certain positions may be elusive, others with greater potential could suddenly open up and some of the earlier disappointments may turn out to be blessings in disguise. With persistence and some fortuitous circumstances, many Fire Pigs will be satisfied with what they achieve. The Goat year could spring several surprises and for work opportunities the months of March, May, June and November are favoured.

Also, all Fire Pigs, irrespective of their present position, should take advantage of any training opportunities that are available. By refreshing their skills as well as learning new ones, they will find they are not only able to make more of themselves but also enhance their prospects.

This theme of self-development could also apply to the Fire Pig's personal interests. By learning new skills and improving his knowledge, he can make these all the more meaningful. Fire Pigs who enjoy creative and expressive pursuits such as art, writing, photography, drama or music should spend time on their interest over the year and possibly consider getting in contact with fellow enthusiasts. Personal interests really can be an enjoyable part of 2003 and in spite of all the other demands on him, the Fire Pig should make sure he devotes some time to them over the year.

As well as his interests, the Fire Pig should also ensure he does not neglect his well-being. To keep in good form, he should take adequate exercise as well as eat a healthy and balanced diet.

As far as financial matters are concerned, this will be a generally positive year for the Fire Pig. Although he will want to do a lot with his money, whenever possible he should set something aside for the longer term. In years to come he could be grateful for savings made now.

On a personal level the Goat year holds much promise. The Fire Pig's domestic life will be generally settled and he will take much interest in the activities and progress of those dear to him, providing encouragement, advice and, in some cases, practical assistance. He will enjoy joining with family members in carrying out various home and garden projects as well as other activities, including social events or travel. The Fire Pig certainly values family life and domestically this will be a rewarding year.

His social life is also favourably aspected and by developing his personal interests over the year he will get to meet others and widen his social circle. In addition there will be quite a few social events that will appeal to the Fire Pig and by going out regularly, he will find his social life will provide an excellent balance to his other activities as well as do him a lot of good. For any Fire Pigs who may start the year feeling dispirited or alone, this is a time to draw a line under the past and move forward. The aspects are favourable and, by going out and keeping busy with interests they enjoy, these Fire Pigs will see a substantial improvement in their situation.

In many respects, 2003 holds much promise for the Fire Pig and it will give him the chance to put his skills and strengths to good use as well as enjoy himself.

Develop your personal interests and talents. These can bring real pleasure over the year.

This will be a constructive year for the *Earth Pig* and will allow him to build on his strengths as well as his recent achievements.

Many Earth Pigs will have seen considerable changes in their work over the last 12 months and taken on new duties or a different role. The Goat year will allow them to settle into their position and master their many responsibilities. By showing initiative and setting about their activities in their usual conscientious way, these Earth Pigs will greatly impress and will enhance their prospects. Indeed, rather than look to the Goat year as a time for rapid advance, the Earth Pig will often gain more by consolidating his present role and preparing for future progress. Also, all Earth Pigs, whether currently in work or seeking it, should take advantage of any training opportunities that become available. Again, by being willing to develop himself and his skills, the Earth Pig will not only benefit from what he learns but also demonstrate his desire and worthiness to progress and this can be to his future benefit. For those Earth Pigs seeking work or desiring a move, keeping their skills up to date will certainly help them in their quest as well as sometimes open up new possibilities for them. In addition, the Earth Pig should also promote any ideas or special talents he has, especially if they are of a creative nature. These, combined with his compelling personality, can make a real impression over the year.

The Earth Pig should also aim to develop his personal interests and if there is a subject that has been intriguing him for some time, this would be a good year to find out more. Again, what he starts now can, in time, become significant. In addition to the satisfaction the Earth Pig's interests will bring, they will also provide an important balance to other aspects of his life.

As far as his finances are concerned, the Earth Pig can look forward to a modest increase in his income as well as benefit from a gift or an additional source of income, perhaps through some freelance or extra work. In view of this financial upturn, the Earth Pig will often decide to spend money on home improvements and comforts as well as other personal treats. By taking the time to carefully consider his purchases, he will be satisfied with what he acquires and may even manage to obtain some useful bargains. If funds permit, he should also aim to save a certain amount for his long-term future.

As far as the Earth Pig's personal life is concerned, this will be an active and potentially exciting year. In particular, a relation dear to him will have some news which will give rise to considerable celebration. Whether this is a wedding, the birth of a grandchild or some other heartening news, the Earth Pig will delight in it as well as be willing to provide help and encouragement. He will also enjoy carrying out activities with others in his household and while sometimes the demands on him will be considerable, by spending time with those who mean so much to him, he can make his home life both rewarding and meaningful. When pressures do mount or there are a great many household chores to be done, the Earth Pig should be forthcoming and ask for assistance rather than soldier on single-handed. Domestically, this can be a pleasing year but, as always, it does require input, communication and mutual support. Fortunately, in this, the Earth Pig is a master.

Socially, too, the year holds much promise. The Earth Pig will enjoy meeting up with friends and going out to some of the events and occasions to which he has been especially invited. For the unattached, a friendship started in the Horse year or a chance meeting in the early months of 2003 could become significant. As far as personal relationships are concerned, this will be a gratifying year and one which the friendly, sincere and outgoing Earth Pig will certainly enjoy.

Overall, the Goat year is a rewarding one for the Earth Pig and it will not only enable him to develop his skills and gain experience but also contain many pleasing occasions. Added to this, the events of the year will often have far-reaching and positive results.

TIP FOR THE YEAR
Be willing to learn and experiment. In the process you can discover a great deal.

FAMOUS PIGS

Bryan Adams, Woody Allen, Julie Andrews, Fred Astaire, Sir Richard Attenborough, Hector Berlioz, David Blunkett, Humphrey Bogart, James Cagney, Maria Callas, Richard Chamberlain, Hillary Rodham Clinton, Glenn Close, David

Coulthard, Sir Noël Coward, Oliver Cromwell, Billy Crystal, the Dalai Lama, Ted Danson, Richard Dreyfuss, Ben Elton, Ralph Waldo Emerson, Sven-Goran Eriksson, David Essex, Henry Ford, Emmylou Harris, Audley Harrison, William Randolph Hearst, Ernest Hemingway, Henry VIII, Conrad Hilton, Alfred Hitchcock, Sir Elton John, Tommy Lee Jones, Carl Gustav Jung, Boris Karloff, Charles Kennedy, Stephen King, Nastassja Kinski, Kevin Kline, Hugh Laurie, David Letterman, Jerry Lee Lewis, Ewan McGregor, Marcel Marceau, Marie Antoinette, Ricky Martin, Johnny Mathis, Meat Loaf, Wolfgang Amadeus Mozart, Camilla Parker Bowles, Michael Parkinson, Luciano Pavarotti, Iggy Pop, Prince Rainier of Monaco, Maurice Ravel, Ronald Reagan, Ginger Rogers, Salman Rushdie, Françoise Sagan, Pete Sampras, Arantxa Sanchez, Carlos Santana, Arnold Schwarzenegger, Steven Spielberg, Suzanne Vega, Jules Verne, Michael Winner, the Duchess of York.

APPENDIX

The relationship between the 12 animal signs – both on a personal level and business level – is an important aspect of Chinese horoscopes and in this appendix the compatibility between the signs is shown in the two tables that follow.

PERSONAL RELATIONSHIPS

KEY

1   Excellent. Great rapport.
2   A successful relationship. Many interests in common.
3   Mutual respect and understanding. A good relationship.
4   Fair. Needs care and some willingness to compromise in order for the relationship to work.
5   Awkward. Possible difficulties in communication with few interests in common.
6   A clash of personalities. Very difficult.

	Rat	Ox	Tiger	Rabbit	Dragon	Snake	Horse	Goat	Monkey	Rooster	Dog	Pig
Rat	1											
Ox	1	3										
Tiger	4	6	5									
Rabbit	5	2	3	2								
Dragon	1	5	4	3	2							
Snake	3	1	6	2	1	5						
Horse	6	5	1	5	3	4	2					
Goat	5	5	3	1	4	3	2	2				
Monkey	1	3	6	3	1	3	5	3	1			
Rooster	5	1	5	6	2	1	2	5	5	5		
Dog	3	4	1	2	6	3	1	5	3	5	2	
Pig	2	3	2	2	2	6	3	2	2	3	1	2

BUSINESS RELATIONSHIPS

KEY

1 Excellent. Marvellous understanding and rapport.
2 Very good. Complement each other well.
3 A good working relationship and understanding can be developed.
4 Fair, but compromise and a common objective are often needed to make this relationship work.
5 Awkward. Unlikely to work, either through lack of trust, understanding or the competitiveness of the signs.
6 Mistrust. Difficult. To be avoided.

	Rat	Ox	Tiger	Rabbit	Dragon	Snake	Horse	Goat	Monkey	Rooster	Dog	Pig
Rat	2											
Ox	1	3										
Tiger	3	6	5									
Rabbit	4	3	3	3								
Dragon	1	4	3	3	3							
Snake	3	2	6	4	1	5						
Horse	6	5	1	5	3	4	4					
Goat	5	5	3	1	4	3	3	2				
Monkey	2	3	4	5	1	5	4	4	3			
Rooster	5	1	5	5	2	1	2	5	5	6		
Dog	4	5	2	3	6	4	2	5	3	5	4	
Pig	3	3	3	2	3	5	4	2	3	4	3	1

YOUR ASCENDANT

The ascendant has a very strong influence on your personality and, together with the information already given about your sign and the effects of the element on your sign, it will help you gain even greater insight into your true personality according to Chinese horoscopes.

The hours of the day are named after the 12 animal signs and the sign governing the time you were born is your ascendant. To find your ascendant, look up the time of your birth on the table below, bearing in mind any local time differences in the place you were born.

11 p.m.	to	1 a.m.	The hours of the Rat
1 a.m.	to	3 a.m.	The hours of the Ox
3 a.m.	to	5 a.m.	The hours of the Tiger
5 a.m.	to	7 a.m.	The hours of the Rabbit
7 a.m.	to	9 a.m.	The hours of the Dragon
9 a.m.	to	11 a.m.	The hours of the Snake
11 a.m.	to	1 p.m.	The hours of the Horse
1 p.m.	to	3 p.m.	The hours of the Goat
3 p.m.	to	5 p.m.	The hours of the Monkey
5 p.m.	to	7 p.m.	The hours of the Rooster
7 p.m.	to	9 p.m.	The hours of the Dog
9 p.m.	to	11 p.m.	The hours of the Pig

RAT: The influence of the Rat as ascendant is likely to make the sign more outgoing, more sociable and careful with money. A particularly beneficial influence for those born under the sign of the Rabbit, Horse, Monkey and Pig.

OX: The Ox as ascendant has a restraining, cautionary and steadying influence which many signs will benefit from. This ascendant also promotes self-confidence and will-power and is an especially good ascendant for those born under the signs of the Tiger, Rabbit and Goat.

TIGER: This ascendant is a dynamic and stirring influence which makes the sign more outgoing, more action-orientated and more impulsive. A generally favourable ascendant for the Ox, Tiger, Snake and Horse.

RABBIT: The Rabbit as ascendant has a moderating influence, making the sign more reflective, serene and discreet. A particularly beneficial influence for the Rat, Dragon, Monkey and Rooster.

DRAGON: The Dragon as ascendant gives strength, determination and an added ambition to the sign. A favourable influence for those born under the signs of the Rabbit, Goat, Monkey and Dog.

SNAKE: The Snake as ascendant can make the sign more reflective, intuitive and self-reliant. A good influence for the Tiger, Goat and Pig.

HORSE: The influence of the Horse will make the sign more adventurous, more daring and, on some occasions, more fickle. Generally a beneficial influence for the Rabbit, Snake, Dog and Pig.

GOAT: This ascendant will make the sign more tolerant, easy-going and receptive. The Goat could also impart some creative and artistic qualities to the sign. An especially good influence for the Ox, Dragon, Snake and Rooster.

MONKEY: The Monkey as ascendant is likely to impart a delicious sense of humour and fun to the sign. He will make the sign more enterprising and outgoing – a particularly good influence for the Rat, Ox, Snake and Goat.

ROOSTER: The Rooster as ascendant helps to give the sign a lively, outgoing and very methodical manner. Its influence will increase efficiency and is good for the Ox, Tiger, Rabbit and Horse.

DOG: The Dog as ascendant makes the sign more reasonable and fair-minded as well as giving an added sense of loyalty. A very good ascendant for the Tiger, Dragon and Goat.

PIG: The influence of the Pig can make the sign more sociable, content and self-indulgent. It is also a caring influence and one which can make the sign want to help others. A good ascendant for the Dragon and Monkey.

HOW TO GET THE BEST
FROM YOUR CHINESE SIGN
AND THE YEAR

To supplement the earlier chapters on the personality and horoscope of the signs, I have included in this appendix a guide on how you can get the best out of your sign and the year.

Each of the 12 Chinese signs possesses its own unique strengths and by identifying them you can use them to your advantage. Similarly, by becoming aware of possible weaknesses you can do much to rectify them and in this respect I hope the following sections will be useful. Also included are some tips on how you can get the best from the Year of the Goat. The areas covered are general prospects, career prospects, finance and relations with others.

THE RAT

The Rat is blessed with many fine talents but his undoubted strength lies in his ability to get on with others. He is sociable, charming and a good judge of character. He also possesses a shrewd mind and is good at spotting opportunities.

However, to make the most of himself and his abilities, the Rat does need to impose some discipline upon himself. He should resist the temptation (sometimes very great!) of getting involved in too many activities all at the same time and decide upon his priorities and objectives. By concentrating his energies on specific matters he will fare much better as a result. Also, given his personable manner, he should seek out positions where he can use his personal relations skills to good effect. For a career, sales and marketing could prove ideal.

The Rat is also astute in dealing with finance but, while often thrifty, he can sometimes give way to moments of indulgence. Although he deserves to enjoy the money he has so carefully earned, it may sometimes be in his interests to exercise more restraint when tempted to satisfy too many extravagant whims!

The Rat's family and friends are also most important to him and while he is loyal and protective towards them, he does tend to keep his worries and concerns to himself. He would be helped if he were more willing to discuss any anxieties he has. Those around the Rat think highly of him and are prepared to do much to help him, but for them to do this he does need to be less secretive and guarded.

With his sharp mind, keen imagination and sociable manner, the Rat does, however, have much in his favour. First, though, he should decide what he wants to achieve and then concentrate upon his chosen objectives. When he has commitment, the Rat can be irrepressible and, given his considerable charm, he can often be irresistible as well! Provided he channels his energies wisely he can make much of his life.

Advice for the Rat's Year Ahead

GENERAL PROSPECTS

The Rat's situation and prospects will be much improved and he should seize the initiative and set his plans in motion.

CAREER PROSPECTS

The year will allow the Rat to make better use of his skills and ideas and to move forward. He should not let himself be held back by past disappointments. By pursuing suitable opportunities and persisting, he *will* make headway.

FINANCE

A much improved year. However, the Rat would still find it helpful to manage his financial situation with care. If he can make provision for his future, it would be to his advantage.

RELATIONS WITH OTHERS

The Rat will be on sparkling form, with his friendly and personable nature being much appreciated. He will win new friends and admirers and can look forward to many interesting and enjoyable occasions with his loved ones. Romance will beckon for some Rats.

THE OX

Strong-willed, determined and resolute, the Ox certainly has a mind of his own! He is also persistent and sets about achieving his objectives with dogged determination. In addition, he is reliable and tenacious and is often a source of inspiration to others. The Ox is a doer and an achiever and in life he often accomplishes a great deal. However, for him to really excel, he would do well to try and correct his weaknesses.

Being so resolute and having such a strong sense of purpose, the Ox can be inflexible and narrow-minded. He can be resistant to change and prefers to set about his activities in his own way rather than be too dependent on others. He should aim to be more outgoing and adventurous in his outlook. His dislike of change can sometimes be to his detriment and if he were prepared to be more adaptable he would find his progress would be easier.

The Ox would also be helped if he were to broaden his range of interests and become more relaxed in his approach. At times he can be so preoccupied with his own activities that he is not always as mindful of others as he should be and his demeanour can sometimes be studious and serious. There are times when he would benefit from a lighter touch.

However, the Ox is true to his word and loyal to his family and friends. He is admired and respected by others and his tremendous will-power usually enables him to achieve much in life.

Advice for the Ox's Year Ahead

GENERAL PROSPECTS
Although the Ox holds some very set views, in the Goat year he does need to show a certain amount of flexibility.

This may not be the easiest or smoothest of years for him, but his accomplishments can still be far-reaching.

CAREER PROSPECTS
The Ox likes stability and control, but the events of the year will lead to some uncomfortable moments for him. As far as possible, he should make the most of the situations in which he finds himself. He should also consider his future, as his actions now can contribute to his future success.

FINANCE
Although the Ox is usually so careful in money matters, 2003 calls for control and the avoidance of risks.

RELATIONS WITH OTHERS
In view of the pressures of the year, the Ox will truly value the support of those who are important to him and any Ox who is alone or dispirited should aim to go out more and meet others. The Ox's personal life can be a particularly important aspect of the year.

THE TIGER

Lively, innovative and enterprising, the Tiger is one who enjoys an active lifestyle. He has a wide range of interests, an alert mind and a genuine liking of others. He likes to live life to the full. However, despite his enthusiastic and well-meaning ways, he does not always make the most of his considerable potential.

By being so versatile, the Tiger does have a tendency to jump from one activity to another or dissipate his energies by trying to do too much at any one time. To make the most of himself he should try to exercise a certain amount of self-discipline. Ideally, he should decide how best he can use his abilities, give himself some objectives and stick with them. If he can overcome his restless tendencies, he will find he will accomplish much more.

Also, in spite of his sociable manner, the Tiger likes to retain a certain independence in his actions and while few begrudge him this, he would sometimes find life easier if he were more prepared to work with others. His reliance upon his own judgement does sometimes mean that he excludes the views and advice of those around him, and this can be to his detriment. The Tiger may possess an independent spirit, but he must not let it go too far!

The Tiger does, however, have much in his favour. He is bold, original and quick-witted. If he can keep his restless nature in check, he can enjoy considerable success. In addition, his engaging personality makes him one who is much admired and well liked.

Advice for the Tiger's Year Ahead

GENERAL PROSPECTS

The Tiger likes activity, involvement and for things to happen fast, but in 2003 he will need to exercise patience and build on what he has. This is a year when he should draw breath and take the time to enjoy himself.

CAREER PROSPECTS

The Tiger may regard his accomplishments in 2003 as modest, but they can have significant benefits in the future. This is a year to develop strengths, gain experience and learn.

FINANCE

A reasonable year, although to benefit the Tiger does need to manage his money carefully and plan his purchases.

RELATIONS WITH OTHERS

By spending time with others, sharing interests and sometimes offering advice, the Tiger will find this a pleasant year. He in turn should be receptive to some of the advice he is given, particularly from those who speak with experience.

THE RABBIT

The Rabbit is certainly one who appreciates the finer things in life. With his good taste, companionable nature and wide range of interests, he knows how to live well – and usually does!

However, for all his finesse and style, the Rabbit does possess traits he would do well to watch. His desire for a settled lifestyle makes him err on the side of caution. He dislikes change and as a consequence can miss out on opportunities. Also, there are many Rabbits who will go to great lengths to avoid difficult and fraught situations, and again, while few may relish these, sometimes in life it is necessary to take risks or stand your ground just to get on. At times it would certainly be in the Rabbit's interests to be bolder and more assertive in going after whatever he desires.

The Rabbit also attaches great importance to his relations with others and while he has a happy knack of getting on with most people, he can be sensitive to criticism. Difficult though it may be, he should really try to develop a thicker skin and recognize that criticism can provide valuable learning opportunities, as can some of the problems he strives so hard to avoid.

However, with his agreeable manner, keen intellect and shrewd judgement, the Rabbit does have much in his favour and invariably makes much of his life – and usually enjoys it too!

Advice for the Rabbit's Year Ahead

GENERAL PROSPECTS
A favourable year which will allow the Rabbit to make the most of his many fine qualities. However, to benefit, he will need to decide what he wants and then go after it. He will also gain from developing personal interests and skills.

CAREER PROSPECTS
With his experience, skills and ability to get on with others, the Rabbit is set to do well in 2003. If he sees a suitable opportunity or is attracted to a certain type of work, even if this means a change, he should take action.

FINANCE

Although the Rabbit's income may improve, financial matters do need extra care. Spending could steadily increase if not watched, and important forms and agreements also need close attention.

RELATIONS WITH OTHERS

A busy but rewarding year. The Rabbit will particularly enjoy the activities he can carry out with those close to him. There is the prospect of new friendships and, for some, significant romance.

THE DRAGON

Enthusiastic, enterprising and honourable, the Dragon possesses many admirable qualities and his life is often full and varied. He always gives of his best and even though not all his endeavours may meet with success, he is none the less resilient and hardy, and is much admired and respected.

However, for all his qualities, the Dragon can be blunt and forthright and, through sheer strength of character, sometimes domineering. It would certainly be in his interests to listen more closely to others rather than be so self-reliant. Also, his enthusiasm can sometimes get the better of him and he can be impulsive. To make the most of his abilities, he should set himself priorities and set about his activities in a disciplined and systematic way. More tact and diplomacy might not come amiss either!

However, with his lively and outgoing manner, the Dragon is popular and well liked. With good fortune on his side (and the Dragon is often lucky), his life is almost certain to be eventful and fulfilling. He has many talents and if he uses them wisely he will enjoy much success.

Advice for the Dragon's Year Ahead

GENERAL PROSPECTS

Although this may not be a year of major developments, it will be a valuable one for the Dragon and he should make every effort to extend his experience. What he accomplishes now will often be beneficial in the future.

CAREER PROSPECTS

This is very much a year for personal development, deciding on future directions and preparing the way ahead. The Dragon should learn more about the different aspects of his work and build up his contacts.

FINANCE

A year for care. Money needs to be managed, spending controlled and risks avoided. Important forms and correspondence need to be handled carefully and promptly.

RELATIONS WITH OTHERS

The Dragon will be in fine form and will enjoy some happy times. His social life and personal interests will provide a valuable balance to his other activities. For the lonely and unattached, the Goat year can bring an important new friendship or romance.

THE SNAKE

The Snake is blessed with a keen intellect. He has wide interests, an enquiring mind and good judgement. He tends to be quiet and thoughtful and plans his activities with considerable care. With his fine abilities he often does well in life, but he does possess traits which can undermine his progress.

The Snake is often guarded in his actions and sometimes loses out to those who are more action-oriented and assertive. He can also be a loner and likes to retain a certain independence in his actions, and this too can hamper his progress. It would be in his interests to be more forthcoming and involve others more readily in his plans. The Snake has many talents and possesses a warm and rich personality, but there is a danger that this can remain concealed behind his often quiet and reserved manner. He would fare better by being more outgoing and showing others his true worth.

However, the Snake is very much his own master. He invariably knows what he wants in life and is often prepared to journey long and hard to achieve his objectives. He does, though, have it in his power to make that journey easier. Lose some of that reticence, Snake, be more open and assertive, and do not be afraid of the occasional risk!

Advice for the Snake's Year Ahead

GENERAL PROSPECTS

The year holds much promise for the Snake, but to benefit he does need to make the most of his experience and often unique skills. This is not a time to go off on completely new tangents or take risks.

CAREER PROSPECTS

There will be good chances to make headway and by following up openings and considering other ways in which his skills can be used, the Snake will be able to improve his position. He should make the most of his creative talents and often innovative approach.

FINANCE

Although income may improve, this is not a year for taking risks. Spending, too, should be watched.

RELATIONS WITH OTHERS

A demanding but pleasurable year. Domestically, there will be happiness, but also pressure, activity and sometimes anxiety. The Snake should be forthcoming and remain his considerate self. Socially, there will also be a lot going on with chances to make new friends and, for some, enjoy the delights of a wonderful new romance.

THE HORSE

Versatile, hard-working and sociable, the Horse makes his mark wherever he goes. He has an eloquent and engaging manner and makes friends with ease. He is quick-witted, has an alert mind and is certainly not averse to taking risks or experimenting with new ideas.

The Horse possesses a strong and likeable personality, but he does also have his weaknesses. With his wide interests he does not always finish everything he starts and he would do well to be more persevering. He has it within him to achieve considerable success, but when he has made his plans he should stick with them. To make the most of his talents he does need to overcome his restless tendencies.

The Horse loves company and values both his family and friends. However, there will have been many a time when he has lost his temper or spoken in haste and regretted his words. Throughout his life, he needs to keep his temper in check and learn to be diplomatic in tense situations. If not, he could risk jeopardizing the respect and good relations he so values.

However, the Horse has a multitude of talents and a lively and outgoing personality. If he can overcome his restless and volatile nature, he can lead a rich and highly fulfilling life.

Advice for the Horse's Year Ahead

GENERAL PROSPECTS

This will be a generally agreeable year and a good one for the Horse to develop himself and his skills. Although

343

actual progress may sometimes be modest, what the Horse learns now will prove a real asset in the longer term.

CAREER PROSPECTS
There will be excellent opportunities for the Horse to use his strengths to good effect and extend his duties. However, he should give thought to how he would like his career to develop and consider future possibilities. Ideas would be worth investigating, with considerable rewards likely to be reaped in 2004.

FINANCE
An expensive year, with particularly high costs connected with accommodation. The Horse will need to manage his finances with care.

RELATIONS WITH OTHERS
By spending time with family and friends, the Horse can look forward to some rewarding occasions. For the unattached, the prospects are excellent for a meaningful romance.

THE GOAT

The Goat has a warm, friendly and understanding manner and gets on well with most. He is generally easy-going, has a fond appreciation of the finer things in life and possesses a rich imagination. He is often artistic and enjoys the creative arts and outdoor activities.

However, despite his engaging manner, there lurks beneath his skin a sometimes tense and pessimistic nature.

The Goat can be a worrier and without the support and encouragement of others can feel insecure and be hesitant in his actions.

To make the most of himself the Goat should aim to become more assertive and decisive as well as more at ease with himself. He has much in his favour, but he really does need to promote himself more and be bolder in his actions. He would also be helped if he were to sort out his priorities and set about his activities in an organized and disciplined manner. There are some Goats who tend to be haphazard in the way they go about things and this can hamper their progress.

Although the Goat will always value the support of others, it would also be in his interests to become more independent and not be so reticent about striking out on his own. He does, after all, possess many talents, as well as a sincere and likeable personality, and by always giving of his best, he can make his life rich, rewarding and enjoyable.

Advice for the Goat's Year Ahead

GENERAL PROSPECTS

The Goat has great talents and ideas and in his own year he should make the most of these. With action and initiative, he can reap significant rewards.

CAREER PROSPECTS

This year the Goat should take the direction of his career into his own hands. By pursuing suitable opportunities, he will make headway and find himself using his talents in a more satisfying way. The Goat's own year is a call for him to take action.

FINANCE

A year spiced with luck and a financial upturn. However, while the Goat is always one to savour periods of financial good fortune, he should not become careless but watch his spending as well as carefully check the terms of any agreements he enters into.

RELATIONS WITH OTHERS

The love, support and friendship of others will mean a great deal to the Goat in his year. By being active in both domestic and social matters, he can make this a happy and busy time. For the unattached, a significant friendship or romance awaits.

THE MONKEY

Lively, enterprising and innovative, the Monkey certainly knows how to impress. He has wide interests, a good sense of fun and relates well to others. He also possesses a shrewd mind and often has the happy knack of turning events to his advantage.

However, despite his versatility and considerable gifts, the Monkey does have his weaknesses. He often lacks persistence, can get distracted easily and also places tremendous reliance upon his own judgement. While his belief in himself is a commendable asset, it would certainly be in his interests to be more mindful of the views of others. Also, while he likes to keep tabs on all that is going on around him, he can be evasive and secretive with regard to his own feelings and activities, and again a more forth-coming attitude would be to his advantage.

In his desire to succeed the Monkey can also be tempted to cut corners or be crafty and he should recognize that such actions can rebound on him!

However, the Monkey is resourceful and his sheer strength of character will ensure he has an interesting and varied life. If he can channel his considerable energies wisely and overcome his sometimes restless tendencies, his life can be crowned with success and achievement. Added to which, with his amiable personality, he will enjoy the friendship of many.

Advice for the Monkey's Year Ahead

GENERAL PROSPECTS

A good year for personal development, particularly work skills, which can help the Monkey's prospects both now and in the future. Travel is well aspected and the Monkey should also set time aside for his personal interests, as these can bring a balance to his life.

CAREER PROSPECTS

The Monkey should concentrate on his true interests and strengths. By developing his skills and widening his experi-ence he will be paving the way for some significant advances later, particularly in the auspicious Monkey year that follows.

FINANCE

A generally favourable year, but the Monkey must not become complacent or too casual when dealing with money matters or entering into important agreements. He should also keep a watch on his spending.

RELATIONS WITH OTHERS

The Goat year offers some happy times, with romance and some personal celebrations in store. However, the Monkey does need to be more open in expressing his thoughts, otherwise he could jeopardize the wonderful rapport he has built up.

THE ROOSTER

With his considerable bearing and incisive and resolute manner, the Rooster cuts an impressive figure. He has a sharp mind, keeps well informed on many matters and expresses himself clearly and convincingly. He is meticulous and efficient in his undertakings and commands much respect. He also has a genuine and caring interest in others.

The Rooster has much in his favour, but there are some aspects of his character that can tell against him. He can be candid in his views and sometimes over-zealous in his actions, and without forethought he can say or do things he later regrets. His high standards also make him fussy, even pedantic, and he can get diverted into relatively minor matters when in truth he could be occupying his time more profitably. This is something all Roosters would do well to watch. Also, while the Rooster is a great planner, he can sometimes be unrealistic in his expectations. In making plans – indeed, with most of his activities – he would do well to consult others rather than keep his thoughts to himself. By doing so, he will greatly benefit from their input.

The Rooster has considerable talents as well as commendable drive and commitment, but to make the most of himself he does need to channel his energies wisely and watch his candid and sometimes volatile nature. With care, however, he can make a success of his life, and with his wide interests and outgoing personality, he will enjoy the friendship and respect of many.

Advice for the Rooster's Year Ahead

GENERAL PROSPECTS

A positive year and by following through his ideas and using his strengths, the Rooster will be pleased with the progress he makes. This is a year to move forward and, particularly for those who may start the year discouraged or feeling in a rut, take decisive action.

CAREER PROSPECTS

This will be a satisfying year for the Rooster and by making the most of his talents he find himself well placed to move ahead. With his prospects showing promise, the Rooster will often be at his best – efficient, motivated and inspired.

FINANCE

With family, social and accommodation expenses, the Rooster will have many demands on his resources. He will need to manage his money carefully and keep particularly firm control over his purse strings.

The Rooster will be in fine form, advising and supporting those around him. Generous and kind natured, he will win the gratitude of many. His social circle is likely to widen over the year and for the unattached, significant romance will beckon.

THE DOG

Loyal, dependable and with a good understanding of human nature, the Dog is well placed to win the respect and admiration of many. He is a no-nonsense sort of person and hates any sort of hypocrisy and falsehood. With the Dog you know where you stand and, given his direct manner, where he stands on any issue. He also has a strong humanitarian nature and often champions good and just causes.

The Dog has many fine attributes, although there are certain traits that can prevent him from either enjoying or making the most of his life. He is a great worrier and can get anxious over all manner of things. Although it may not always be easy, the Dog should try to rid himself of the 'worry habit'. Whenever he is tense or concerned, he should be prepared to speak to others rather than shoulder his worries all by himself. In some cases, they could even be of his own making! Also, the Dog has a tendency to be rather pessimistic and he would certainly be helped if he were to look more optimistically on his undertakings. He does, after all, possess many skills and should justifiably have faith in his abilities. Another weakness is his tendency to be stubborn over certain issues. If he is not careful, this could at times undermine his position.

If the Dog can reduce the anxious and pessimistic side of his nature, then he will not only enjoy life more but also find he is achieving more. He possesses a truly admirable character and his loyalty, reliability and sincerity are appreciated by all he meets. In his life he will do much good and befriend many – and he owes it to himself to enjoy life too. Sometimes it might help him to recall the words of another Dog, Winston Churchill: 'When I look back on all these worries I remember the story of the old man who said on his deathbed that he had had a lot of trouble in his life, most of which never happened.'

Advice for the Dog's Year Ahead

GENERAL PROSPECTS

This will be a demanding year and to get results the Dog will need to show persistence and determination. However, what he does accomplish will often be to his longer-term good and he will gain a great deal by drawing on the help of those around him.

CAREER PROSPECTS

This is not be a year for major advances but rather a time to gain experience, develop existing skills and learn new ones. In 2003, the Dog will be positioning himself for the successes he will enjoy in the near future.

FINANCE

Accommodation matters will involve considerable expense and the Dog will need to watch his financial situation carefully.

RELATIONS WITH OTHERS

Despite the year's many demands, the Dog's personal life will be of great value and he should ensure he makes time for his social life and personal interests as well. His relations with others really will benefit him over the year.

THE PIG

Genial, sincere and trusting, the Pig gets on well with most. He has a kind and caring nature, a dislike of discord and often possesses a good sense of humour. In addition, he has a fondness for socializing and enjoying the good life!

The Pig also possesses a shrewd mind, is particularly adept at dealing with business and financial matters, and has a robust and resilient nature. Although not all his plans may work out as he would like, he is tenacious and will often rise up and succeed after experiencing setbacks and difficulties. In his often active and varied life he can accomplish a great deal, although there are certain aspects of his character that can tell against him. If he can modify these or keep them in check, his life will certainly be easier and possibly even more successful.

In his activities the Pig can sometimes overcommit himself and while he does not want to disappoint, he would certainly be helped if he were to set about his activities in an organized and systematic manner and give himself priorities at busy times. He should not allow others to take advantage of his good nature and it would be in his interests if he were sometimes more discerning. At times the Pig can be gullible and naïve; fortunately, though, he quickly learns from his mistakes. He also possesses a stubborn streak and if new situations do not fit in with his line of thinking, he can be inflexible. Such an attitude may not always be to his advantage.

The Pig is a great pleasure-seeker and while he should enjoy the fruits of his labours, he can sometimes be self-indulgent and extravagant. This again is something he would do well to watch.

However, though the Pig may possess some faults, those who come into contact with him are invariably impressed by his integrity, amiable manner and intelligence. If he uses his talents wisely, his life can be crowned with considerable achievement and the good-hearted Pig will also be loved and respected by many.

Advice for the Pig's Year Ahead

GENERAL PROSPECTS

The Pig will enjoy the Goat year, particularly as it will give him the opportunity to advance his talents and, on a personal level, be in demand. For Pigs who may have had some recent difficulty, the Goat year offers real hope.

CAREER PROSPECTS

There will be plenty of opportunities for the Pig to extend his experience over the year and obtain a greater satisfaction in his work. For those seeking to move on, there could be some surprises in store with the Goat year offering a possible change in direction.

FINANCE

A generally positive year, but the Pig's commitments will mean he will sometimes draw heavily on his resources and he would be wise to keep a close watch on his financial position. If he is able, he should set something aside for the future.

RELATIONS WITH OTHERS

An excellent year, with the Pig's domestic and social life going well. For the unattached, the prospects are highly favourable for romance. The Pig has always been a great pleasure-seeker and in the Goat year, he will experience pleasure aplenty!